THE OLIVE BRANCH

An Evangelical Anglican Doctrine of the Church

A Latimer Monograph

FOR ANN

THE OLIVE BRANCH

An Evangelical Anglican Doctrine of the Church

TIM BRADSHAW

Published for Latimer House, Oxford
by
THE PATERNOSTER PRESS
CARLISLE

A Latimer Monograph

Latimer House, Oxford is a centre for study and research. It is committed to the ideal of creatively applying Biblical and Reformation theology to the ongoing life of the Church of England and the Anglican Communion. This book is one of a series of occasional studies on theological subjects sponsored by the Latimer House Council, which bear on issues of importance for Anglicans.

British Library Cataloguing in Publication Data

Bradshaw, Tim
The olive branch
1. Church of England
I. Title
283.42

ISBN 0–85364–512–4

Typeset by Photoprint, Torquay, Devon
and Printed in Great Britain for The Paternoster Press,
P.O. Box 300, Carlisle, CA3 0QS
by The Guernsey Press Co. Ltd., Guernsey, Channel Islands.

CONTENTS

INTRODUCTION

The churchyard of a Bristol Anglican parish contains a plaque commemorating some Nonconformists who were executed for their faith by the church authorities three hundred years ago. This was told me by an elderly Free Church lady for whom the spot still bore memories of persecuted nonconformity, her own tradition, at the hands of the ruling established church. All the Christian denominations, including those who do not consider themselves denominations, will have similar historic memories burned deep into their souls and occasionally surfacing to cause pain. Church history has come a long way since the very earliest years when mutual love and care marked out the Christian community and communities.

This book aims to give an account of various major interpretations of the church, interpretations which often trace back to the bitter divisions of the past, however much the emotional acrimony has died and rises only at certain times and places. The academic name for such study is ecclesiology. All Christians have an ecclesiology: whether implicit or consciously held, all have an idea of the church's place and nature, all have an opinion over the way the official and the spiritual relate in the church. Ecclesiologies abound today, from the highest Roman Catholic view to the charismatic house fellowship, and most claim scriptural support as well as that of custom and tradition. I will concentrate on stating the positions largely but not exclusively as they exist within the Anglican Church, where the catholic, the charismatic and the evangelical coexist with the liberal and the liberationist. It is a particular concern to offer an evangelical account of the doctrine of the church, something lacking in the Anglican context for some time.

The subject is of key importance for the ecumenical process, for the ways in which the ministry and mission of the church will develop and hence for the impact of the church on society. The game is worth the candle; we do need to think hard about the nature of the church. The melting pot of inter church discussion and negotiation will produce change of some kind and it is vital that this change is for the better, and not a reinforcement of beliefs and practices which are less than helpful in spreading the faith of Christ in a needy world. A critical appraisal of current ecclesiological options hopes to contribute to clarity of thinking in this process of change. Changes in attitudes continue apace in the process of theological revaluation and ecumenical negotiation, and in the grass roots common life and worship now being enjoyed increasingly between denominational groupings. The statement issued by the representatives at the Swanwick Conference 'Not Strangers But Pilgrims' was a determined expression of churches to cut through the red tape of historical and administrative differences in order to re-establish a common, visibly united church. The new 'Ecumenical Instruments' have been set up to take this process forward, Roman Catholics now included.[1] The Anglican Roman Catholic International Commission (ARCIC) agreed statements, however, have attracted much attention and deserve a full appraisal as representing to many an ecclesiological consensus.

I would be sorry if this programme limited the band of readership to Anglicans and European Roman Catholics, because the reports represent the general ecumenical consensus. The former Archbishop of Canterbury, Dr Robert Runcie, in General Synod, said of the World Council of Churches Report, *Baptism Eucharist and Ministry*, and of the first ARCIC Report, that they are as alike as two peas in a pod. The ARCIC material develops a fuller theology to justify its conclusions than its WCC sister document.

The theology of liberation, another crucial issue today, is not a truly new phenomenon in the church if we take account of figures such as the priest John Ball, who served as chaplain to Wat Tyler in the Peasants Revolt, and theologians like F. D. Maurice who sought for a theological Christian socialism in Victorian England. Now these concerns are irrepressibly vocal on the ecclesiastical scene, with an official Anglican statement in the ACUPA Report *Faith in the City*, and this ecclesiology will be explored as a topic in its own right. This whole concern and awareness of the character of the church as in some way determined by a distinctive attitude to the under-privileged of society must not be ignored in any contemporary treatment of our understanding of the church, her structures, ministry and mission. Of all the voices which protest against any split between the church as a visible entity from the church as a spiritual reality, the theology of political and social concern calls out the loudest against playing down the earthly form in favour of an invisibly spiritual centre. The complex question of formulating the relationship of the outward and visible to the inwardly spiritual will not go away and it lies at the heart of many ecclesiological disagreements existing between and within denominations.

Church life has to be practical if it can properly deserve the name. Theology of liberation claims to define the church; the 'preferential option for the poor' is no optional ecclesiastical extra but belongs to the very essence of the church. The challenge to a proper Christ-centred ethic for life is properly made. Richard McBrien in his book *Do We Need the Church?* tellingly quotes Karl Barth on this whole area:

'Is there not also an astonishing disparity between what is important, discussed, and more or less victoriously put in action in theology, and the errors and confusions, the sea of suffering and misery prevailing in the world that surrounds theology? . . . *There,* amidst the world, is the still 'unconquered past' of the madness of dictators . . . *There* are the murderers and the murdered of the concentration camps. *There* are Hiroshima, Korea, Algeria, and the Congo. *There* is the undernourishment of the greater part of mankind. *There* is the cold war and the sinister threat of a 'hot' one, which might very well be the last. In other words, there is stubbornly promoted the end of all life on our planet.

'*Here,* however, in the realm of theology, is a little demythologizing in Marburg and a little *Church Dogmatics* in Basel. *Here* are the rediscovery of the 'historical' Jesus and the glorious new discovery of a 'God above God'. *Here* are the discussions on Baptism and the Eucharist, Law and Gospel, Kerygma and Myth, Romans 13 and the heritage of Dietrich Bonhoeffer. *Here* are ecumenical discussions and Church councils. But *Kyrie Eleison*! —what is the real relationship to everything that simultaneously happened *there*?'[2]

The powerful emergence of such intensely practical views of the church, views which attack a 'spiritual' Christianity without Christlike fruits in society, underscores the pressing need to formulate a doctrine of the church which does justice to the earthly dimension. What is spirituality for the Christian if it is not at the one and same time practical, sacrificial and therefore bodily commitment to the way, the truth and the life? Both evangelical and catholic wings of the church have to listen to this call. The former continue to wrestle with their commitment to conversion, sanctification and justification with reference to the definition of the church and the sacraments; how is the visible, tangible and historical phenomenon of the church to be related to the grace of God in Christ Jesus? The latter stress the place of the visible church in mediating salvation, but it is a narrowly defined, cultically determined idea of the visible church that often emerges. A theology of the church visible, which seeks to remain in touch with the tenor of the New Testament, cannot surely rest content with an exclusively cultic definition. *Which* visible aspect constitutes the church? What kinds of feature should we be looking for in forming a judgement on the question?

This treatment of the subject contends that one such basic feature is that of teaching or doctrine. This contention flies in the face of much commentary on the matter at present and I think that the counter position badly needs restating. The Christian faith does have content which can be understood by the mind, and this content is a vital part of the church's self-definition. Indeed the ecumenical agreements reached so far have been at pains to set out the doctrinal points held in common and these are the bases of the joint statements. ARCIC, for example, stated that the sacrifice of Christ had been made once and this is a doctrinal affirmation which it claims to rest on the witness of the New Testament. Here is a clearly understandable statement vital to the Christian faith: would the church be Christian without this commitment to the centrality of the historical atonement of Calvary? A Christianity without a cognitive content understandable to the mind, like the chameleon changing colour on the leaf, becomes vulnerable to having the doctrinal void filled by the latest cultural secular bright idea in theological dress. Interpretations of the faith that cut away doctrinal content in fact smuggle in revelation in sieved, reduced form. Such a theological approach, like jealousy, 'mocks the meat it feeds on.' The church has its governing doctrinal core, however unacknowledged this may be. The writer is well aware that he is rowing against the stream in making this point, a point which goes back to the understanding of the scriptures as revealed fact and interpretation. This attracts considerable hostility from the more respectable and fashionable theological salons of the day. We cannot separate this issue from our understanding of the church and it cannot be avoided. The question of doctrinal authority in and over the church is part and parcel of ecclesiology.

Today's church in the West shows signs of exhaustion, despite pockets of clear bright light and life. The way, the truth and the life, each facet of the faith, seem in general depressingly pallid and dilute across the denominations. The church in a context of material well-being, in a context of mass education and apparently inevitable secularization, is often reduced to uttering shy, apologetic echoes of current social orthodoxy, while presiding pastorally over gradually diminishing congregations. The tired, cynical West can look to the newly evangelized and evangelizing African church for an example of hope and life, but also an example of sacrifice and faith under persecution. If the West needs to set her face towards the long march of renewing herself as the church, that march needs prior ecclesiological map work as part of setting a straight course in accord with the will of her head. If the exploding growth of the African church is to become secure for the future she too must set her compass and plot her course in order to indigenize the gospel in a catholic and apostolic way, and in order to cope with the inevitable intellectual challenges latent in the increasing spread of mass education across a continent whose soul Lenin and Mohammed are aggressively and intelligently seeking. Young churches in the third world will have to go through at least the intellectual and cultural fires endured by the western and must be theologically deep enough to withstand them.

Churches both old and young need desperately to dig into the treasure of the gospel and the Christian past in order to become renewed and established as visible, practical and as audible: we must aim to produce an ecclesiology of the word in the several theological senses belonging to that term. We must insist on the centrality of the Lord of the church, on Christ crucified and risen, the head of the covenant community indwelt by his Spirit and obedient to him; but also we must be aware of the fact that our knowledge of him cannot do without the witness of scripture with all its richness and roundedness. I believe that the apostolic interpretation of Jesus, taken with the vast testimony of the Old Testament, is sufficient for the church to sort out primary from secondary questions, while affirming the real importance of the secondary. I believe that there is a general tenor and shape to the message of the New Testament as a whole, as well as the now much emphasized diversity of expression and context. These documents naturally show signs of developing thought and practice, but not of self contradiction, and the current tendency seems often to rule out an appeal to scripture on the grounds of possible conflicting interpretations, as if the whole, overall, were thoroughly unclear. Such sceptical presuppositions need resisting in the church. The Anglican evangelical, pressed on both wings by his Anglo-Catholic and his Restorationist brethren, rightly disturbed by radical political claims for the poor, has rarely more needed to appraise the scriptures wisely and historically; and to appraise the use of scripture by such persuasive groups. But the heart of the evangelical method commits itself to reformation, to fresh explorations of scripture and correction of received traditional interpretation. Listening to the range of voices in the Christian family is vital to this process and we shall therefore seek to listen carefully and charitably before making our conclusions.

END NOTES TO THE INTRODUCTION

1. See *Churches Together in Pilgrimage* (CTS/BCC, London, 1989).
2. R. P. McBrien *Do We Need the Church?* (Harper and Row, Evanston, 1969) p. 23, quoting Barth *Evangelical Theology* p. 125.

1

THE HISTORICAL COMMUNITY OF CHRIST

The image of the olive tree, used for example in Paul's epistle to the Romans, will recur in our thinking on the nature of the church through the book. Paul in Romans combines the two themes which will be set out in this first chapter: the historical, continuing community and faith in Christ. Both together define the church. It is the shape of this combination which lies at the heart of ecclesiological debate and thought. This chapter will run through the outline of the problem before giving a review of how two great thinkers take up different ends of the combination and try to link them in a satisfactory way; these two will be the Nineteenth century English catholic John Henry Newman and the Swiss evangelical Karl Barth. They are men whose personal stories and theologies go hand in hand, and are probably the most formative minds for the catholic and evangelical wings for our century. They will serve as the best possible way in to our subject.

1. The olive tree

A. COMMON HISTORICAL ROOTS

All church people if asked would in some sense wish to claim an inheritance going back to the time of the apostles and to Jesus himself. Historically each Christian person owes his or her position as a member of the church to their preceding generation. In what particular sense this is true remains to be probed later. But in the widest and most general sense we would all say that a pre-existing historical tradition was handed on to us. A Roman Catholic or Greek Orthodox will perhaps see this very immediately and obviously: we were nurtured in the faith of our fathers by the mother church, from infancy we were taken into the sacramental system and taught the faith. But it is also true for the evangelical and indeed the liberal wings of the church. If we were converted to Christ as a result of the preaching of the gospel, that was a spiritual reality not reducible to purely historical cause and effect at all, but usually this will have been through someone who actually and historically did the preaching or the witnessing to Christ; or it may have been through reading a 'concrete historical' book of some kind, a text which will have an origin in the world of space and time. The person who witnessed, or the writer of the book, also received the gospel from some other identifiable source in the stream of time.

The witness to the gospel of God witnesses to Emmanuel, God with us. The witness comes to us in human historical conditions, concerning the God who revealed himself as a human being in a real place at a definite time in history. The testimony comes in space and time; we actually hear or see or touch or sense the contacting agent, usually personal, at a certain time in our life and in the life of the witnessing person. In this way the church, represented by this individual, has brought the saving gospel of Christ to us in many and various ways. For example it may, and certainly sometimes ought, to happen as a result of Christian people, the church, living out the gospel and drawing others to the Lord. The church serves as the indispensable visible and audible instrument for spreading faith in Christ. God works through the human and fallible efforts of his people, in and through the very particular circumstances of personal histories.

The church in the Soviet Union has demonstrated the power of both the Orthodox and Baptists, one church emphasizing its ancient and historic past, the other stressing the courageous witness to the word in the power of the Spirit. But the former is also spiritual and the latter is also audible, visible and historical. Both are tangible, real communities, with a past inheritance. Both refused to become silent and from both martyrs arise who are prepared to make the final sacrifice in order that the gospel be not rendered invisible and inaudible. The very meaning of martyrdom is of proclamation and witness, of refusal to be silenced, of death precisely for the highest possible profile of Jesus Christ. The martyr visibly and audibly witnesses to the universal gospel: privatized and purely inner, unexpressed, invisible, inaudible faith would not produce the martyrs known in all strands of Christianity. This point will be shown later to have relevance in the debate over the significance or otherwise of doctrine in Christian faith and church definition.

The fact that all groups of Christians can only trace their historical roots back in some way through conflicts, splits and expulsions does not cancel the historical links with their past. The Hutterite Brethren and the Mennonites, for example, will see themselves historically as being persecuted by the main denominations of the Reformation era; the Anglicans as having reformed the English church tradition; the Greek Orthodox as having been illegitimately put out of communion with Rome: the story of the church provides many examples. We are for the moment bracketing the question of the reasons for the parting of so many ways, the justifiability of these partings and the counter claims of denominations to 'legitimacy' as churches. Let us for the moment focus on the fact that all Christian groups, whether they stress the visible, institutional dimension or the invisible, spiritual dimension, all can trace their ancestry back and back to the very earliest Christian era. The way, the truth and the life has been handed on through time humanly and historically. No Christian group will settle for this as a sufficient definition of the church. Not only is it true for all denominations but for individuals that they have a past in the history of the faith once delivered to the saints, a pedigree transcending denominational bickering.

Let me repeat my plea for the reader's patience: I am not denying that individuals and denominations more importantly have their spiritual origin and background in the election and love of God, as the Epistle to the Ephesians tells us with such clarity. For the moment, however, the historical pedigree of all church people in the world is being emphasized. Indeed the unseen cloud of witnesses, the church now worshipping in glory, each one also has an earthly tale to tell of the way faith was begun and nurtured by fellow Christians around and before them in space and time. No church is pure spirit if it contains human beings, because we live in time; this is not just worldly common sense, but it is theologically given that mankind lives an earthly and historical life. The church can be likened to a tree with increasingly wide branches as it grows older: branches divide and re-divide but they all, even the tiniest twig, stem back to the trunk and common roots.

Whatever the disagreements between the branches, historically all come from the same stock. In discussing the relationship of ancient Israel with the church, Paul uses the picture of the olive tree, saying that the new believers, the Gentile Christians, were grafted into the old trunk as wild cuttings into a cultivated plant. He sees a deep continuity between the ancient people of Israel and the Messianic church: the one tree continues, but with the Gentiles brought into the ongoing history of the people of God. Paul agonizes over the mystery that the Jewish people are not accepting the Messiah Jesus, since this is the very destiny of the cultivated olive tree. Our point here is that the apostle interprets the church as one with Israel. The roots of the church must be acknowledged as going back, therefore, beyond the time of Pentecost and of Jesus, into the long history of the covenant between God and His ancient people. Christians stand in the tradition of Abraham and are children of promise, together constituting their vast array, as many as the sands on the sea shore or the stars in the heavens.

B. DIVIDED HISTORICAL BRANCHES

What we have said so far is purely descriptive. It describes the whole historical church in the most inclusively general and uncritical terms. In a way it simply states the problem: of course there are links back to the past, but what kinds of links are valid for defining the church? Clearly the synagogue, according to the picture just painted, would be included in the church; and perhaps the household of Islam also could count itself as an offshoot rooting back to the church and to the history of Israel. Purely historically connected bodies continue to proliferate on the edges of the tree: the Mormons, for example, stem from Christian beginnings, call their organization a church, and give some priority to Jesus Christ. How are we to proceed? Denominational groups today travel along pathways which go back to earlier forks in the road where decisions to part were taken for various reasons. Those reasons must form part of our discussion. We will try to take sections through the now great historical tree to get at what is going on inside and what is essential to its life.

But are we wholly mistaken to assume that the image of the single tree is a correct means for describing the historical church? Are there not many separate trees, and has this not always been the case? Historically even the one people of Israel split into North and South, a divide whose legacy in the New Testament writings we glimpse in John's Gospel chapter 4, with Jesus' encounter with the Samaritan woman at the well. She tells us that her tradition worshipped at Mount Gerizim whereas the Jews had their temple at Jerusalem. As for the Samaritans and the Jews, is the problem faced by the Christian faith not so much the plurality of churches as their hostility and non-acceptance of each other? Can we not be happy that there is a World Council of Churches which extends an invitation to all churches claiming to be Christian? Given the differences in the human race and national characteristics, are we not bound to expect differences between Christians and therefore between churches? Even inside the same denomination there will be a great range of belief and practice; many will have more in common with members of other denominations in terms of theology and style. There are bound to be enormous differences and contradictions within churches as well as between them. Why not settle for a multi-coloured ecclesiology and aim to be more fraternal one to another?

This question contains its own presupposed answer: if there are different churches rather than one church then why bother to seek fraternity unless, that is, there is a higher and prior norm which demands fraternity? Here we can no longer simply be descriptive, be content to describe the way the branches of the tree descend as a matter of historical cause and effect into a unified origin. Theology becomes essential. History alone leads us beyond description to interpretation of the description, and in particular to the tenor of the New Testament which cannot possibly be described as suggesting purely private, individual religion. The gospels and epistles presuppose a united church as the norm. Paul writes with several goals in mind, but one of them is to secure unity. Division in Christ is an abomination, an idea from which he recoils: is Christ divided? The reason why wars of Christian religion are so awful is that really the church is the church of Jesus Christ. Above and below the separations of the Christian denominations is the reality of the Lord of the church and his ever present Spirit. Violence upon the Donatists supported by the 'Catholics', the Eastern Greek Christians by the crusading Latins, the Anabaptists by the Reformers, such action makes us cover our eyes and ears not only for its general brutality but also because it offends the very idea of church, the idea for which the action was taken, since church inherently implies Jesus. The holocaust in this century, with the very mixed performances of the churches in that blasphemous obscenity, reminds us that we can cast no moralistic stones in terms of wars and persecutions, whatever our tradition. That we know such deeds contradict the essence of the church tells us already that deeper unity is the only possibility if the church is seeking to be the church, to live out its own way, truth and life. The church is not meant to fight internally, to be divided, any more than the gospel was ever to be spread by force of arms while remaining the gospel.

The church is the church of Jesus Christ and all individual Christians are united in him. This statement would be accepted today across the range of theological and denominational opinion. For Paul the church was the church united in Christ in the Holy Spirit, in all her diversity of gifts. The historical olive tree is in Christ and yet continually needs to be reminded, called back to that constant fact. The image of the vine in John's Gospel chapter 15 is used to spell out the union of the faithful in Christ as the essential core of spiritual life. It is this theological fact, rather than a humanistic summons to the fraternity of all mankind, which imposes upon us the need to work for visible reconciliation and to heal the wounds of history. The history of the self-understanding of the very earliest apostolic church takes us into the depths of the Christian gospel and its theological implications. Then the church wrestled with the unheard of fact that Gentiles were being grafted into the tree by faith, as the Holy Spirit moved outwards into universal humanity. What could have been an easier option than fraternal separation? This might have let the Hebrew believers have their group and the Gentiles theirs, which would have stopped the need for any debates or disputes over whether the Gentiles needed to be circumcised and be under the law. But it never occurred to either party in the debate to advocate fraternal separation into two camps, the Holy Spirit providing the bridge between different communities. Paul, in Galatians especially, showed that the implications of the gospel of grace freed the Gentiles from the Jewish law, since salvation was by faith in the Messiah. But the unity of all believers was also perceived to be another theological implication flowing from the death and resurrection of Christ and the coming of the Holy Spirit. The cross recreated humanity into 'one new man', as stated in Ephesians 2:15; violence and division were absorbed into the sacrifice of the suffering servant, the second Adam, the new beginning to humanity. Divisions in Christ therefore are a contradiction.

Jesus, the Messiah who brought in the kingdom of the end-time in his person, ushered into the old world of violent hatred the new order of love, in which the lion and the lamb lie down in peace. Selfishness, disobedience, bitterness and hard division within this new order are crimes against this new humanity and the apostles could not finally entertain fudging arrangements permitting friendly separation.

This point could be developed by linking salvation from sin achieved by the cross and resurrection, with the constitution of the new humanity and the spirit of the new man Jesus in the hearts of the new race, the church. Are the evangelicals correct in coming at the gospel so much in terms of 'Jesus Christ came into the world to save sinners', and to set that somewhat apart from the teaching of the new humanity formed in the second Adam, whose obedience made him the new head of a wholly new line of human existence, the church? As will be seen in the next chapter, theologians such as Michael Ramsey compel the evangelical to attend to the church in the gospel, and not as a second level doctrine.

The church, then, cannot for long be considered apart from the theological fact of the crucified and risen Christ at her centre, the heartbeat of her history. Gospel and church distort when barriers are set up within the church again after the cross has removed them. Such behaviour betrays the Lord who not only broke bread and fish to feed all, but gave his own body to be broken for all. When the church strays from her Lord's ambit she is less the church, and this was so in the apostolic age, right back, for example, to Peter's confession, and his denial, of Jesus seen in Mark 8:29 and 14:66.

C. INGRAFTING INTO THE GREAT CHURCH

New Testament writers, working out practically the truth of the saving gospel of the Father, Son and Holy Spirit, reject today's situation of varying degrees of mutual lack of fellowship among churches. The section through our historical tree of the church reveals that its core of life is Christ. The community is the community of Christ. But history remains world history and the people of God live historically, not free from sin nor error, despite structural arrangements that have been tried to insure against them. The church historically has performed what is impossible theologically and split apart the one new man. This makes a definition of the church in terms of the two clear aspects so far identified, that of the one historical tree and that of the inner core, which is Christ who forms the new humanity, a paradox and a contradiction. The fall has entered into the world of the church, and things are out of joint. It is often said on the catholic wing that the church is best described as a mystery.[1] I beg to differ and to call her a contradiction! In this respect at least, and it is no minor matter, the church is constantly called to bring her own true self into being.

The problem of a modern definition of the church, taking account of the realities of past history as well as theological norms from the scriptures, lies in relating the invisibly present Lord to the history of the church as denominational churches. That there is one church, 'the great church', is agreed: how to formulate this united church is not. The church from the divine standpoint is definable as the company of the faithful, those who truly are in covenant with God. Among all the churches and outside them are the truly spiritual Christ-centred people of God. This may be despite the ministrations of the churches. The historical churches are not identical with those known of the Lord. 'The ecclesia is just as ambiguous a phenomenon' comments Bultmann of the testimony of the New Testament, 'as the cross of Christ: visible as a worldly fact, invisible—yet to the eye of faith also visible—as a thing of the world to come.'[2] The church has this double aspect.

Yet the 'earthly' church, to use crude shorthand, is no optional extra for any Christian, and this view deeply mistakes the basic character of Christianity. As was pointed out descriptively at the start of the chapter, a Christian has a past and future of an historical and spiritual kind which are not easily divorced, so now theologically it can be shown that the spiritual birth and life of the Christian is inseparable from membership of the church, of the Body of Christ, the community of the Spirit. The two events are simultaneous, are a single spiritually historical reality.

Here the Anglo-Catholic theologian R. C. Moberly was correct in his reply to Edwin Hatch around the turn of the century, when he rejected Hatch's notion that the early church was primarily a voluntary association of Christian individuals who might prefer to remain out of the church. Moberly comments: 'When he says, "There were many who stood apart: and there were many reasons for doing so", the first thing we want to be told is "Were there ever any who were *allowed to* stand apart? Were there, or could there have been, any *lawful or adequate* reasons for their doing so?"' 'He adds', continues Moberly, '"A man might wish to be Christ's disciple and yet to shrink from hating father and mother and wife and children and brethren and sisters, yea and his own life also". Of course he might. But Dr. Hatch does not say a word as to whether he might *legitimately* so wish. Still less does he make a point of reminding us that in these very words which he is in fact quoting, Christ himself had laid down long before sub-apostolic times, that upon such conditions a man "cannot be my disciple."'[3]

These remarks seem justified. The church, the ecclesia of the New Testament, both in the historical and the doctrinal passages, does not seem to be a nice organization to join so much as a God-given body in which we are privileged to share, into which we are elected by the grace of God; the body for which Christ died and at whose centre he stands. The church's unity is, putting it crudely, 'from above' first and foremost, by the activity of God's saving work. Moberly was an influential and polemical Anglo-Catholic thinker of great subtlety, but his point about the unity of the church as a New Testament theological and historical fact would be agreed on by evangelicals across the denominations. The quotation from Bultmann above has already shown that the church was the end-time community of the Spirit for the apostolic writers. One of the finest British evangelical minds of the century explicitly takes the same line as Moberly against Hatch. P. T. Forsyth, in what is a sadly neglected book outside the Free Church constituency, states the case with his usual clarity and force: 'The ecclesia was the gathering of a *people*; Hort . . . makes this quite clear. It was not in the nature of a club, guild, or association. Hatch's line has not been adopted. It was the New Testament Israel, the Israel of God in Christ, (Galatians 6:2), the New Testament *people* of God, the landless nation, God's vis-a-vis for the new age as Israel was for the old. It was the New Covenant people, resting, not on an act of association, but on a divine call and corporate creation. It was Christendom. It was the assembly of all Christians with God and before God.'[4]

Forsyth teaches that the church of the New Testament is the one great church, the unique reconstitution of Israel under the hand of the Lord. God created a people: 'Once you were no people, now you are God's people' says Paul to the Gentile Christians in Rome, using the words of the prophet Hosea (Romans 9:25). Even the glimmerings of a grasp of this would revitalize church life across the denominations in the West, in all its coldly secular individualism. It is not that Christians *feel* warmth and oneness one with another as one people in their local or national church life, although that is the ideal subjective state for church members. Rather it is an objective truth that we are in Christ as one spiritual community, that this is given and we must live accordingly, seeking to make real this spiritual fact in the realm of our hearts and minds, our homes and cities and communities.

Individual Christians then, in belonging to Christ, belong inseparably to the church: they are his, his church. In the New Testament, local groupings are also called churches, the church that meets in the house of a local Christian, for example. Forsyth convincingly states the relationship of local churches to the universal church when he says that the local church is not primarily the empirical, social grouping of individuals: 'It means not the group there but the one community of faith everywhere which crops out there.' This rests on the fact that where two or three are gathered together Christ is in the midst of them (Matt 18:20), not in such a way that three believers make up *a* church 'but that where there are three such people there is *the* church, that three with Christ draw thither spiritually the whole church.'[5] Forsyth's language of the local church as the outcrop of the one great church catholic is clear and helpful; this seems to be the way the writers of the New Testament envisage the matter. Earlier in his book he asks us to imagine that we are strangers from another country visiting Cambridge. The visitor, after viewing the colleges, then asks to see the University. He is puzzled to be told that it is not the Senate House, not the Library, not the Lecture Halls. Nor is it the collection of the colleges and other offices. 'It has a personality of its own; it is not a mere group, or sum, or amalgam. It has a history, a tradition, a life, a power, a spell, which is not simply the added-up history and influence of the colleges. To the curious stranger you cannot show the University—which yet is Cambridge. Who can deny the University? It is a great reality, a great spiritual reality, in which its colleges inhere. It gives the colleges their true value. It is that which they serve. It is the one spiritual corporation in which the palpable sodalities of the colleges hold together. It dignifies them all. It is the mother of them all from above.'[6]

The church is properly seen as one church with many local manifestations, not so much an amalgam of individuals who have contracted in, as a living organism whose life is given to its members rather than drawn from them. The first chapter of the Epistle to the Ephesians testifies to this view of the church, emphasizing the heavenly origin of the church of Jesus Christ. By grace Christians are chosen, thrown into, find themselves in, the church. They have this 'thrust upon them' in the mercy of God. Being in Christ in the church, is all of grace. In reviewing our spiritual experience we can perceive the grace of God leading us to himself, never apart from the church. D. M. Baillie's great book *God Was In Christ* spells out this 'paradox of grace': human decision and activity are really and fully involved in our spiritual walk at every point, and yet the paradox is that as we look back we see that it was the grace of God going before us which was most ultimately responsible for such decision and activity. This is a deeply moral paradox since we attribute our sinful deeds and thoughts, says Baillie, to ourselves alone: we trace them down an earth wire back to our own hearts; but the good we do as Christians we attribute to the grace of the Lord, and this is the paradox. 'By the grace of God I am what I am, and his grace toward me was not in vain. On the contrary I worked harder than any of them, though it is not I, but the grace of God which is with me.'[7]

This Pauline teaching rings true in our own Christian experience. We can apply this to our doctrine of the church as we consider the nature of the connection between the great church and the individual, and further of the connection between the church in its local manifestations and the individual. It would be the ecclesiological version of the Pelagian heresy to regard the church as an optional society which might help my personal spiritual life, which I as a Christian am therefore free to take seriously or not. Just as Pelagianism taught that humanity saves itself by its own moral uprightness arising from the unaided will of the individual, so to see our participation in the church as a choice which is left to our own discretion is to miss the point of divine grace. We are grafted into the church as the shoots are grafted into the olive tree. Not only is that so, but the Holy Spirit has given gifts for the upbuilding of the whole church, and to fail to participate in the life of the church is to bury talent, to lack faith in oneself as a child of God as well as to disobey the thrust of the teaching of the apostles.

It is not for us to decide whether or not to 'join' the church. As Christians we are already in the church of God and, as Moberly protested to Hatch, failing here is a grave fault in discipleship, something to grieve the Holy Spirit. The New Testament has no idea of believers coolly deciding whether to join as they might a useful organization or club. The notion of a voluntary contract springing from the mind and will of the individual is foreign to the vision of the eschatological ecclesia of God, meaning the end-time community of those decisively 'called out'. The church, following the meaning of the New Testament term ecclesia, are those called out, called from darkness into light. Once they were 'no people', now they are God's people. This is crucial for apostolic ecclesiology. It was true for Israel of old as for the ecclesia of the New Testament, both Jew and Gentile. Grace, the merciful act of God, is prior to our decision, and this applies ecclesiologically: the church is a God-given reality in which it is our destiny to share. The 'you' of the New Testament Epistles is always plural, and their language of election expresses this very point about divine calling of the person into the one end-time community, the church, as we see, for example, in Ephesians 1, Romans 8 and 1 Peter.

The theological fact of the one great, catholic church into which we as individuals are grafted of undeserved grace as we receive Christ, relates not only to the local churches which manifest the church, but to their state of being split into denominations that were apparently unknown in the apostolic age. The branches themselves, in Paul's image of the olive tree, were the Gentile believers as a whole and not several denominational groupings. The message Paul addressed to the Christians in Rome applies therefore all the more powerfully to us in our fragmented state:

> 'But if some of the branches were broken off, and you a wild olive shoot were grafted in their place to share the richness of the olive tree, do not boast over the branches. If you do boast remember that it is not you that support the root, but the root that supports the branches. You will say, "Branches were broken off so that I might be grafted in." That is true. They were broken off because of their unbelief, but you stand fast only through your faith. So do not become proud, but stand in awe. For if God did not spare the natural branches, neither will he spare you.' Romans 11:17 ff.

The fact of being part of the structure of the historical tree was not enough to prevent part of Israel 'being broken off' and the fact of being in historical continuity alone will no more prevent the same happening to the Gentile church and, all the more, to the Gentile church in the form of one of its fragmented parts. Interestingly, Paul clearly teaches in his parable that the tree itself existed before the Messianic community of Jesus; it is not that a completely new tree has been planted, the old one having been destroyed. Israel continues in the community of faith, whether Jew or Gentile. The Old Testament often portrays a picture of the faithful within the whole people of Israel, in particular of the remnant faithful to the God of Israel. Forsyth pithily has it that 'no one can be saved by a denomination as such, but only by what Church there is in it',[8] echoing Paul in the passage from Romans just quoted. The church is the church of God through history, and she cleaves to her Lord by faith and obedience. Reliance on the formal institution alone is failing to be the church and risks the judgement of God.

This corresponds with a motif found in the Old Testament, that of the Lord's disconcerting habit of allowing the most sacred items of the Israelite religious life to be captured or destroyed: the Ark of the Covenant for example was taken by the Philistines, the city of Jerusalem with the Temple itself was taken and sacked twice, the people of the Northern Kingdom were carried into exile and never returned. Often this was associated with unfaith: the people failed to obey their Lord and became complacent, coming to rely on their historic status and cultic artefacts rather than on the Lord, to whom they were intended to point. The result was a lesson in true faith and destruction of what displaced the Lord from central worship. This can happen to the evangelical in terms of replacing the Lord with an idea, however true that idea may be, in particular the idea of justification by faith; when it is severed from the ongoing relationship with the living Christ then it is a form of idol and hardens the heart away from its personal source and goal. The Ark of the Covenant was the God-given aid to worship and assurance for Israel, but in and of itself it was dispensable. Justification and the Bible are even more vital gifts of God, but they are not ends in themselves: it is unbiblical to think that they are. Likewise the structures and forms and pedigrees of the church, let alone any one denomination, are means and not ends. Isolated from the giver these gifts will wither in the recipient, and the branch will be broken off.

The picture of the vine and the branches in John's Gospel is not so different after all from from Paul's parable of the olive tree. The pressing need is for real personal faith, holding fast to Christ within the historical church. But it seems foreign to biblical thought to pit faith against the historical community as alternatives. John's Gospel seems to come closest to this possibility in such passages as Jesus' statement that true worship after his ministry will be in spirit and in truth, freed from geographical location at the Temples of Jerusalem or Mount Gerizim; and the insistence that God can raise up sons of Abraham from the very stones in the absence of true faith among the people of Israel, the natural sons of Abraham. For John emphasizes the fact that what is born of the flesh is flesh and what is born 'from above' of the Spirit is spiritual. In John's Gospel the words from the cross and the post-resurrection Jesus' commands to fish and to shepherd the flock show that an historical living community from the people of Israel is wholly intended, rather than an individualist religion of pure spirit, a community bound to the Lord by the Spirit in faith.

2. Historical process and the risen Christ: Newman and Barth

Are we left with a contradiction? On the one hand we have seen that the real, historical community is the church with a very long ancestry indeed, and on the other hand that the church is herself as she abides faithfully in the vine, which is Christ. Another contradiction is that we have concluded that there is a church, the great church, the people of God down the centuries and yet there are many separate churches, denominational branches rather than individuals grafted into the old stock. If the church is historical and if it is one then where is it to be found? Where can we visit this church? Can we be sure that our particular denomination is part of the one great church? Is it 'Christian' to break away and set up a new church? Down the centuries these questions have prompted some of the major theological suggestions in the history of Christian thought, and distinctive families of view have developed.

Sykes uses three basic models to clarify the nature of 'the identity of Christianity' in its 'inner' and 'outer' dimensions. These may be helpful to us in clarifying interpretations of the relationship between the inward and the outward aspects of the church. These models, which correspond quite closely to important options in models of the church, can serve as useful markers for discussion. As Sykes says, these types or models do not provide solutions to the key issue of the relationship of the spiritual and formal aspects of being the church; his types do, however, ensure that the key issues are raised and that major theological efforts at treating them are taken seriously. They also ensure that we will not divorce theological essentials of Christianity from our consideration of the church.[9]

The 'foundation-superstructure' model sees the base of the church in early doctrinal and ministerial fundamentals, to which she must refer back for her authority and on which she builds. This model teaches a spiritual golden age of the apostles as the authoritative yardstick for today's church and the pedigree with which she proceeds on her path into history with the correct means of grace. The second type on Sykes' list, 'the spirit-body' model, relates the inner to the outer in the more dynamic manner of the living organism. Invisible, spiritual life fuses with the bodily, visible, institutional church. Growth and development play an important part in this model, providing its great strength for interpreting the ongoing changes in the life and thought of the church. This development in time resembles the development of a human person, for whom the soul and body are not separable. The third type is the 'centre–circumference' model, and this takes up the theme that the church is most truly the church when and where her heart is closest to her Lord; the church and her Lord are more definitely distinguished by this model, or at least the focus is on their covenant relationship rather than their identification. These models state the problem in different ways, rather than providing solutions, and it will be instructive to follow the grain of two great church thinkers as they wrestled with these issues and models in their personal pilgrimages, pilgrimages which have influenced ecclesiology very much in this century.

A. JOHN HENRY NEWMAN 1801–90

Firstly a figure vital to the formation of the contemporary Roman Catholic position will help us appraise the contradiction, tension or paradox between the spiritual and the historical, as well as, and at the same time as, that between the one church and the several denominations. John Henry Newman's view of the church travels from an early evangelical faith, through a high church Anglican phase and finally into an anticipation of a modern Roman Catholic position.

As a Tractarian Anglican, Newman believed, along with the

Oxford Movement, that the Church of England was a middle way between the Protestant and the Roman churches, a middle way which represented the true church. He held, at that time, a version of what Sykes called the 'foundation-superstructure' model. The Oxford Movement rejected Protestantism on the grounds that it failed to use the first four hundred years of church life and doctrine, the crucial era of filling out the interpretation of Christ and the scriptures. The Reformation, in its concentration on scripture as the supreme norm for faith, had cut itself off from the twin source of truth, the early tradition. Therefore the Protestant churches of the West were not, it was argued, authentically part of the historic great church, they lacked catholicity, the authenticity of the one historic church, in their teaching and also in having broken with the line of consecrated bishops coming from the very early church.

But at the other extreme the Roman church was also defective, although she was in continuity with the line of duly appointed bishops, because she had added considerably to the apostolic and patristic teaching and practice of the early church. Roman medieval beliefs and customs formed a shell of distortion around the pearl of pure early catholic Christianity. Anglicanism was a middle way between Protestant and Roman extremes, based on scripture and early tradition.

But Newman increasingly came to doubt this position. He looked about him in the Church of England and saw conflicting theological and liturgical views and customs where he wanted to find clear, authoritative catholic doctrine. His own opinions were publicly refuted by Anglican bishops. His theological interpretation of the Church of England seemed increasingly to be artificial and unreal, not corresponding to the facts on the ground in parishes up and down the country. In marked contrast, when he visited the continent of Europe he was deeply impressed at the extent of a uniform pattern of Roman Catholicism and its hold on the lives of ordinary working people. Here was a universal faith across geographical and social borders.

As he studied and explored Roman Catholicism, Newman felt that his own spiritual life deepened. This blending of the moral or spiritual with the intellectual is recognized as a feature of Tractarian thought and is clearly present in this crucial phase of his reflections.[10] He was a master of the history and doctrine of the patristic writers and continued to mull over these with his piercingly logical catholic mind. Newman was shifting his ground and coming to, what was for him, an inescapable change of heart. His Anglicanism of the middle way was untenable. It did not work in theory or in practice. He was searching for the church which was sure of her identity as the authoritative catholic and apostolic church, the place where he could confidently rest his soul, secure in the knowledge that it was the one church of Christ. There had to be a church which was the one church, since Christianity spiritually and doctrinally was one faith. His heart was restless until it could find its rest and security in the one concretely real church. Only then and there would he have the absolute ground for an absolutely certain faith.

Newman, then, required an existing historical church to equate with the great church. Both his heart and his head told him that it was to be found in the Roman Church. He was received into the Roman Church in 1845 and wrote his most well known work to explain himself to his Tractarian friends from whom he was parting. His task was to show why he had changed his mind about Rome and specifically why the Tractarian objections to Roman additions to the faith were fallacious. The massively influential notion which he brought to bear on the issue was that of development. The title of his book was *An Essay on the Development of Christian Doctrine: an hypothesis to account for a difficulty*. After rejecting the Protestant, biblically based, position as untenable and contradictory in view of the conflicts of fact and interpretation which he perceived in the canon of scripture, he skilfully attacked the weak point of the Tractarian, or Anglo-Catholic, position in a critique which has been much admired by its recipients but never seriously answered. The simple question he put to them was to ask why the first four centuries of Christian tradition should constitute a normative block of teaching. What criteria were used to select only this block of tradition rather than a longer span of time? Newman rejected the very notion of scribing a line at any particular point in the historical development of the tradition in order to gain an authoritative section of dogmatic interpretation. Such a procedure was merely arbitrary. The old foundation-superstructure model would not serve its purpose, since it was impossible to define a separable foundation era.

Newman proposed a different understanding of developing normative tradition to enable him to identify the true church as coming through the ornate Roman ecclesiastical evolution. He moved to a very organic, biological model of the church and her authenticity. Instead of the long held Roman Catholic and Anglo-Catholic model of a church built on the solid rock of its foundational apostolic ministry and teaching, enshrined in the Bible and interpreted by the early creeds and councils, a church whose teaching and practice was *'semper eadem'*, always the same, he adopted the model of a spirit filled, living organism growing through time. Whereas the old model stressed the fixity of the faith and order, the new one stresses the inevitability of living development. Christianity is an 'idea' which evolves in time with its historical form. Developments, for the earlier type of view, were acknowledged as logical deductions from the given premises of the early centuries; for Newman's modern view, development is more historical in character. A development is not simply logical outworking of what was given earlier.

His coup is to take the apparently hostile phenomenon of historical change in doctrine and turn it into an ally of faith. To try to stay exactly the same is really misguided and unhistorical, it ends up by fulfilling a death wish of being 'set in amber' or fossilized. If we are speaking of any living beings or societies, to remain the same involves adaptation and change.[11] Newman endeavours to couple the historic faith to the train of modernistic historical thought, in an effort to overcome the severe problems posed by such thought to the classical static foundational models of church doctrine. He moves from the idea of logical ground and consequent deduction to that of historical cause and effect; or rather he seeks to run these two ways of thinking together.

Lash, a Roman Catholic commentator, correctly states the change involved: 'Criteriologically there is indeed a shift of emphasis from the normative function of antiquity to that of the living voice today.'[12] From the fixed foundational type of catholic system, Newman shifted to an evolutionary historicist type of model. The Roman church could not validly defend itself from charges of adding to the patristic deposit of faith by appealing back to the early centuries as if they constituted an available yardstick. It was undeniable that big changes had taken place as the church entered the middle ages and customs unknown to the apostles or the first centuries of tradition had become official Roman dogma. But he argued that changes were only natural and to be expected in Christianity as it filled itself out and developed into full bloom. The Holy Spirit was promised to lead the church of Christ into all truth. Newman envisaged the true church to be the historical organ of the Spirit, developing in many ways and senses under the hand of God and indwelt by the Spirit as she walked through history. There was only one church and therefore only one true belief system, 'we must have a whole doctrine stated by a whole Church.'[13] The church was the infallible guide, the definitive interpreter of revelation.[14]

The church guarantees what is a true doctrinal development by way of her teaching office. One would expect an infallible interpreter to be provided providentially, and the Papacy, a final arbiter, is therefore a natural development out of the whole college of bishops. The church develops her doctrine through the minds of her theologians whose work is then validated or rejected by the official episcopal and papal office. The Spirit continually breathes through this process of the church's reflection on the revelation given her to keep and interpret. The organic, historical church provides the living voice today which we can consult for firm guidance. Only in the Roman church is there unity of teaching in developmental continuity down the ages. Newman argued that what he had formerly taken to be exotic superstitious ideas in the Roman church were in reality proper and natural developments from the earliest days of the church. One must choose from among all the denominations which is in line with the one great church, and of all the claimants the one whose face has the family resemblance with the ancient church, and can best claim the pedigree, is the Roman face.

For Newman there can be only one church which itself is the great church. The physical, historical and social reality of this church is the Spirit-breathed catholic and apostolic church. Other bodies are splinter groups and all in error in some way or other. The fullness of catholicity is in the Roman communion only. Like a great tree in full leaf, with all the richness of its colours and blossom, Roman Catholicism is properly developed Christianity. Like any living idea, Christianity will continue to grow and fill out as time goes on. The Roman church is the divine society governed by the successors of the apostles, 'As creation argues continual governance,so are Apostles harbingers of Popes.'[15] Historical development, to meet naturally arising church needs, coupled with argument from analogy, gives Newman his method.

Newman's position expresses an evolutionary spirit-body model. For him the spirit indwells the church, the historical

Roman church. The continuing instititutional church is inherently spiritual; the Holy Spirit works through the 'prophetic' office of the church, giving fresh, living interpretations of the faith for today. The 'episcopal' office of the church possesses the gift of discerning which prophetic theological insights are correct and authentic. The spiritual and the institutional, the prophetic and the official, unite in the divine society, as the spirit breathes life in the body.

Newman then envisages one spiritually historical church, one tree of faith and one alone, identifiable as the Roman church. There true grace and authority are fully to be found. In this theory providence unites with grace to produce an organic revelatory and saving stream of embodied, sacramental, ecclesial history.

B. KARL BARTH 1886–1968

Barth's life, like Newman's, represents a theological story of enormous importance. The careers of both were conditioned in a remarkable way by their theology, and their theology in turn has had great impact on the Christian church. The story of Barth's theological development forms an essential component in a theological education, and although it has probably been repeated unnecessarily often in theological texts, yet its relevance to the doctrine of the church has not fully been brought out, except at times by Barth's Roman Catholic dialogue partners.

Barth was born in 1886 into the family of a Swiss Reformed pastor. After a theological education imbuing him with anti-supernaturalist theology, he was ordained and took pastoral charge of Safenwil, a small Swiss village. Here he began to question his liberalism and to seek God's majesty and transcendence. He wished to recover the God who reigns in unknowable otherness and judges the earth. Barth moved from a position founded on human reason or feeling to one trying to base itself on God's grace and revelation coming to fallen humanity. But Barth succeeded in re-establishing the transcendence of God so much, in his *Romans* of 1922,[16] that he ended up with a God who was out of contact with humanity. It was the classical understanding of the incarnation of God's Son which enabled Barth to reunite God and creation without, this time, defining divinity only in terms of human ethics, religion, or reason.

Barth's theological journey is well charted in many books,

perhaps Nicholls[17] gives one of the most vivid portrayals. He describes the plight of the pastor, expected to bring the word of God to the people Sunday by Sunday, but left by the dominant liberal tradition with only the word of man. From here he moved to a position which acknowledged the objective reality of the sovereign Lord who does break in to address man in an act of grace.

Barth, in other words, moved into a type of evangelicalism, stressing Christ's coming to the believer, and the Holy Spirit imparting Christ to us as we adopt a worshipful, obedient and faithful attitude. Our knowledge of God comes from the miracle of grace. The objective reality of revelation is Christ, the subjective reality of revelation, our human apprehension of Christ, is the Holy Spirit, without whom we could not begin to relate to God. Knowing God is knowing the supreme Lord and nothing less. Theology and church have to circle around God's revelation in Christ, and not around the dubious products of human cultural effort. The church is the community formed by the Word becoming flesh and must listen to him. Theology must adjust its methods to its object, God. But this object really is the subject who searches our hearts and minds, and the only proper way of thinking about this object is prayer, worship and obedience.

Barth developed his theology in the light of the unique revelation of Jesus Christ, but saw this not in individualistic terms so much as in church terms. His first effort at a systematic theology was called *Christian Dogmatics*, 1927, but he deliberately revised this title to *Church Dogmatics* for his major classical work. That is, he wanted to do theology from within the community of faith in Christ. The church is the community which worships God in Christ in the power of the Spirit.

The church defines herself by finding herself defined by Christ, the constant centre of her being. The normative witness to him are the canonical prophets and apostles, who point us to him by their written testimony. As we attend to their voices in faith and expectancy, the Holy Spirit brings the message to life and we receive the living Word. 'God has sent the Spirit of His Son into our hearts whereby we cry "Abba, Father!"' Barth insists that the church must take the witness to Christ by the apostles as utterly binding. God has guaranteed to bring himself, in his living Word Jesus, by his Spirit to humanity through the scriptures and through the proclamation of the church as it is based on these normative scriptures. The Word forms, informs and reforms its community, the church.

Since God is the sovereign Lord, he can and may mediate himself to people through other means: 'If the question what God can do forces theology to be humble, the question what is commanded of us forces it to concrete obedience. God may speak to us through Russian Communism, a flute concerto, a blossoming shrub, or a dead dog. We do well to listen to Him if He really does. But unless we regard ourselves as the prophets and founders of a new church, we cannot say that we are commissioned to pass on what we have heard as independent proclamation.'[18] The church lives by Jesus Christ, measures her proclamation by the message of the prophets and apostles, the Old and New Testaments, and proclaims this gospel. This witness forms a tangible, visible authority at the very centre of the church. As she proclaims Christ according to the written word, the church becomes a form of the word, bringing the living Word himself to humanity. In this ministry she always depends on God's action by the Holy Spirit.

The three mutual elements, the revealed Word, the proclaimed word of the church, and the scriptural written word, coalesce under God to bring revelation to us. The first, the living Christ, is served by the other two, which point to Christ. Proclamation and Bible serve Jesus Christ, they come to life as the elements in the triangular relationship unite dynamically to bring human beings to a knowledge of God in Christ. This happens when God so ordains and faith responds.

The Bible functions along the lines of eucharistic reception, as taught by Calvin and Cranmer, according to which we 'feed on him in our hearts by faith with thanksgiving' as we receive the bread and the wine. Likewise the text of scripture is the visible medium through which Christ comes to the faithful heart. Barth gives the church a higher priority than some seem to realize. She supplies the voice of witness to Christ today and so becomes a 'form of the threefold word'. Yoked to the Word, she exists as the visible community to speak of Jesus and live for him in history. Christ, the living Word, defines the church.

Barth launched penetrating criticisms of the liberal and the Roman Catholic positions in expounding his theology of the Word. He brands both as guilty of the same kind of error, one on the left of the church and the other on the right. That error was to cut free from revelation and replace the divine Word with human experience or human religious practices. Liberal theology had refused to acknowledge the objective revelation given in Christ, through the scriptures, preferring instead to focus on human possibilities, whether rational, ethical, aesthetic or pietistic. These high human ideals, argued Barth, are distilled into the divine.The liberal approach displaces attention from the objective word to what is only human.

Roman Catholicism, on the right wing, commits the same kind of error exalting ritual and cult, a humanly developed phenomenon, and identifying this with the revelation of God. For Barth, the Roman religion is the 'naturalization of grace', the domestication of God by hierarchy, ritual and various kinds of sacramental system. Barth has argued with great power that our religious intuitions and cults must be submitted to the judgement of the word of God. Ecclesial tradition does not stand exempt from this scrutiny.

The rise of Nazism tested Barth's Christological doctrine of the church. Barth fiercely rejected the theological infiltration of anti-semitic Nazi doctrines of creation ordinances into the German churches. The sharp focus on Christ as the centre of the church provided a clear criterion with which to judge the Nazi German church. Alien bacteria were being injected into the Body of Christ, and his condemnation of that alien theology eventually cost Barth his Professorship in Germany and led to his expulsion to his native Switzerland. Christ as Lord: this was the very centre, the heart of the church and her faith. Barth's summons lay behind a minority Christian protest, the Barmen Declaration of 1934. This served as a rallying call for the relatively few Christians of any denomination who would listen. Barth and Barmen summoned the church away from any treaty with poisonous racist ideas incompatible with Christ's gospel. The Barmen Declaration became an important basis for the small 'Confessing Church', the movement often associated with Bonhoeffer and his resistance to Nazism. This was the context of the rather bitter debate Barth had with Emil Brunner, also Swiss, over the capacity of 'natural man', unaided by grace, to receive knowledge of God. Barth, all too mindful of the consequences in Nazi Germany of admitting any such 'natural' capacity outside of the grace of Christ, took a sharply hostile view of natural theology and its potential.

This brings us back to Sykes's models of the identity of Christianity. The model of the 'centre and the circumference' appears to be essentially what Barth taught, and this Christocentric model had a great strength in the Nazi era. When the church is faced with crisis, heresy, confusion and persecution, the message that Christ, God and man, constitutes the church as the church judges and clarifies the situation. When the Nazi pressure was on the church, where was the 'true' church? Where was the church truly the church, or most truly so? The answer seems to be where it was clinging most closely to Christ, her true centre, in an obedient and costly way. Where her witness to the gospel was faithful, there at that time was a true outcrop of the church of Jesus Christ; there the great church was manifest in the tiny minority of Christians, and manifest under the cross of Christ in suffering witness. The church was and is most clearly and really herself when concentrating on the centre, drawing teaching and strength from her heartbeat. This is Barth's 'Christocentric' view of the church's being.

Throughout Christian history persecution has drastically influenced understandings of the church. The Roman Empire required its citizens to toss a pinch of incense into the fire beneath the pagan statue of the emperor god. Were those who conformed, and for the sake of peace formally went through these motions of allegiance to emperor worship, to be accepted as inside the church? Was holding fast to the good confession, that Jesus is exclusively the Lord, all that important? Was a silent, purely mental assent to the gospel sufficient, under hostile interrogation? The book of Revelation is very rarely taken into account by current ecclesiological writers, although many African and Soviet Christians, for example, will even now be able to testify to its relevance in time of oppression. The opening letters to the seven churches are inescapably clear in their challenge to compromising and lukewarm churches. The summons is to hear the judgement of the Lord of the church on the church, the call to move closer again to the centre, back to the strength of the first love. Being committed to the inner heart of the church, however, cannot mean only a commitment which remains 'inside' privately; the word must also be audible from the church in, and at times against, the world.

The church is the church of Jesus Christ, and when other loyalties blur this focal point of reference, then the church somehow becomes less than the 'great church' and is merely a religious association. Barth reacted so acerbically to Brunner, over the possibility of natural man being able to say something about God outside the revelation in Christ, because he saw so clearly how importations into theology from outside the gospel can produce terrible distortions of the faith, can lead the church into foreign and evil bondage, can unchurch the church by tearing her away from her centre.

Barth insisted that the centre of the church is not the church's possession but her possessor and master. The Lord of the church speaks to the church and the church witnesses, proclaims not herself but Christ. The heard word, rather than the seen institution, forms the main burden of this ecclesiological understanding. The church listens and proclaims on the basis of what she hears. It seems untrue that this view of the church is that of the invisible church only. Sight is only one of the senses, hearing is another, and language is a fashionable sociological category. The church is the *church audible*, voicing the message of Christ, the kerygma, the martyr, or witnessing, church.

Avery Dulles classifies Barth's model as 'the church as herald', and, for Dulles, it fails to do justice to the ongoing historical, physical church as a reality.[19] Certainly Barth and the word models of the church work with the idea of the repeated event of Christ's presence to and with the church as she awaits in faith the guaranteed comings of her Lord. Is the church still the church as she prays in faith and expects the renewing presence of Christ? Von Balthasar, a leading Roman Catholic interpreter, neatly comments that in Barth's thought the church is the body of Christ but not sufficiently the bride of Christ.[20] Is the church always fully constituted as the chosen partner through history, come good times and bad? Theologically Barth replies to this charge, of what is technically called 'occasionalism', by saying that his evangelical hold on the reality of justification by grace through faith means that for him the church is never out of the covenant. The circumference-centre model, while pressing the speech of the Word to the church, does not necessarily unchurch the church pending this speech. The word of God is objectively available and the church, echoing this word, is ever to conform herself to the word, to Christ, as she looks and speaks outwards from herself to the world. The word model of the church therefore is not necessarily pietistic and inward looking as a kind of soul culture. The centre is not properly understood as invisible and therefore inaccessible. The gospel word is quite concrete and available, which is why this notion of the church proved to be an important theological corrective and rallying point against the Nazi infiltration.

Barth's theological contribution, according to Sykes, is a radical example of the 'inwardness tradition'.[21] Christ, this inner reality, gives life to the outer, visible structures of the church. 'In everything that we have to say concerning the Christian community and Christian faith we can only move within the circle that they are founded by the Holy Spirit and therefore that they must be continually refounded by Him, but that the necessary refounding by the Holy Spirit can consist only in a renewal of the founding which He has already accomplished . . . and where He is really expected, where there is a desire to receive Him, that is the work He has already begun, the infallible sign of His presence.'[22] The church cannot be defined in terms of the normal distinction between event and being, act and essence, the static and the dynamic: these differences are overcome in the continual miracle and mercy of her existence. God is not subject to such philosophical classifications and distinctions. The Word constitutes the church invisibly and visibly since the Word has a twofold character: the living Christ and the written word, collected and handed down as the Bible which is the visible basis of the visible church. Barth therefore finds the formulation of the Augsburg Confession satisfactory: 'The Church is the assembly of believers in which the gospel is taught in all its purity, and the sacraments administered,'[23] familiar to Anglicans as part of their understanding of the church visible, stated in article 19 of the Thirty Nine Articles.

This brings out the main thrust of Barth's position as a restatement of an evangelical ecclesiology resting on the word and the priority of divine grace. Roman Catholic theologians have found it presents the church as an insufficiently permanent partner for God. Surely the church is always the church whether she is wholly in tune with the divine will or not? If she is not the church even outside the moment of inspiration, then who is doing the waiting and praying and expecting for this moment to recur? Even as a rebellious proud sinner, is not the church still the church? Barth will reply that the nature of the church is never to achieve existence independent of her centre, Christ.

Barth's Roman Catholic critics do appreciate the priority he accords to the church over the individual Christian. He echoes Forsyth: 'What we have to do with in the New Testament is the individualizing of a corporate salvation, not the incorporation of an individual.'[24] Christ is the centre of the church, not just of the believer. But again, does Barth's view allow scope for the church's, and the individual believer's, moral and spiritual progress in history, for sanctification? Does Barth allow room for this if the church seems always waiting for grace rather than walking confidently into the challenges of life knowing that the Holy Spirit is always within, as promised to the believer? This is the conservative evangelical criticism of Barth, and it is the same point as the Roman criticism. That the church, by her very nature, can never be autonomous, remains the abiding and tested contribution of Barth's ecclesiology. She is the church of the risen Lord and always exists only from, in and through his Holy Spirit. That she must never shirk living out and telling out her gospel audibly, follows from the nature of this Christ. Therefore Barth can resist the criticism of representing a *purely inward* tradition, as his contribution to the church in the 1930's shows.

C. CHURCH HISTORY AND THE HOLY SPIRIT

Reviewing Newman and Barth sharpens the issues concerning the nature of the church. Newman felt the need for one visibly united, historical and infallible church, and he rejected the distinction between the spiritual and the institutional churches. He identified this one spiritually social body as the Roman church. His thesis on the development of doctrine was necessary to justify his changed understanding of the nature of the church's progress in the course of time. Rather than recognizing a norm external to the life of the church, he envisaged this ecclesial life as a process gradually developing the interpretation of revelation in the historical, social, philosophical and political circumstances of each generation and culture. We might use the analogy of the English law: the law develops case by case in response to new cultural and social factors, but the judges would claim that this development happens on the same common law principles of the need for justice, equity and the common good.

This analogy might even be pressed further in that the judges lay down the law in dialogue with the lawyers, who argue the merits of the applications of different cases and opinions to the present facts. This parallels Newman's idea of the church's episcopal office listening to and adjudicating the opinions of the prophetic office. The church's very essence is that of an historical community possessing all the facets of any such institution, while at the same time being the divine society, the school of grace. Barth, with the protestant tradition, also says that the church is a living identifiable community, identifiable by her proclamation and her sacraments of Jesus Christ, both resting on the canonical scriptures as the guaranteed access of Christ. The church is measured by her obedience to the word. The canon of scripture, using all the necessary critical historical interpretative means available, is the church's final arbiter and judge.

Barth suspects Newman's type of modern Roman Catholic developmental system of a kind of man-centred idolatry: 'Instead of bearing witness to the authority of Jesus, it invests itself with His authority, attributing absolute perfection to its order and ministry, cultus and dogma, and interpreting historical evolution as the automatic development of the divine truth incarnate in itself.'[25] For Newman, the Bible as an authority does not fulfil the task, and he felt himself driven to seek an absolutely authoritative interpreter of the canonical scriptures. He insists that the scriptures must be interpreted in a mystical sense to produce the traditional dogmatic trinitarian system now accepted by the church. To appeal simply to scripture is to appeal, he says, to the opinions of the destructive biblical critics. Meaning cannot simply be extracted from the text by ordinary grammatical and historical means. Scripture must be interpreted symbolically by the mind of the inspired church, which already knows the truths of the catholic tradition in broad overall shape. For Newman the Bible functions by providing analogies: as certain events happen in the church now, so we can perceive analogies of similar developments in the text.

Neither of these two thinkers can be accused of trying to state just one side of the case. Newman regards the inner life of the church as the prophetic Holy Spirit inspiring and indwelling the whole process. The outer form is not without the inner Spirit. Barth rejects individualism and 'ecclesiastical docetism', the idea that the external physical side of the church does not matter since it is only an appearance and not the spiritual reality. The church is the visible community of faith gathered round, and living out, the Word. Very much like Forsyth, for whom redemption is primarily corporate and then individualized, Barth teaches that the church is the elect in Christ as a whole, before individuals come into the church as a conglomerate. The church is the covenant people of God, the elect, who realize that the source and centre of their life is Christ and that their presence in the world is a light to lighten the Gentiles, a visible beacon to tell out the glory of the Lord. Both theologians, representing either wing of the church in the West, can be said to use the models outlined by Sykes above in different ways.

The real difference between them, and perhaps between the two wings of western tradition, catholic and evangelical, may be their different readings of historical progress and divine presence.

Inheriting the foundation-superstructure model, Newman refashions it so as to try to prevent the past being used against the church of the present in a critical way. The Bible or the early Fathers are not to be held as a corrective to the present theology or practice of the one historical and inspired church. The foundation is not foundational in the sense of being separable from the superstructure, any more than the roots of a plant are separable from its shoots, they constitute a natural whole. The sap flows progressively throughout the one system. Barth, on the other hand, insists that the church is built around the central witness of the apostles and can deviate from that witness, as happened in the Hitler years. The canon of scripture does therefore form a criterion, a yardstick separable from the whole historical development of the church. For the Swiss theologian there is a point, a critical point, needing to be inserted into the process of church history to test and check the straightness of the plant. The English thinker sees no such need or possibility, holding the canon as the product of the ongoing community of faith and needing that community as its interpreter. The process as a whole is one holy, catholic and apostolic, from the start of the church to the finish. The Bible cannot be fruitfully interpreted outside the living and true church, they are linked together in the very life of the church and it is inconceivable to set one against the other.

The spirit-body model fits Newman's notion of Christianity as an idea which develops in the historical community of the church. The mind, government, and practices of the church are informed by the growing idea, just as, for example, the Soviet empire has been shaped by, and has embodied, the Marxist idea in a developing way over the years. Christianity is no inner pietism but a flesh and blood religion involving the incarnational principle initiated by Jesus. Spirituality for the church concerns not only prayer life but very visible and physical things. The spiritual and the bodily are at one in Christianity, and this holds true for the church: she is a spriritual institution dispensing grace to her adherents through her properly appointed agents and agencies. Spirit and matter, in the one true and Roman church, coalesce. As no person can be without a body or an inner animating soul, so with the church.

Barth insists likewise, as we have seen, on the church

visible, the church whose inner motive power is Christ himself. The community of faith waits as the eschatological church for the repeated, but guaranteed, coming of the Lord as the Holy Spirit works this miracle. It is always the Spirit who acts in this event, the church does not 'have' the grace of God at her disposal. Yet in the mercy of God the community of faith is assured of this divine action through the word and sacraments. Only in the person of Christ can we speak of the identity of the human and the divine, for Barth. Only in that human and historical life was there a permanent, constant identification of the earthly, temporal with the divine.[26] The unity of the church with God is of a different order to that of Christ with God. Barth draws on the analogy of the Trinity, unity embracing distinction, to explain the relation of the divine Son to his humanity, and again the relation between Christ and his church. In each case the Holy Spirit miraculously bonds in unity a differentiation. In the case of the relation in distinction between Christ and the church, the Spirit characteristically brings into union what naturally should be apart, the holy God and the sinful church. This relationship stands wholly on the mercy of the atoning Lord. Whenever and wherever the event of this visitation occurs and Christ becomes present in, with, and under the words and deeds of the church, he is united to his covenant people, while not being identical with them.

Interestingly both theologians relate the divine Spirit with the earthly historical form dialectically, that is by way of an interactive conversation between two poles. But they work their dialectic out very differently. For Newman the spirit works in the church through theologians whose efforts 'bring forth in speech', or focus, the church's spiritual experience in words and concepts. These suggestions interact with the official jurisdiction of the bishops and Pope as the final head. Out of these dialogues the developing life and thought of the church proceeds, gaining ever wider and deeper syntheses of the truth. The process itself is filled with the Spirit and always moves positively forward, never incorporating error.

The philosophical background to this process is Hegelian thought, which identified the developing historical process as the unfolding of the divine Spirit or Mind. Ever deeper, richer syntheses of meaning grow from the knitting together of thesis with antithesis in the history of thought. Likewise, for Newman, the nearer to the spring, the muddier and shallower is Christian doctrine, but later on a broad, deep river bed provides for a clearer, wider body of water. The one true church, grows spiritually and triumphantly into the future. The dialectic of the spiritual and the official works within the continuum of the church's life process.

Barth teaches that the church has her being from outside herself, that she is in a sense 'eccentric'. This dialectic unites the church to Christ in the Spirit, or brings the word to the church, often a word of judgement as well as of grace. The revealed Word identifies himself with the church, but not in a permanent identity of being, so as to divinize the church herself and her historical evolution. Christ is not without his people for Barth, but never in such a way that the distinction between them is in danger of being compromised. That which is born of the Spirit is Spirit, for John the Evangelist and for Barth, and that which is born of the flesh is flesh. The real spiritual core of the church is the freely acting Lord. Whereas for Newman the Holy Spirit constantly indwells church history, for Barth the accent is on the sovereignty of the Spirit over the church, imparting renewal to her in particular circumstances. The Spirit is not immanent in the life of the structures of the church without prayer, faith and expectation.

The model of the centre and the circumference plainly applies most obviously to Barth's version of dialectical understanding. He envisages movements toward and from the spiritual centre of the church, Christ. The church can and does err and stray from her way like lost sheep, she needs often to repent and to open herself again and again to the voice of her Master. She has nothing in her hand to offer to God except the fact that they are empty and in need. Newman sees the whole church, and especially her official structures, more optimistically. But even his school of thought has a place for differentiating the church aglow with the Spirit from the merely nominal Christian. Möhler, whose doctrine is virtually identical to that of Newman, goes so far as to say, 'It is not to be doubted that Christ maintains His Church in spiritual energy by means of those who live in the faith of Him, who are spiritually united to Him; that in these lives His truth, which otherwise would be forgotten, or degenerate into an empty form. Yes; these who are transformed into His image, are the true supporters of the visible Church, whereas mere outward professors would not for a day maintain it even in its outward forms.'[27] Here is a statement fitting exactly into the centre-circumference model from a writer whose position, to say the least, formally does not leave much room for the distinction between the form of the church and her spiritual heart of real faith in Christ.

If Newman over-identifies the historical process of the one church with the divine, Barth fails sufficiently to give spiritual value to the historical church. The historical community becomes the true church as she prays and expects the Spirit, although even taking up this attitude means the Spirit is present. Outside this event of grace, the church is a rag bag of humanity as the Bible is a dubious collection of ancient near eastern texts, hoping for God to visit and reconstitute the earthly form with the suffusing grace of Christ. Newman, with modern catholic critique, rejects this as a punctiliar, intermittent view. Does it leave the church like an electric light bulb, switched on and off repeatedly? But instead Newman seems to commit the equal and opposite mistake of extending the point of 'becoming', when the Spirit comes to the church, into the centuries-long process of infallible Christian, or Roman Catholic, development.

If philosophically Newman resembles a form of Hegelian thought Barth's position retains something of Kierkegaard's 'infinite qualitative distinction' between God and history. This results in the 'mathematical point' being the nature of the relationship between God and human history, in distinction from Newman, who comes close to an idealist blending of history and spirit, the church as the historical unfolding of the spirit. Although the theory is that revelation itself does not develop, only its interpretation, yet in reality Owen Chadwick is right in saying that 'Newman's theory, like that of Suarez, is dependent upon the contention that definition by the church is equivalent to revelation.'[28] Where Barth seems to lack confidence in the historical community, Newman's theory goes to the opposite extreme and virtually deifies the stream of Roman Catholic history and thought. To Barth this theology amounts to the 'secret identification of God with man', with the Roman Catholic historical institution, in this case.

It is a sad fact that the church has in her past frequently masked and even reversed the gospel of Christ, has sinned and needed to repent. These have been points in history when the Christological corrective has been needed against the church's ongoing development. When the people of God have become turned in on themselves, then the Word of God has to break in again. There is no escaping this critical factor in framing our understanding of the church, the point of crisis, of judgement, needing radically to cut in to the process of church history to return her to her Christological centre. The course of church history is not inherently Spirit-filled, either in terms of life or in terms of teaching.

On the other hand, the church is the church even in her sin, sinners justified by grace through faith. The church is the people which may have fallen but can still repent. God calls the church to turn back to Christ and live, although the possibility of divine rejection is very real scripturally, according to the book of Revelation, if spiritual and moral failure concretize into a hardening of the heart and a rejection of God. If the inner heart becomes so hardened or lukewarm as to destroy genuine love for the Lord, then official status and historical pedigree will not suffice to save us from judgement.

As regards her teaching the church may make errors of understanding, but remains the church. Barth regards formulated doctrine as far less important than the person of the living Christ who visits and sustains his church. Correct teaching, for Barth, apart from the affirmation that Jesus is Lord, has not the place it has in traditional evangelical faith. Newman and Roman Catholicism distinguish between the officially structured church and individual members: it is the officially constituted organs of the church which are preserved from error as they act in accordance with their duly formed ecclesiastical procedures. Even if a bishop or pope were in a condition of sin within himself, that would not affect his function at the formal level in the official scheme of things, any more than the moral failure of the priest would invalidate the sacrament administered by him. Whatever the spiritual or moral condition of the personnel at any particular time, that does not alter the fact that there is still a divinely constituted visible church, with sacramental means of grace. The structures remain divinely ordained and for Newman, the Roman structures are infallibly preserved from error when due process is observed.

It will be noticed that the official validating agencies of the church are not, for Newman, themselves susceptible to further radical change once in place. The ecclesiastical structures and procedures evolve historically in the Spirit and, having been completed by the emergence of the Papacy, the system for validating developments is fixed in place, no longer subject to change. The arbiters of true development, having themselves evolved, become a fixed, system of control. Having evolved, the defining structures are abstracted from the process of historical development and become the mouthpiece of the Spirit to the church as the needs arise. The ecclesiastical forms gain the status of guaranteed bearers of doctrine and of sacramental grace, but, interestingly, there is something of the Barthian intermittent and punctiliar structure embodied in the process. Sacramental grace needs to be administered at points in the historical process; there are occasions when the sacraments are not being activated and hence when grace is not issuing forth. Newman's system in fact proves to be more static than has seemed the case. Grace-bestowing and truth-bearing in the church flow from or through fixed structures. For Barth the written word is the guaranteed medium of truth and revelation as the Spirit brings it to life. For Newman the official episcopal ecclesiastical forms stand in this place, the divinely developed and now fixed channels ready to mediate grace and truth to the church.

For Barth the written word is a fully historical document, the product of all kinds of ancient near eastern influences and errors, yet to the eye of faith and in the miracle of the Spirit it unites us to Christ. The Bible functions as the great sacrament, always with the guarantee and promise of being brought to life at the touch of the Holy Spirit. This written witness to Christ serves as the focus for the church, around which the church gathers and waits and listens. There is a fascinating area of common ground with a catholic view of things in his notion of the sacramentality of not only scripture but the whole of creation. As we saw, Barth in his first volume of the *Church Dogmatics* tells us that God can reveal himself in a Mozart concerto, a summer's day, a blossoming shrub or a dead dog, should he so choose.[29] His fourth volume develops this idea so that creation can be ordained to the ministry of the word of God, in other words that the natural realm can reflect the divine revelation at God's good pleasure. The world is sacramental, God can always ordain or baptize it.[30] This has been likened to the car's headlamp beam hitting the 'cats' eyes' on the road at night, grace lighting up nature and commissioning it to tell of the creator. This is a point of contact with Newman and catholicism which focuses on sacramental means and medium of grace for the church's life. The very great difference remains that for Barth the initiative of grace lies with God, for Newman the church is entrusted to administer the divine gifts and sacraments bearing grace.

The modern catholic stance, represented and pioneered by

Newman and Möhler, has not altered its notion of the church as the divinely ordained and formed institute. What has changed is the rationale for her creation in history. Instead of the once-for-all creation of the older theology, the church now is said to have developed organically over the centuries under the guiding hand of the Lord and indwelt by the Holy Spirit. The church has become the living institute of salvation and God has set up all the necessary agencies in ministering the salvation entrusted to her care. In the Old Testament God gradually led his people and gave them an ordained priesthood and cultic form, so by analogy we should not be surprised at similar developments in the church. To be sure of salvation we need to unite ourselves to the one true church. Newman ends the revised edition of his *Essay*, written after some thirty years as a Roman Catholic, with an appeal to the reader to ensure his eternal destiny, presumably by joining the church he has just been presenting in the book.

Barth reflects the Reformation unease with the view of the church as a kind of mediator, acting for Christ in dispensing truth and grace. This 'naturalization of grace', according to Barth's critique, attributes to the church what is only Christ's, that is the power to forgive sins and to baptize with the Holy Spirit. Not only does this seem to absolutize the institutional church in the sense of making her structures divinely perfect and her decrees free from mistake and misinterpretation, but, even more seriously, this view of the church fails to acknowledge direct access to God in the Spirit of Christ.

Barth's doctrine of the church emphasizes that her real essence and mission is to serve and point to Christ in dependence on Christ; to awaken the church from complacency and self-adulation; to prevent reliance on the past displacing trust in herself; to prevent, as Forsyth put it, 'the tortoise being absorbed by the shell'![31]

Barth in effect repeats the critique of official catholicism made by Dostoyevsky's Grand Inquisitor. This figure represents a cardinal castigating Jesus, who has returned unexpectedly as a weak human again. The churchman accuses Christ of stirring up trouble and unrealistic expectations among poor weak mortals with ideas of free access to God by personal faith. Such ideas were, according to the cardinal, cruel and romantic. But the church has overturned such unrealistic folly and reinstituted a proper religion, with a cult and hierarchical orders of priests. Herd-like humanity can manage this type of religion, but not notions of direct relations with the Almighty. Christianity is a fascinating and colourful authoritative religion based on a rigid imperial organizational structure, not living personal faith.[32]

The parable attacks the official, structured religious institute in the name of Jesus and simple faith. Dostoyevsky, who influenced Barth's early development, makes the same kind of rejection of religious cultural system as Barth makes, and indeed as Kierkegaard, another influence on Barth, made against the official, highly systematized, state Lutheranism of his native Denmark in the nineteenth century. Barth can argue that Jesus himself made this protest against the morally impressive religious system of his day.[33] Newman's contribution must add, however, that reform and renewal should come within the existing, historic church body, if endless breakaway movements, in the name of personal faith, are to be avoided. Gospel and church go together.

3. Setting an agenda

Both Barth and Newman, however, insist that the church is the work of the Holy Spirit. They provide us with apparently polar opposite ideas of this spiritual creation, the evangelical and the catholic. From this appraisal of their work we can set an agenda for the following chapters.

(i) The basic issue remains that of the relationship of the outward to the inward aspects of the church, the historical to the spiritual. Perhaps the more biblical and profound polarity exists between sin and grace, and this moves the issue towards setting the visible church in tension with the holy church. The church reconciled to God in Christ's death and resurrection remains fallen and imperfect, always the repenting church. The appropriateness of the visible structures for this gospel at the heart of the church must be of key importance in appraising any ecclesiological view. This relates to the crucial issue of how the risen Christ comes to the church and remains immanent in her, the question so crucial to the conflict of views between Newman and Barth. This will be a major item to look for in our continuing exploration into Anglican ecclesiology, the relationship between the Christological heart and the members of Christ.

(ii) Newman's essential point was that the church is the living church of changing history, of the process stretching back to Pentecost and beyond to Abraham, the church is 'diachronic'. This historical church is one church logically but, more importantly, one church theologically. Here the aspect of the church as historical society presents itself as an inescapable item on the agenda, an item which the evangelical wing cannot ignore. If this is a theological given, we are still left with the question as to how to define and evaluate this 'horizontal' historical process, in all its naturalness, theologically. How legitimate is it to form a new church, splitting from the existing body? Another main issue in the life and theology of the church at present comes from the changed perception of the ministry of women in the church; history and sociology have moved on and the church has had to address her interpretation of scripture afresh in the light of changed cultural understanding. This example must especially be discussed.

(iii) Perhaps the most urgent issue in the life of the Anglican church follows from the previous two, that of authority for belief: what are the theological norms for the church? Barth has spoken mightily for the canon of scripture as her central point of theological and spiritual reference, with tradition as the very important secondary source. His criticism of liberalism thundered even more loudly than his criticism of Roman catholicism. Newman insisted on authority in the church, by the church, for the church, and this roots back to the Roman idea of authoritative interpretation of the faith by the episcopate and papacy. Can normative authority be reclaimed in the Anglican church, as well as her well known respect for diversity of opinion? I will argue that the biblical authority is binding on the church, that the church, as the community of the Holy Spirit, is the proper keeper and interpreter of the apostolic teaching, and that the current vogue for claiming an endless relativism of interpretations, a basic unclarity of scripture, is a false view. Would recovery of clarity here prevent the tendency of evangelicals to split, in the name of a purer gospel?

(iv) The social issue, I argue, is vitally on the agenda of the church, and interestingly, Barth's theological approach has provoked much discussion of the matter. He undoubtedly influenced Bonhoeffer, who later developed his idea of 'religionless Christianity' for industrial 'man come of age' now living in 'his strength' and not in need of any ennervating summons to repent. This theology holds sway in much Anglican teaching and action in diocesan industrial ministries. The *Faith in the City* report[34] raised the question of the 'relevance' of the church to a materially needy society. How the church relates to this challenge must be part of any Anglican ecclesiological discussion.

(v) *Seeing, hearing,* and *doing,* these three facets focus the differences in ecclesiological approach among the various families of theology we will discuss. The visible, historic, sacramental church is the focus for the catholic; the word-centred theology for the evangelical; and 'praxis', or practical social concern, for the radical liberation theologian. All parties include all these aspects, but treat them very differently. The final analysis found in my closing chapter restates the importance of the word in all its richness, complexity and authority as being the most modern and, more importantly, most apostolic, category with which to express the Christian understanding of the church and interpret the foregoing issues.

END NOTES TO CHAPTER 1

1. Avery Dulles *Models of the Church* Gill and Macmillan, Dublin, 1974 p. 7.
2. *Theology of the New Testament vol. 1* p. 308.
3. *Ministerial Priesthood* John Murray, London, 1897 pp. 12–13.
4. *The Church and the Sacraments* Independent Press, London, 1917 p. 65.
5. op. cit. p. 66.
6. op. cit. p. 49.
7. 1 Corinthians 15:10. D. M. Baillie *God Was in Christ* Faber and Faber, London, 1948.
8. op. cit. p. 54.
9. S. Sykes *The Identity of Christianity* SPCK, London, 1984 pp. 235–8.
10. See for example Newman's letter to his sister Mrs Jemima Mozley, March 15, 1845; 'From the time my doubts (about Anglicanism) come upon me I begin to live more strictly; and really from that time to this I have done more towards my inward improvement, as far as I can judge, than in any time of my life . . . And how is it that I have improved in other points if in respect of this momentous matter I am so fearfully blinded?' *Letters and Correspondence of John Henry Newman during his life in the English Church* edited by Anne Mozley vol. 1 Longmans, Green and Co, London, 1898 p. 411.
11. *An Essay on the Development of Christian Doctrine: an hypothesis to account for a difficulty* Longmans, Green and Co, London, 1891 8th edition, p. 40.
12. *Newman on Development* Sheed and Ward, London, 1975 p. 132.
13. *Essay* op. cit. p. 14.
14. ibid. pp. 86–9.
15. ibid. p. 86.
16. *The Epistle to the Romans* OUP, London, 1933 (1972).

17. *Systematic and Philosophical Theology*, The Pelican Guide to Modern Theology vol. 1, Penguin books, Harmondsworth, 1969 ch. 2.
18. *Church Dogmatics* vol. 1/1 T & T Clark, Edinburgh, 2nd edition, 1975 p. 55.
19. op. cit. pp. 80, 142.
20. *Karl Barth* Holt, Rinehart and Winston, New York, 1971 p. 291.
21. op. cit. chapter 2.
22. *Church Dogmatics* 4/1 p. 647.
23. *Church Dogmatics* 1/1 p. 72.
24. op. cit. p. 5.
25. *Church Dogmatics* 3/2 p. 510.
26. *Church Dogmatics* 1/2 pp. 162–3.
27. *Symbolik* p. 49.
28. *From Bossuet to Newman* CUP, Cambridge, 1957 p. 160.
29. See note 18 above, *Church Dogmatics* 1/1 p. 55.
30. *Church Dogmatics* 4/3 p. 164.
31. Forsyth op. cit.
32. *Brothers Karamazov* 'The Grand Inquisitor', Penguin, Harmondsworth 1958 p. 288.
33. Jeremias on the Pharisees repays study, for example, in *Jerusalem in the Time of Jesus* SCM, London, 1969 p, 246f.
34. ACUPA *Faith in the City* Church Information Office, 1985.

2

THE ANGLO-CATHOLIC SYNTHESIS

1. The apostolic structure of the church

For the Anglo-Catholic or high church Anglican the outward form of the church is no accidental matter. In his criticism of Hatch, cited earlier, Moberly not only insists that membership of the visible church is part and parcel of being a Christian, but also argues that the structure of the church's ministry is essential to her very being. This structure, as all agree, developed in the generation after the days of the apostles. The threefold ministry, of bishops, presbyters and deacons, and the continuing tradition of this ministry, according to Moberly, determines the proper order of the church. The bishop, tracing his pedigree back through his former bishops, continues the function of the apostles in providing the authoritative source of validation of ordination to the ministry and of handing on that authority to the next generation of bishops. Bishops provide the God-given, outwardly historical and official point of reference for deciding whether a priest has been properly ordained and whether the consecrating bishop also was properly in possession of authority to ordain.

The bishop serves as trustee, holding the title deeds of the property which is not his but belongs to a higher and wider ownership. He uses the rights temporarily vested in him to maintain and develop the whole estate in ways laid down by the trust. He then hands on his commission to a successor who acts in exactly the same way. The bishop is the officially appointed administrator or guardian, who works with a panel of others to oversee the good growth and development of the entrusted estate. The Greek New Testament word for bishop is *episcopos*, literally 'overseer', and it is from this early origin that the office was founded and grew in the plan of God.

Episcopal order, accordingly, is not optional, but forms an unchangeable and necessary structure of the church of Christ. It will be noted that the gospel of life-changing salvation in Christ need not be compromised in this pattern. The line of bishops, begun with the apostles, ordains the ministry to proclaim Christ crucified and risen, justification by grace through faith and the sanctifying presence of the Holy Spirit in the believer. None of these evangelical truths need be evicted from the household of God as governed by the succession of trustee bishops.

Episcopacy is more than a tried and tested form of government, it is the God-given pattern of the continuity of the church and of her form of ministry. As we have seen from our brief rehearsal of Newman's ideas, there are different ways of interpreting the creation of this official episcopate. It can be seen as a matter of straight commission from Christ to his apostles and from them on to their successors, the bishops. This is a foundation-superstructure picture: on top of the foundation of the apostles stand the bishops. But it can also be understood as having been developed over the course of history in the providence of God. The apostles and the church came to realize their own place in the scheme of things under the ministry of the Spirit. But this distinction applies only to the order of knowing: some might hold that the system was clear to the apostles from the first, others that their understanding of their position developed and expanded as guardians of the faith and delegates of Christ to ordain each new generation of priests. The office of bishop itself, it can be argued, was given by Christ after his resurrection, but the full meaning of this commission was only understood and applied in the church later.

Whatever the precise view of what actually happened to achieve the original commissioning, the Anglo-Catholic view claims that episcopacy was given to and imposed on the church 'from above' by divine ordinance. It must therefore be strictly kept. The 'historic episcopate' constitutes a vital part of the very make-up of the church. Not only is it Christ's sign and sacrament of the unity of the church, it is simply commanded by God, therefore is non-negotiable. Outward and visible it is, but that is no reason to undervalue the episcopate and no warrant for disobeying God's chosen pattern. God knows that we all need structures and forms to live life, and the church is no exception.

Protestant rationales for the church are rejected as tainted with unbiblical dualism. This can be either a Greek type, divorcing matter and spirit, or Cartesian type, between subjective thought and objective reality. 'At the time Descartes was writing, Puritan reformers were smashing the pictures and statues with which their Christian ancestors had filled the churches, writes De Waal.[1] De Waal regards evangelical disdain for the church visible as directly linked to the dictum of Descartes 'I think therefore I am,' according priority to inner thought. Puritan vandalism tried to strip away the visibly objective side of the faith, leaving only a bare subjectivist religion of the mind and spirit. In the same way the evangelical doctrine of the church distorts and neglects the necessary outward, structural side of the church of Jesus Christ. This church, after all, centres on the *incarnate* Word, not on some abstract invisible message. Structures, like things in creation, are not inherently evil! The one church of Christ needs them and was given them. It would be unbiblical, indeed, to reject the gift and command of God concerning episcopal structures. Disaster awaits the church if she decides to do what is right in her own eyes and develop her own patterns.

This gift of the threefold order of bishops, priests and deacons is the gift of apostolicity, the living ongoing apostolicity of guidance and oversight in the whole church of God. 'Christ,' for Moorman, 'gave two things to his Church—the means of grace (word and sacraments) and the ministry of grace (the apostles and fellow workers). It was the apostles and their successors, the bishops, who were responsible for the proclamation of the word and the administration of the sacraments.'[2] This ministry forms part of the very fibre of the church's being. It can no more be taken away and replaced than can the skeleton or blood vessels from a living human being! It is the means of her continuity over the centuries. The bishops themselves form a human chain back to Christ, a vital, real, flesh and blood link to guarantee the future of the church in the correct form. Reference can always be made to the episcopal network by anyone seeking the church with the proper title deeds from the original builder of the house of God. Only from the true church can the grace of Christ be guaranteed, therefore we cannot separate official church structures from salvation and access to God.

To settle for a local pastoral ministry, whether networked together or not, without the third level of bishops does not provide sufficient warranty for a church's genuine Christian character and status. In the days of the apostles local elders or presbyters were established but under the overall reference of the apostles, or their delegates. Churches were not independent congregations so much as parts of a network, parts which had to keep in tune with apostolic guidance and supervision, and whose ministers were appointed or ratified by the apostles.

Paul's Epistle to Titus plainly shows this. There Paul tells his agent, Titus: 'The reason I left you in Crete was that you might straighten out what was left unfinished and appoint elders in every town, as I directed you.'[3] Bicknell speaks for Anglo-Catholic theology by concluding that this exemplifies the normal threefold pattern operating in the church: the apostolic authority laying down and ('episcopally') supervizing the local pastoral presbyterate or eldership. On revisiting the Galatian cities of Lystra, Iconium, and Antioch, Paul and Barnabas representing apostolic authority 'appointed elders for them in each church with prayer and fasting.'[4] This again illustrates that the presbyterate came from the apostolic authority, authority now existing in the line of bishops.

The episcopate came from the commission of Christ to the apostles and from this apostolic episcopate the local ministry originated. The flow is 'from above', from Christ to the apostles and their successors, the bishops, who in their turn ratified the pastoral ministry. Grace and authority do not flow 'from below', from the local assembly of the faithful upwards. Rather the apostolic government of the church has always been responsible for her ministry, and this pattern of ministry actually defines her to a very important extent. Therefore ecclesial structures belong to the very *essence* of the church, they are no accident of history but divinely ordained and vital for the whole church.

Episcopal ministry traces back to Christ's apostles in an unbroken line of consecration down the centuries, and this historic chain of succession is indispensable. It means that the church is indeed one whole community through time and space. The episcopate is specifically 'the historic episcopate'. The historical continuity of the chain ensures unity and the binding together of the whole body, across space and time. The fact that the episcopal line has this historic character means that other churches, formerly without bishops, which decide to adopt the episcopalian structure of church order, do not automatically gain access into the apostolic network. They may share the right structure now, but this does not mean that they stand in the apostolic succession, not unless they accept consecration by the bishops already in the historical network. This drastically demonstrates the nature of episcopacy as uniting historical life through time, as well as a contemporary life linking the church together across the face of the earth. Time and space relate as one in Anglo-Catholic ecclesiology. No merely external guarantee of the pedigree of the true church, the episcopate fulfils its role as the duly appointed channel for the ministration of grace in the historic community.

The Anglo-Catholic theology makes the form of ministry decisive for the very being of the church of Christ, and that form was developed by the first four centuries of church life. It is fundamentally a form of foundation-superstructure model, because the first four centuries of teaching and ministry provide the norm for what follows. Ministerial succession, following the early foundation pattern, determines where we find the true church. This pattern of ministry is part of the whole church but also in a real sense stands over against the rest of the church while defining her and serving her. This chain of ministry interprets the faith for the church, using both the scriptures and decisions of the early great councils of the church before the great split between East and West, formalized in 1054.

It must be stressed that Anglo-Catholicism sees itself as biblical. It also looks to the early councils and great patristic theologians, but regards these as interpreting scripture aright, not as creating new truth. We have shown how the claim to continue the apostolic ministry builds on scripture. There have been several rationales for this view, but none so determinedly scriptural as that offered by the former Archbishop of Canterbury, Michael Ramsey in *The Gospel and the Catholic Church*.[5] Ramsey argues that the high church Anglican view is no mere compromise between Rome, with her bishops and pope, and protestantism, with the preaching of the gospel and dependence on the Holy Spirit. Rather, the Anglo-Catholic believes that the apostolic succession is vital to the evangelical nature of the church.

Ramsey takes us to the crucified Jesus, the representative of old Israel and the start of the reconstitution of Israel, who died for all to form a new humanity. All can share in his life by sharing in his death; Jesus 'died for all, that those who live should not live for themselves but for him who died for them and was raised again.'[6] Ramsey pierces deep into the atoning gospel of redemption in thoroughly evangelical manner. His theological exposition continues by relating this gospel to the life in the church. Union with Christ is beset by the temptation to sin and especially the sin of pride, pride in being one of the redeemed, the temptation to individualistic faith. Belonging to the one body, the church, offsets this peril and was always intended by the Lord of the church. Christ died and rose, giving his life to redeem the church. The sacraments of baptism and eucharist entail joining ourselves to the sacrifice of Christ in total self-giving. But this self-giving also means giving up my individualism, being a member of the one body in humility and service. The Christian therefore places himself, or finds himself placed, in the church under the delegated apostolic ministerial authority. He finds himself under the proper authority of the bishop and the presbyter or priest, and not as a totally free agent adrift from the visible body of Christ. The whole historic shape and order of the church hold together for the welfare of all Christians. The episcopal structure does not dominate but forms one of the ligaments in the overall, spiritually healthy, visible body. Visible authority may be anathema to modern secular individualists, but the gospel and church reversed any notion of humanity as purely autonomous individuals, a law unto themselves.

Scripture, episcopal order, sacraments and creeds form a beautifully coherent pattern of the organic, historically living organism, together telling forth the saving gospel of Christ and his one body. They must be seen in mutual harmony and if one element gains disproportionate attention distortion arises; but 'deliverance', from such imbalance, 'comes not by discarding the gift of God which has been misused but by recovering its true relation to the other gifts. The remedy for a misuse of Creeds is to see that Creeds are a signpost to scripture and accordingly to turn to scripture; but scripture will be misused unless the Episcopate points us to the continuous life of the one Body in which scripture emerged. And the Episcopate will be perverted unless it knows itself as nothing in isolation and as significant only as an organ of the one Body, which, by the healthy relation of all its parts, sets forth the gospel.'[7]

Ramsey elegantly sets out the best Anglo-Catholic vision of the church of Christ. Newman likened the ministry of the official church to the story of the conversion of the Ethiopian eunuch in the book of Acts. This Ethiopian, while travelling through the desert reads the prophet Isaiah. He finds himself puzzled and needs someone to interpret the text. Philip, representing the apostolic church, serves this purpose, explains the gospel and then baptizes the believing African dignitary.[8] This episode, for the catholic mind, exactly mirrors the integration of church with gospel: the scriptures, interpreted by living apostolic authority of the body, bring about the sacramental act of baptism so incorporating a new member into the body of Christ. The very gospel itself demands the catholic, episcopal, sacramental structure of the church. 'But meanwhile it must be insisted that neither the apostolic nor the sub-apostolic ages nor the period in which Creed, Canon and Episcopate emerged knew the see of Rome as having any monarchical place in the one structure. How far the Papacy expresses this main fact or distorts it is a subsequent historical question.'[9] The catholic structure is historically episcopal, but not necessarily papal, for Ramsey and the Anglo-Catholic, in close agreement with the ecclesiology of the Eastern Orthodox.

This ecclesiology obviously resembles that of Newman in his early Tractarian phase, but Ramsey invests the basic foundation-superstructure model with a greater warmth and life than some explanations have achieved. He has a deep sense of the living community, structured in the ancient episcopal fashion, living as the body of Christ in history. Perhaps there is also some influence from the later Newman and his organic vision of the church. While the parallel with the Newman line, Tractarian and Roman is plain, it may be interesting to pause and relate Ramsey's vision to Barth's evangelicalism.

Barth's doctrine of revelation incorporates a powerful place for the church. Christ, the Johannine revealed Word in person, comes in the Spirit through his church as she takes seriously the witness of scripture. Ramsey teaches a dynamic fourfold interlocking pattern of church life. The church is the body of Christ, sacramentally mediating Christ afresh to her members. Church, proclamation and scripture are the 'forms of the Word' for Barth, whereas the order of ministry and the sacraments serve that purpose for Ramsey. Both these theologians are deeply Christ-centred in their doctrines of the church, both in a way which seems most indebted to John's Gospel. One might even say that Barth's Christocentric ecclesiology in the Nazi years can be matched by the Anglo-Catholic Christocentric opposition to apartheid in South Africa. The Swiss Reformed theologian with his focus on the 'heard' revelation, and the English Anglo-Catholic, stressing the visual and tangible, may have far more in common in ecclesiology than is often thought.

They differ particularly over the significance attached to the precise *structure* and order of the audible and visible church in her witness, worship and teaching. Ramsey claims to be Anglican, catholic and evangelical, insisting that the gospel and the canon are normative foundations. The episcopacy, creeds and canon all had to develop but, unlike Newman, Ramsey insists that these developments had to be tested against the yardstick of apostolic foundations. Again there is a strange degree of similarity with Barth on the nature of this process of ratification. The scriptures combined with the gospel function as the key yardstick: 'The tests of a true development are whether it bears witness to the gospel, whether it expresses the general consciousness of the Christians, and whether it serves the organic unity of the Body in all its parts. These tests are summed up in the scriptures, wherein the historical gospel and experience of the redeemed and the nature of the one Body are described. Hence, while the canon of scripture is in itself a development, it has a special authority to control and check the whole field of development in life and doctrine.'[10] Barth would not agree to the coordination of these criteria, being particularly suspicious of the 'general consciousness' test, but the overarching control of scripture and gospel of Christ means that Ramsey can claim to represent a catholic evangelicalism.

2. The eucharistic body

Ramsey's Christological grasp prevents him from following the view that the threefold line of apostolic ministry stands wholly independently over against the church. He criticizes some of the Tractarians of the last century and their successors who 'were led into a view which is Augustinian and "clericalist" rather than Catholic, and which treats validity of orders as in itself the first basis of the Church's life, and even as the sole test of membership in the Church of God.'[11] Ramsey relishes the early Greek patristic writers, theologians such as Irenaeus and Athanasius, whose focus was Christ and who wrote before the church was fragmented between East and West. These writers envisage the church as the body indwelt throughout by Christ. The incarnation of the Word in humanity centres the whole Eastern Orthodox tradition in terms of religion and spirituality. The church is the body of Christ, indwelt by Christ throughout her whole being. The apostolic ministry subserves this community united in Christ, and cannot be regarded in opposition to the church or over against it. Living unity, dedicated to worship, suffused by the mystical presence of the risen and ascended Christ, dominates the idea of the Eastern Orthodox understanding of the church, and Ramsey shares the vision. Once again we can point to a parallel with Barth's theology and its focus on the incarnation of the Word, much influenced by Athanasius. Religiously and spiritually Ramsey works with this centre-circumference model; it is the structures of the church that he bases on the early patristic era, and, as he is to argue, these relate to Christ as organs of his body on earth.

The unity in worship and adoration of Christ centres on the sacraments of baptism and the eucharist. Both include the recipients into the one body of Christ. Both focus on the one redemptive sacrifice of the Second Adam into whose death and resurrection we are baptized, and which we celebrate eucharistically. The eucharist especially forms the very core of church being. Here the one body re-participates in the sacrifice of Christ and unites her sacrifice to his. Here eternity exists in time, our history is taken into the depth of the glory of Christ, crucified and risen, the exaltation in the redeeming humiliation. Here we all die anew into the sacrifice of Christ and in that death we are profoundly one, for Christ's death created the unheard-of, end-time event of 'one new man': 'For He is our peace, who has made us both one, and has broken down the dividing wall of hostility by abolishing in his flesh the law of commandments and ordinances, that he might create in himself one new man in place of two, so making peace, and might reconcile us both to God in one body through the cross, thereby bringing the hostility to an end.'[12]

The church participates sacrificially in Christ crucified and risen at the eucharist, as the new, end-time community. Sacramentally the church dies into the death of Christ so as to live in him. The Anglo-Catholic and the Eastern church actualize the New Testament teaching on our sharing in Christ crucified and risen at the eucharist, which for them is the corporate proclamation and reappropriation of Christ.

Perhaps Christ's transfiguration serves as a type of the church for this family of theology. Certainly it was central to Ramsey's theology. The man Jesus, aglow with a transforming brightness, the glory of the Lord shining with a radiance of holiness in true humanity, there is the analogy of Christ in his church. The church is one holy, catholic and apostolic as the living embodiment, the sacrament, of grace. She unites grace and earthly nature, eternity and time, as did Christ, while she is wholly dependent on Christ for her mysterious, divine yet human, essence.

A. SCHISM

Ramsey's work exudes this spirituality. For him the Anglo-Catholic is free to regain the riches of this early treasure, treasure unmarked by the later characteristics of Latin western Christianity. The Latin theology, developing after the Greek theologians, had to wrestle with concrete problems of church order, with disputes and splits, and in the context of an increasingly large and respectable Christianity which was to become the officially accepted religion of the Roman Empire before long. The Latin fathers, notably Cyprian and Augustine, North African bishops, had to make decisions on hard cases regarding recognition of Christians who decided that they had to separate off from what they considered to be a spiritually bankrupt, compromising line of bishops.

These situations arose out of persecutions of the church, during which Christians were compelled in some way to pass a test of loyalty to state religion by renouncing their Christian faith and making a token sacrifice to the pagan gods. In the Decian persecutions of 250 A.D. everyone was required to produce a certificate that he had offered sacrifice to the pagan gods in front of state officials. Thousands of Christians complied with this threat to escape torture and death. Cyprian, bishop of Carthage on the North African coast, himself escaped and, when the persecution ceased, was faced with the aftermath. Many Christians had not complied, preferring imprisonment and suffering torture in order to maintain the good confession that Jesus Christ alone is Lord.

They were called 'confessors' and were regarded as specially filled with the Holy Spirit and authoritative on account of their stand. Large numbers of the lapsed, those who had compromised, sought reinstatement and forgiveness after the ordeal was over. Great dispute arose over the ease of readmission to the fellowship of the church and therefore to the sacraments and forgiveness. Also at issue was the question of who might grant such readmission. The 'confessors' granted forgiveness to the fallen, but Cyprian said that the 'power of keys', the right to grant admission to the church, was given utimately to the bishops, however much they could be advised by the holy 'confessors'. This view provoked resistance and a rival bishop was chosen in Carthage, Fortunatus, whose church group insisted on the right of the 'confessors' to reinstate the lapsed without further reference to the bishop.

At the same time the church in Rome experienced a parallel problem after the persecution. Novatian held that the church had no power to remit grave sins such as forswearing the faith in time of trial, and that such fallen sinners could not be admitted into the church. Cornelius took a more practical line, in view of the great number of the fallen, and taught that forgiveness was possible after repentance. The Novatianist church demanded actual purity of life and saw itself as the community of the holy and re-baptized members from the other church under Cornelius.

Cyprian, having re-established his position, united with Cornelius rather than Novatian and when members of the Novatianist group applied for readmission to Cyprian's, he ruled that Novatianist baptism was not baptism because it was not administered by the one true church. For Cyprian, the 'schismatics' were no church at all, but were outside the gifts of the Spirit and not able to confer them. Therefore Cyprian insisted on re-baptizing those from the 'heretical' congregations. In this view he was opposed by his brother bishop Stephen of Rome, who argued that the sacrament belongs to Christ rather than to the church and that its administration depends on its proper form rather than the person administering it. With this view the North African church later agreed.

Cyprian formed the understanding that there was one church only and therefore only one community in which the Spirit of Christ was at work in the ministry and the sacraments. He exalted the role of bishops in this understanding. However much the holy spiritual 'confessors' might advise the episcopate, the latter had the final authority as to membership of the church. For Cyprian the bishop is not only the officially appointed successor to the historical apostolate and therefore an authentic teacher of the apostolic faith, he is also an inspired prophetic figure gifted by the Holy Spirit to rule the church. Cyprian held to the collegiate nature of bishops: the conference of all the church's bishops forms the flat top of the pyramid of the ecclesial structure. To be in communion with this bench of bishops is an essential part of being in the church: the episcopate is the bond holding the church in unity. Rebellion against the bishop constitutes not merely an offence against the outer order of things but a rebellion against God: the schismatic is in sin, is a heretic outside the realm of the church, her ministry and sacraments.

North-African ecclesiastical turmoil continues this story which is in itself crucial to the development of the doctrine of the church. The persecution of Christians under the emperor Diocletian and his successors from 303 A.D. led to similar problems to those just described. Bishop Mensurius of Carthage and his archdeacon Caecilian cooperated with the authorities in handing over some theological writings as decreed, although not the Bible itself; likewise in Rome bishop Marcellinus followed a policy of not aggravating the situation by flagrant defiance of the authorities and of formal compliance. In Carthage the 'confessors' in prisons denounced the bishops as compromisers, prompting Caecilian to try and stop food getting to them in the prisons. Again the church divided into the stricter and the laxer parties, the spiritual and the official, and when Caecilian was consecrated bishop after Mensurius, an assembly of 70 bishops in Carthage declared the consecration invalid. They appointed Marjorinus bishop instead, and Donatus succeeded him. Two lines of church tradition therefore emerged in North Africa, the 'Catholic' and the 'Donatist'. This split lasted for more than a century and up until the flood of Islam into the area, both maintained a presence.

The Donatists considered themselves the true heirs of Cyprian in their view of the sacraments. They held that there was one church and one realm in which sacraments were valid. Since the episcopal line of Caecilian had been contaminated by unholy compromise his church was not the church, neither were its sacraments nor ordinations valid. Augustine, bishop of Hippo in North Africa since 395 A.D., had to wrestle with this terrible and bitter dispute from the catholic side, and strove to bring about reconciliation. Since the Council of Arles in 314 A.D., the catholic side had agreed to drop the Cyprianic doctrine of the sacraments which denied validity to any outside the one church, and agreed with Stephen that the sacraments belong to the Lord's command to baptize in the name of the Father, Son and Spirit. Augustine, in line with this, accepted that Donatist sacraments were valid, that re-baptism was not necessary for a Donatist coming into membership with the Catholics. Despite his efforts the rift did not heal and eventually Augustine agreed to the use of force against the Donatists by the state power to solve the problem, perhaps his greatest mistake of judgement.

The brief snapshot of the African church feud shows how the theology of the church was dragged into the seedy area of dispute and definition, of law and jurisdiction. Sins, not only in individuals faced with torture, but in uncharitable reaction to these, ever more bitter personal vilification and community hatred, split the people of God apart. The twentieth-century church has no standpoint from which to criticize. For theology, however, the difference between the old Cyprianic view and the subsequent Augustinian, causes the Anglo-Catholic some ambivalence. Ramsey commends the warmer broader Augustinian view which recognizes sacraments in other bodies outside the church proper. But he thinks there is a perilous cost to this charity. The effect seems to be that of allowing the sacraments to be separate from the church, since they now can exist elsewhere. Schism now seems rather less serious, the seamless fabric of the one visible church becomes less sacred. A scar tissue will grow over the split leaving its ugly wound mark, but with life continuing to flow through it.

B. EPISCOPACY AND ECUMENISM

Regarding the church as one holy visible community, structured episcopally according to the gospel, the Anglo-Catholic faces major problems over interpreting the divided episcopal church. Such divisions occurred early in the church's history, as we have just seen. Ramsey points to the general acceptance of Augustine's policy, against Cyprian's, as the root of future problems because developments after Augustine led to what had previously been regarded as 'schismatics' coming to be regarded as sacramental communities and so as churches with an episcopal pedigree. 'But if this new view was "broader",' he says, 'it contained the seeds of much perversity in later history. For while the Cyprianic view makes orders utterly dependent upon the Church and validity a part of the Church's single life in grace, the Augustinian view leaves room for thinking of orders as valid apart from the Church's corporate life and for the idea of succession by orders as a single and isolated channel to grace. S. Augustine has "broadened" church theory; but he has opened the way for a line of thought which glories in the name of Catholic but which severs the doctrine of orders from the doctrine of the Body of Christ.'[13] Ramsey feels that Augustine's interpretation of 'validity' sacraments outside the single 'catholic' church, because of their being ministered by validly ordained priests, opens the way to acknowledging groups which have split off as 'church' rather than as schismatics. This can lead to several lines of 'valid' episcopal ministries sustaining different churches with valid sacraments.

This could serve as the epitaph for the theology of the church which concentrates on the historic pedigree of episcopacy as the test of a true church. The historic episcopate itself now separates, like a river delta into different streams, yet still is claimed by the Anglo-Catholic theology to be of the very essence of the one visible church.

Newman saw this and criticized what was termed the 'branch theory' of episcopal authenticity on his move to Rome. 'It may possibly be suggested,' he says in discussing the unity of the church,

> 'that this universality which the Fathers ascribe to the Catholic Church lay in its apostolical descent, or again in its episcopacy, and that it was one, not as being one kingdom, or *civitas*, at unity with itself, with one and the same intelligence in every part, one sympathy, one ruling principle, one organization, one communion, but because, though consisting of a number of independent communities, at variance (if so be) with each other even to a breach of communion, nevertheless, all these were possessed of a legitimate succession of clergy, or all governed by bishops, priests and deacons. But who will in all seriousness maintain that relationship, or resemblance, makes two bodies one? England and Prussia are both monarchical, are they, therefore, one kingdom? England and the United States are from one stock, can they therefore be called one state? England and Ireland are peopled by different races, yet are they one kingdom still? If unity lies in the apostolical succession, an act of schism is, from the nature of the case, impossible; for as no one can reverse his natural birth, so no church can undo the fact that its clergy have come by lineal descent from the Apostles. Either there is no such sin as schism, or unity does not lie in the episcopal form, or in episcopal ordination.'[14]

Newman leaves the Anglo-Catholic theology on the rack, opting for the Roman solution to the problem: the Papacy as the guarantor of the only true episcopal lineage for the only true church.

Anglo-Catholic ecclesiology has wrestled with this question of episcopal schism, of churches accepting one another as 'valid' and 'fully catholic', while not being 'in communion with' each other. Ramsey finds the legal 'branch theory' insufficient. Clerical pedigree alone does not define or validate the church. The church must also be defined as the Christocentric Body of Christ, the one eucharistic body as a whole. Ramsey prefers ancient Eastern Orthodox stress on the church as the adoring, worshipping body, to the legal, Latin definitions:

> 'Neither the massive polity of the Church, nor its devotional life, nor its traditions in order and worship can in themselves ever serve to define Catholicism; for all these things have their meaning in the Gospel, wherein the true definition of Catholicism is found. Its order has deepest significance not in terms of legal validity but in terms of the Body and the Cross . . .'[15]

Ramsey wishes to ground episcopacy in the Athanasian vision of the church as the body of Christ.

Anglo-Catholic ecclesiology struggles to mesh the theology of episcopal order with the theology of the whole church of Christ. Neither Roman nor Orthodox catholicism have this problem, since each regards theirs exclusively as the only truly authentic church. If the historical episcopate is the church's criterion of authenticity, then Newman's critique stands. By moving from the Tractarian foundation model to his living organism model of the church, with its papal organ to preserve unity and exclude schismatics, Newman resolved his ecclesiological problem. For the non-papalist Anglo-Catholic, things are not so simple, since the early united foundation rock of episcopal order has several deep fissures. The problem is whether this weakness can be overcome by reference to the church as Christ's body across history, to complement transmitted episcopacy and to ground it in a grander unity.

The foundation centuries of the undivided church of Irenaeus and Athanasius provide the origin of episcopacy and the ideal model of what the church should be like, both in terms of doctrine and church order. Ramsey insists that the ancient threefold order of bishops, priests and deacons is of the very essence (*esse*) or being of the church. Historic episcopal order is more than a venerable, tried and tested structure which has proved itself as important for the church's well-being (*bene esse*) only, as the traditional evangelical Anglican interpretation has it. Episcopal order was given to the church and is part of her very self.

Canon Oliver Quick, another Anglican on the catholic wing, took the view that the church as a whole is in a state of schism within herself. He rejects the clericalist episcopal branch theory, which 'involves the paradoxical consequence that, whereas great Protestant Communions have no valid sacraments except baptism and are outside the body of the Catholic Church, nevertheless "a wandering bishop", who has received the episcopal character but holds no office or authority in any Christian body, can confer the orders of the Catholic Church upon anyone he chooses, and thereby starts a new "branch" of the Catholic Church itself.'[16] But Quick also regards episcopal order as of the essence of the church. He teaches that churches with episcopal succession should continue to prize it. At the same time they must recognize that the ordinations and sacraments of all churches are defective, because all are involved in the scandal of schism. Validity of ordination depends on the unity of the whole church, therefore all ordinations now are compromised, in these days after 'the fall', the splitting of the churches.[17]

William Temple, perhaps the most eminent Archbishop of Canterbury this century, disagreed. He could not accept that the disunity of the church prevented valid apostolic authority being transmitted through the historic threefold ministry in albeit divided churches. 'Our claim is that where a living Church acts through duly consecrated Bishops we have assurance that there Christ bestows His commission, which is a commission to act on behalf of the universal Church.'[18] The threefold ministry, for Temple as for Ramsey, is the duly appointed means of handing on the authority to oversee the whole church of God, whether some fail to recognize this or not. Quick's criticism, that this excludes too many churches and includes eccentric 'wandering bishops' as embodiments of new branches, is countered by the appeal to the living church. A bishop is not simply an individual but represents the church and must be set in the context of the church.

Anglo-Catholic ecclesiology today follows Temple and Ramsey in wanting to distance itself from a purely legal pedigree view of episcopal succession. In a recent symposium we read, 'At its heart is precisely the recognition that the special ministry (episcopacy) is a gift of God to, and in, and through, the Church, and that continuity in office and responsibility is one of the signs of continuity of the whole Church in the faith and witness of the apostles.'[19]

Temple appeals to the action of the 'living church', represented by the bishops, to counter Quick's more pessimistic view. The church is the living, single body of Christ which does work through the appropriate and ancient apostolic organ, the threefold ministry, despite the divisions of history. The episcopate is part of Christ's body and this cannot be divided. The historic line of episcopacy is not reducible to simply an external legal pedigree but it forms an integral aspect of the whole living body of Christ. The bishop therefore acts for Christ in the church on the authority of Christ transmitted through the channel of the episcopate. He is not merely representing the aggregate of all Christians in all churches now. For Temple, followed by Ramsey, therefore, Quick's idea that all orders are invalid, because schism afflicts all churches, fails to touch the Christ-bestowed consecration exercised in the body of Christ today.

Temple employs an idea of the church as a single spiritual organism against Quick's pragamatic interpretation of the church as thoroughly split. For Temple

> 'Every priest who by virtue of his ordination celebrates the Holy Communion acts not for the congregation there present, nor for all Christian people then living on the earth, but as the organ of the Body of Christ, the ministerial instrument of Christ active in and through His Body; so that though no more than two or three persons be actually assembled, yet the congregation at the Holy Communion is the Communion of Saints, with which the persons present, be they few or many, are there conjoined. Here therefore, as in the Incarnation itself, we find the eternal in the midst of time, the secret of a fellowship against which the gates of hell cannot prevail.'[20]

Temple and Ramsey seem content to say that the church of Christ ordered with its ancient threefold ministry is a metaphysical unit, whatever the historical appearances to the contrary; certainly the theological reality is one episcopally ordered church, although the historical reality fails to reflect this.

An implicit understanding of the invisible church here replaces the failure of the 'historic episcopacy' as a means and sign of ecclesial unity. The Anglo-Catholic appeals to the historic episcopate as part of the whole reality of the body of Christ, a body both spiritual and temporal. This appeal, however, on its own, fails and needs to appeal to an invisible reality called the catholic church which, to use Forsyth's term, 'crops out' at focal points under the ministry of the historic episcopate. Humanity is guaranteed contact with this reality at the divided river delta of episcopal churches. We may possibly, in the mercy of God, receive contact at other points also, in non-episcopal churches on the edges of the delta, where the proper channels have become silted up.

This view has become in effect the official Anglican stance toward other denominations. The famous 'Lambeth Quadrilateral' (endorsed in 1888 by the bishops of the Lambeth Conference) lays down four bases for reunion: the scriptures, creeds, two sacraments of baptism and eucharist, and the historic episcopate. The history of ecumenism in Britain has shown that the last leg is treated by the Church of England as being absolutely vital in defining the church. Churches in the Free Church tradition which have offered to come into this historic episcopate have failed to gain entry unless they have been prepared to have their ministry re-ordained by Anglican bishops. This remains true despite official Anglican protestations of acceptance that Free Church ministries are blessed by the Holy Spirit and bring their members to a saving and full knowledge of Christ. This ambivalent attitude results from the ambiguity inherent in the Anglo-Catholic position, the weakness long exposed by the logic of Newman. Twice the Methodists in Britain have offered to take up the episcopal system but twice been rejected over the issue of re-ordination into the historic line of ministerial succession.

Lesslie Newbigin wrote a telling critique of this Anglican episcopal position from his place as a bishop in the Presbyterian church involved in the formation of the Church of South India in 1947. There the Free Churches undertook to join with the episcopal Anglicans and to adopt the episcopal order, but not necessarily to have their own leaders consecrated separately by Anglican bishops, since this would have given the impression of something lacking in their previous ministry. Still forty years later, the official Anglican stance toward the Church of South India, now a totally episcopal church, remains one of non-recognition; there will be official communion between the two bodies when a handful of elderly, ex-Free Church, bishops are no more. At that point, when the remnant of ministry without the historic, (which is the word to be stressed), episcopal pedigree has gone, then that church can come into full communion with the Anglican communion. According to this view, the line of ordained ministry defines the church.

Notwithstanding beautifully wrought and aesthetically moving theological statements affirming the wholeness and spiritual nature of the catholic church, and of the presence of the Holy Spirit in Free Church life, this family of ecclesiology in practice is trapped into a peculiar, probably unique, exclusivist clericalist definition of the church. In this it reflects the aspect of Augustine's ecclesiology encountered above, as against the Eastern Orthodox more Cyprianic view, and against the logic of the legal Latin monolith of the Roman church, which crowns her episcopate with a topstone to avoid any possible confusion.

But there can be no doubt that the work of this family of theology, non-Roman western catholicism, has served its vocation of calling for one visible church. It refuses to accept complacent notions of an existing single spiritual church as not sufficiently close to the New Testament. Many now would agree that 'a divided Church is a contradiction of its own nature as Church; it is witnessing to a falsehood. Its evangelism cannot be effective.'[21] Whether the dominating theological principle for a reunited church should be that of Anglo-Catholic theology is another matter, and we now examine the distinctive heart of this principle, sacramental grace.

3. Priesthood and sacrifice

A. SACRAMENTAL GRACE

For Anglo-Catholic ecclesiology the 'historic episcopate' guarantees the duly appointed means of receiving divine grace and forgiveness in the sacraments. Indeed full membership of the church requires confirmation by a bishop, after which a person can receive holy communion.

The sacraments of baptism and the eucharist were ordained by Christ as the chief means of the church's contact with her Lord. They are to be celebrated by the duly appointed ministers of the church and of Christ in the church. These ministers are presbyters appointed in the proper manner by the successors to Christ's apostles, the bishops. Church order, as we have seen above, is no matter of convenience or accident but specifically given and imposed, patterned on the gospel, by Christ. This network through time forms the theological, not just the legal, instrument by which the Lord of the church repeatedly bestows grace upon his children. The ordained ministry of presbyters, continually renewed through the agency of the consecrated ministry of the episcopate, unites the faithful to Christ sacramentally. There is no room here for a division between salvation and the church's sacraments nor between an invisible and a spiritual contact with Christ. The visible sacraments are essential means of grace. The sacraments cannot, therefore, for this family of theology, be regarded as merely symbolic of a more real grace: they actually effect what they show forth, a rebirth or washing and a feeding.

Baptism brings about not merely a formal membership of the community but an actual regenerative event in the life of the candidate, whether infant or adult. This is argued on biblical grounds, for example Paul speaks 'of all of us who were baptized into Christ Jesus' being 'buried with him through baptism into death in order that, just as Christ was raised from the dead through the glory of the Father, we too may live a new life' (Romans 6:3). This is realistic rather than symbolic language apparently, speaking of a genuine change in the believer. But also, and in particular for the baptism of infants, baptismal regeneration is argued on the grounds of early church tradition. The general rule is that baptism be administered only by episcopally ordained priests, but as with Augustine and Stephen in the turmoils of schism, baptisms by other churches are recognized as valid, if not ideal, ways of entering the church, although needing to be fulfilled with continuing reception of the eucharist from the hands of the episcopal tradition.

The complete incorporation into the life of the body of Christ needs episcopal confirmation to complement baptism, and confirmation enables the candidate to receive the eucharist. Eucharistic contact is not available, in properly gospel form, from the hands of Nonconformist ministers without the benefit of episcopal ordination, although God in his mercy can and does use such ministries for bonding people to himself. Here we meet another facet of Anglo-Catholic ambivalence. One sacrament seems efficacious from other churchmen and even in emergency from lay people, such as the midwife baptizing a dying infant. But the eucharist is zealously fenced about from other ministries, however spiritual, and from lay celebration. The eucharistic ministry has become the testing point for inter-church relations. Priests ordained by Roman and Orthodox bishops are not re-ordained if they enter the Anglican ministry, whereas this is not now the case with ordained ministers from Free Church denominations.

The eucharist, linked to the historic episcopate, plays a dominating part in defining the function of the ordained presbyterate or priesthood. The notion that the local priest celebrates the eucharist as the representative of his bishop is also found in this tradition, an idea deriving probably from the early church after the age of the New Testament. Ignatius of Antioch, martyred between 110–115 A.D. wrote: 'Let no man do anything pertaining to the Church apart from the bishop. Let that eucharist be considered valid which is under the bishop or him to whom he commits it.'[22]

For the Anglo-Catholic tradition, the New Testament and the development of the canon have to be read in the light of the very earliest post apostolic age, as a living body of church life closest to the days of the apostles. The authority of scripture and that of the apostolic ministry coalesce to form one body of scripture and interpretation. 'The NT writings must be understood historically, that is in relation to a development which emerges into clearer daylight in the time of St Clement of Rome or St Ignatius of Antioch: the living tradition of developing church order is 'inspired' by the Holy Spirit as well as the writings that were later collected in the NT canon. The writings are to be interpreted by the organic development of the Church's life, not received as divine oracles that have miraculously dropped down from heaven without any reference to the Church as it came to exist in the second century.'[23] This is a key methodological point, and the same method of interpretation leads to the understanding that the sacrament of the body and blood of Christ, duly performed under the apostolic institute of bishop and priest, embodies the whole gospel including the self giving of the church in responsive sacrifice into the sacrifice of Christ.

B. MINISTERIAL PRIESTHOOD

The precise relationship between the ordained ministry, the church, and Christ remains to be explained. The priestly ministry, under the episcopate, constitutes Christ's ordained instrument for overseeing the church. The ministry serves the church 'ministerially'. It is a necessary organ of the whole body: 'The very point of the ministerial principle is this,' according to R. C.

Moberly, 'that whilst it is always the corporate church which acts through its representative instruments, it is only through instruments, empowered to represent, that the corporate church does act.'[24] The ministry acts only as representing the whole church, not as if it were separate from her. But the ministry is the only appropriate organ of the church for its particular function. This activity of oversight includes general pastoral care, teaching and proclaiming the faith, and celebrating the sacraments. This last commission most profoundly incorporates and sums up all the ministerial functions since the sacraments, particularly the eucharist, uniquely embody the gospel in the church. Because the presbyter, under the oversight of his bishop, celebrates the eucharist, blesses the people and pronounces absolution from sins, he is in some important sense a priest according to this theological view. But the interpretation of this priesthood is quite sophisticated and needs careful clarification.

Although the New Testament does not lay down in mechanical terms a blueprint or list of instructions for the priesthood of the presbyterate, nevertheless the living truth crystallized clearly that a priestly ministry was and is the true gospel means of grace in Christ. This priestliness arises from the priesthood of the whole church. Because Christ, according to the New Testament, is the high priest, his church is priestly. In 1 Peter 2:9 we read that she is a 'royal priesthood', in parallel with the ancient description of Israel as the 'kingdom of priests' (Exodus 19:6). The church of Jesus Christ has this unique privilege of priesthood 'to offer up spiritual sacrifices acceptable to God through Jesus Christ' (1 Peter 2:5). Her new status in Christ brings the church into this special relationship of holy, costly love with God, based solely upon the priestly, self-sacrifice of Jesus. The church relates to God no longer on the basis of the repeated sacrifices of bullocks and goats, as under the mechanical system of the old dispensation. Rather the whole church is priestly, having the impress of Christ's sacrificial character, called and empowered by the Holy Spirit to offer herself as a living sacrifice day by day (Romans 12). The very life of the church of God is the way of the cross, self-giving, living out the spirit of Calvary, following her shepherd who gives his life for the sheep. Self-identification with Christ crucified, in response to Christ's identification with us, is the heart of the church's royal priesthood.

Given that the life of the whole body reflects this priestly sacrificial character, then outwardly, in her gospel celebration of the eucharist, she also must be called priestly as she celebrates and proclaims this spiritual gift in the body and blood of the Lord. The eucharist unites the inner and the outer, the spiritual and the corporate, in the great gospel sacrament of the life-giving death of the Lord. In the celebration of the eucharist the church ceremonially enacts the priestly sacrifice of Christ and in so doing makes her own self-consecration, dedicating herself to die into Christ's one perfect sacrifice. The church's identity, as the eucharistic body under the cross in Christ, expresses itself most fully as she unites herself into the great atoning act, as she makes her priestly sacrifice. Baptism ordains all church people to the royal priesthood of the church, all share in the eucharist, all join in worship and offer spiritual sacrifices of thanks and praise. The Epistle to the Hebrews tells the whole church: 'Through him (Jesus) let us offer up a sacrifice of praise to God continually, that is the fruit of lips which make confessions to his name' (Hebrews 13:15). The Christian sacrifice offered by the priestly people is self-sacrifice, always in Christ's sacrifice.

If the whole body is priestly and sacrificial in this Christ-dependent sense, that means that the duly appointed ministerial organ of the church, the ordained ministry, acts on behalf of the whole body at the eucharistic celebration. Therefore this ordained ministry is in a special way priestly. The priesthood of all believers does not mean the priesthood of every believer. Responsibility for celebrating the sacraments falls to the ordained ministry and it was only natural that the church's priesthood in Christ should gradually be represented in the person of the celebrant, that the ordained ministry therefore be called priestly. 'If it once be admitted that the "breaking of the bread" was the essential Christian service from the first, and that it meant, and was, the Church's identifying with the body and blood of the Lord, everything follows in order from this one fact', explains Moberly.[25] Given that celebration of the sacrament inherently lies in the task of the presbyterate, then logically, and theologically, we are compelled to acknowledge a priestly presbyterate.

The presbyterate alone possesses the right to perform, amidst the whole church, on her behalf, the Christian sacrifice. Therefore, although the New Testament never applies the term 'priest' (*hiereus* in New Testatment Greek) to the presbyter, it was a purely natural development that this redefined, purified, notion of a priesthood after the model of Christ should have emerged very early after the New Testament era. This is just what we find indeed in the writings of Clement of Rome roughly at 96 A.D.[26] It was only natural, perhaps inevitable, and in the providence of God, that 'hieratic' priestly language should have become attached to the eucharist and the celebrants.

While upholding the sufficiency of Christ's one perfect sacrifice, a dependent or subsidiary priesthood of the ministry has been constructed from the priestly church as a whole. The method of exegesis hinges on reading the New Testament in the light of the early developments in church order after the close of the age of the apostles. Richardson argues that Luke's account of the Last Supper constitutes an 'ordination charge' to a new priesthood, the apostles: 'The appointment of places at the table of the Lord means that Christ is consecrating a new priesthood of those who will share in his *hierosune* (priesthood), and who will offer through his priesthood the Church's oblations. Christ is thus represented as consecrating the apostles as ministers of the eucharistic feast, at which he himself will be present (Luke 22:18), those who are to break the bread and pour the wine, the priests of his *Basileia* (kingdom), of which the Church on earth is the eschatological sign. They are the *leitourgoi* (servants or priests) of the new royal priesthood which is formed by the whole *ecclesia theou* (church of God).'[27] Richardson rebuts anticipated criticism: 'If to anyone today this interpretation of Luke 22:14–38 seems far-fetched or artificial, let him ask himself what else these verses could mean in the light of the developing eucharistic worship and episcopal-presbyteral church order of the later years of the first century. . . .'[28] Anglo-Catholic exegesis typically reads the New Testament as a phase in church life, a phase to be interpreted with strict reference to the developments in early church life and worship. Christ instituted the apostolic ministry which rapidly emerged as necessarily priestly as a result of eucharistic presidency.

This view of priesthood preserves the pastoral aspect of the ordained ministry. The inner heart of the presbyter is self-giving and pastorally caring, the inner being outwardly manifested in the sacramental priestly role. 'True priesthood is pastorate and pastorate based on priestliness . . . cure of souls is so really a sacrifice, and intercession an Eucharist, that the very ministry of the Eucharistic sacrifice fails to understand itself, if it find no corresponding utterance, in the secret chamber at least, as divine love and "cure" of souls.'[29] Rejecting at the outset the strong protestant distinction between the visible and the spiritual aspects of the church, Moberly interestingly reintroduces a different version of the distinction which envisages the "inner" as pastoral and personal, and the "outer" as the ceremonial and official, both united in the person of the priest, who reflects the humble character of the priestly Christ. The priestly ministry of intercession for the flock of God is also a theme of the pastoral function of the ministry.

C. EUCHARISTIC SACRIFICE

Christ ordained, more or less directly, the official ministry as representative of the whole church's priesthood. The Christian church has been given by historical development a notion of ministerial priesthood which rejects the Old Testament Mosaic idea of a priest standing between God and the people, making atonement for them. Rather priesthood is ecclesial and Christological. The one perfect sacrifice has already been made by Christ at Calvary. For Bicknell, in the last Anglo-Catholic exposition of the Thirty Nine Articles 'The one view that contradicts all Scripture teaching is to maintain that our Lord's death is in any sense repeated.'[30]

As we learned from Ramsey, the church is the visible, eucharistic body of Christ, the whole which goes beyond the sum of its parts, the spiritual and sacrificial community of the gospel. Now the nature of the priestly ministry as instrumental for the whole church has become clear: the ministerial priesthood, in total harmony with the church whom it serves, represents her eucharistic, priestly nature both ceremonially and pastorally. This priesthood therefore is not really vicarious, performed instead of the whole body, but expresses what the whole priestly, eucharistic, historic community already is. The priesthood is the organ of the body. 'What is duly done by Christian ministers, it is not so much that they do it, in the stead, or for the sake of, the whole; but rather that the whole does it by and through them.'[31] Given this interpretation of priesthood, how is the eucharist to be described as in some way sacrificial?

Christ's sacrifice, the decisive event of redemption, is celebrated in the eucharist which renews the church's participation in this saving event. But Christ's work of redemption did not terminate at Golgotha. Anglo-Catholic theology strongly emphasizes that Christ is now at the right hand of God and is continually offering his sacrifice in favour of the church. There is a movement of saving action from the Son to the Father in which the Son does not repeat his sacrifice but pleads it for the benefit of mankind. Hebrews 10:21 speaks of Christ as our great high priest over the house of God, and Hebrews 7:25 of Jesus living forever with an eternal priesthood who 'is able to save completely those who come to God through him, because he always lives to intercede for them.' The book of Revelation tells of the 'Lamb, looking as if it had been slain, standing in the centre of the throne' and receiving the praise and worship of the 'twenty-four elders' who represent the church (Revelation 5). We need to regard the sacrifice of Christ in a wider perspective than merely that of his death; this perspective must take in the incarnation and the heavenly priesthood which continues the offering of the once-for-all historical sacrifice.

At the eucharist the church not only recalls the historic act of atonement, but brings into the present the whole saving work of Christ and re-presents this, along with her own self-offering, always in Christ, to the Father. The Church in a sense offers Christ to the Father, joining with the eternal movement of Christ's self-giving. 'Through the commemorative thanksgiving the Church cooperates with the eternal act of His will and offers Him to the Father. Our Lord, as the Lamb that hath been slain, is an eternal and abiding sacrifice, interceding for us by His presence in Heaven. In the eucharist we on earth join with Him in pleading His sacrifice, even as He pleads it above.'[32] The Anglo-Catholic understands the church to offer Christ but not as if she were apart from Christ. The whole Christ offers the whole Christ, that is the Church already in Christ participates in his eternal self-offering. Christ brings before the Father not only his own offering but included within it the self-giving of his priestly people.

> 'Not only do we commemorate all that our Lord has done for us, but in and through Him we offer ourselves to the Father. Our Lord in Heaven presents to the Father not only Himself but His Body, the Church. . . . This is the culmination of the Eucharistic sacrifice. Not the mere presentation of Christ's sacrifice as something done for us or outside of us, but rather our own self-identification with that sacrifice.'[33]

Perhaps the stress on the fact that the Body of Christ includes his church can help in our understanding of this sophisticated theology of priestly eucharistic sacrifice: Christ's offering includes ours, ours is never apart from Christ's.

In this theology the notion of *anamnesis* has played a peculiarly important role, developed notably by Gregory Dix, one of the several brilliant Anglo-Catholic theologians in the first half of this century. The Greek word *anamnesis*, remembrance or memorial, is found in the key text, 'Do this in remembrance of me' (1 Corinthians 11:24), and has been found by this school of theology to have the dynamic meaning of 'bring into the present' or 'make present' the redeeming effect of the cross by means of the action of the eucharist. The eucharist therefore perpetuates the eternally accepted sacrifice of Christ in time by way of repeated anamnesis. Dix claims that this theology reflects the early patristic doctrine of the eucharist, 'whose key thought is that the action of the earthly church in the eucharist only manifests within time the eternal act of Christ as the heavenly High Priest at the altar before the throne of God, perpetually pleading His accomplished and effectual sacrifice.'[34] Anglo-Catholic theology believes that both Roman and Reformed Western doctrines of the eucharist have narrowed into an undue stress upon the unique event of the cross of Christ. Rome, with the medieval development of the unbloody reiteration of Calvary at the mass, and the Reformed view emphasizing the 'proclamation of the death of the Lord until he come', each lacks a sufficiently rounded understanding of the eucharistic celebration of Christ's ongoing heavenly priesthood for his church.

The priestly work of Christ did not finish at his death but goes on in heaven. According to the book of Revelation Christ, the Lamb, stands as if slain in the middle of the divine throne and evokes the worship of the twenty-four elders, representing the church, who say 'worthy art thou for thou wast slain . . .' H. B. Swete interprets this as the elders, the church, recognizing the abiding sacrificial value of the Ascended life; while on earth the church by Christ's ordinance commemorates the sacrifice under the form of bread and wine. 'The presentation in heaven and the commemoration on earth will go on simultaneously up to the moment of the Lord's Return.' The eucharistic commemoration is not, indeed, described in scripture as a presentation of our Lord's sacrifice to God: Paul's proclamation (*kataggelete*) refers rather to the witness borne by it to the world and the church. 'But,' continues Swete, 'our solemn memorial is assuredly made in the presence of God, and before all the company of heaven; and it proclaims the death of the Lord not as a past event as we might commemorate the death of a martyr, but as a sacrifice which lives on and is perpetually presented by Christ Himself in heaven. We have an altar (Hebrews 13:10) which answers to the heavenly Altar at which the Great High Priest officiates. The eucharistic rite is the nearest approach which the priestly Body of Christ on earth can make to a participation in the High Priestly self presentation of her Head in heaven.'[35] Or, using Bicknell, 'In the eucharist we on earth join with Him in pleading His sacrifice, even as He pleads it above.'[36]

Texts referring to the heavenly Christ bolster an understanding of the pleading of the sacrifice of Calvary by Christ and, derivatively, by the church. Offering the consecrated bread and wine to God, the earthly priest offers Christ's sacrifice and presents on earth what Christ is eternally offering to the Father. The priest, on behalf of the church, faces toward the Father with the memorial, making present, of the great sacrifice of Christ. At the same time the priest faces the church as the representative of Christ, feeding the faithful with the bread and wine, now become Christ's body and blood. The priestly pleading and feeding is primarily Christ's, the church uniting herself in this action, through the service of the ordained ministry.

This traditional Anglo-Catholic understanding of eucharistic sacrifice and priesthood has very recently received endorsement by the influential Faith and Order Advisory Group of the Church of England in its report, *The Priesthood of the Ordained Ministry*.[37] This report argues that the mainline Anglican position on the priesthood of the ordained ministry is that just outlined. This document runs over the history of the priesthood and the Anglican usage of the term and the great debates involved. It seeks to be guided by scripture using the Anglo-Catholic method of interpretation: 'We have taken account of the normative witness of Scripture as it has been understood in the life of the church.'[38]

The result of the historical and theological exploration is that right up to the Reformation, 'the theologians interpreted the eucharist as a renewed apprehension and application of the past event of the sacrifice of the Passion, in which the risen Lord himself, as the head of the Church, now pleads his self-offering before the Father and brings his people with him into the holy of holies. The priest played an essential part in the eucharistic celebration at precisely this point. Here the priest both represents Christ to the people and the people to God in union with Christ.'[39]. Because the Anglican ordinal has kept the word 'priest', because of the Tractarian re-statement of priesthood, and because of converging ecumenical agreements, the official Anglican position ought to be along this line. Moreover, the priesthood of the ordained ministry 'is not simply derived from the priestliness of the whole community. Rather, the common priesthood of the community and the special priesthood of the ordained ministry are both derived from the priesthood of Christ.'[40] This line of interpretation is quite a strong strain of Anglo-Catholic doctrine, separating out two lines of priestliness stemming from the one great high priest, Christ, a lay line and a clerical line, notwithstanding the acknowledgement that the New Testament itself does not apply the term to the ministry. The justification for this distinct and special priestly line is precisely that of Moberly: 'the difference is that their ministry is an appointed means through which Christ makes his priesthood present and effective to his people.'

D. BAPTISM AND ABSOLUTION

Baptism can in an emergency be administered by the layman or woman and therefore entails a less exclusive view of ministerial priesthood than applies to the eucharist, exclusively confined to the ordained priesthood. Indeed, traditional Anglo-Catholic theology rejects women as possible priests on the ground that in the eucharist the priest, representing Christ and his apostolic priesthood, must therefore be male as were Christ and the apostles. The priesthood has an exclusive ministry of reconciliation, of pronouncing and conveying absolution from sin.

Baptism acts as an 'effectual' sign and not merely a symbol without substance. In baptism an individual becomes part of the church body and is incorporated into Christ. Baptism actually conveys saving grace to the candidate, who needs however to maintain this process in the life of the church's sacramental ministry. The Anglo-Catholic insists that the sacraments of the church are objectively effective: they do not depend for their power on the faith of the recipient but on the power of God who has guaranteed to work in and through properly celebrated sacraments. Grace mediated through the outward and visible sacraments of the church life plays perhaps the major part in spiritual life.

As regards forgiveness of sins, which baptism initiates, the church has been given the ministry contained in the words of Jesus to Peter: 'I will give you the keys of the kingdom of heaven, and whatsoever you shall bind on earth shall be bound in heaven, and whatsoever you shall loose on earth shall be loosed in heaven' (Matthew 16:9); the same command being addressed to to the disciples in general, without the 'power of keys' statement (Matthew 11:18). The Anglo-Catholic interpretation stresses the ministry as the church's instrument for exercising this role of ruling the church and absolving from sin. This absolution can be granted with the imposition of a penance after private confession of sin to the clergy. The clergy have the power to exclude the sinner from the fellowship of the church, in exercising the keys of the kingdom, and to re-admit, but they seek to rely on the Holy Spirit's guidance rather than regarding themselves as acting as independent agents.

This ministry is not understood as delegated from the whole body of the church to the clergy, but rather delegated by Christ to the twelve who in turn handed this to the episcopate and clergy. The ministry of absolution or reconciliation is seen as part of the oversight of the church, performed by the appropriate part of the whole body, but which received its commission from the Lord rather than as a democratic convenience 'from below'.

Theologically the official pronouncement of absolution comes from Christ through the properly appointed ministerial channel stemming from the twelve, the apostolate now continued in the historical episcopate. Anglo-Catholic thought envisages the heard word of pardon from Christ to the penitent through the priest as coinciding with the spiritual reality of forgiveness from God. The Epistle of James teaches Christians to confess their sins to one another: the priest, the agent of the church, also represents Christ's words of pardon to the sinner.

4. An Evangelical critique of the Anglo-Catholic ecclesiology

A major concern with this theology of priesthood and eucharist is that exegetically it seems weak. In particular the appeal to the notion of an ongoing pleading of Christ's sacrifice in heaven rests upon weak New Testament evidence, only strengthened with the addition of the glue of some parallel patristic interpretation. The appeal to the epistle to the Hebrews, in particular, needs thorough investigation. Alan Richardson, an Anglican

Biblical sholar not unsympathetic to the high church scheme of things, is quite emphatic. According to him, the interpretation that the author of Hebrews

> 'teaches that Christ in heaven is continually offering himself (or his blood) to God is based on a falsely Platonizing interpretation which ignores the kephelaion—'the chief point' (8:1)—which the writer himself wishes to make: because of the one, perfect, unrepeatable sacrifice of Calvary, "we have a great high priest who sat down on the right hand of the throne of the Majesty in the heavens" (8:1). Christ is seated in the seat of the Vizier, not standing in the posture and place of the suppliant. He intercedes for us, but with the effective power of the co-ruler seated on the right hand of the sovereign God. Because of what he has done in history there is no more offering for sin (10:18).'[41]

For Richardson the epistle as a whole teaches that the ascension 'is the moment of the completion of Christ's atoning work, the presenting of the blood in the heavenly tabernacle,'[42] the moment when the true sacrifice made on the cross was offered as Christ entered the 'holy of holies', heaven itself.

The doctrine of the eucharistic offering or pleading of the once-for-all sacrifice by this school of theology underlies its picture of the ministry as priestly and its ecclesiology as primarily sacramental. But there is great difficulty in deriving it plainly and clearly from the New Testament. The high priesthood of Christ as intercessor from the throne of grace is clear, but notions of ongoing pleading in the eternal realms are not. In an authoritative commentary on the Epistle to the Hebrews we read this observation on chapter 8 verse 3:

> 'we may note that it is not implied that Jesus is continually or repeatedly presenting His offering; this is excluded by Ch. 7:27, which contrasts the daily sacrifices of the Aaronic high priests with the offering which the Christians' high priest has already presented once and for all. The tense and mood of the Greek verb "to offer" in this clause (8:3) also exclude the idea of a continual offering; indeed, NEB suggests in a footnote a rendering which would make the situation completely unambiguous: "this one too must have had something to offer".'[43]

It seems exegetically doubtful whether the notion of an ongoing offering of the sacrifice can be sustained. This relates to the issue of the distinctive Anglo-Catholic method of theological interpretation, which co-ordinates the New Testament with patristic doctrine, never allowing the former to criticize the latter.

Both Hebrews and Revelation associate the slain and risen Christ with kingly rule and a priestly intercession rather than with any idea of eternal pleading of his sacrifice. Christ has 'sat down' in the royal position, he is the lamb in the middle of the throne, interceding for his people from the position of having completed making atonement, both as regards the act of dying and of offering that death. Christ's continuing ministry is not that of pleading his sacrifice but rather, on the basis of his accepted sacrifice, taking royal, priestly intercessory interest in his people. The imagery of Hebrews is that of the Old Testament Day of Atonement on which the victim was slain in the court of the sanctuary and its blood presented inside the sanctuary; Christ's death on the cross parallels the former, his appearance at God's right hand the latter, also a decisively completed event. Because of this completed atoning work, the church, seeing she has a great high priest who has passed into the heavens, can draw near with full assurance of faith to the throne of grace, enjoying the extraordinary privilege of access to God.

'We must not think,' says Bruce, 'that because our author speaks of Jesus as having "passed into the heavens" and having "sat down at the right hand of the throne of God" he thought of the heavenly sanctuary as being, in reverse, a glorified replica of the sanctuary on earth, established in perpetuity on some higher place.'[44] This would be a platonizing interpretation of a text whose true background is Jewish eschatological expectation. The true interpretation is that a new spiritual order now exists wherein true worship, the spiritual sacrifice of praise, is now possible.

Aulen points out the risks of connecting the high priesthood of Christ in heaven with the eucharist on earth. This connection tends to divert attention from the radical change effected by the cross of Christ and to obscure the divine verdict, made once and for all, by the resurrection. The resurrection means that the sacrifice does not need to be pleaded because the verdict of the Father has already been given decisively to the sacrifice.[45] These are very telling points from the heartland of basic New Testament doctrine. Pannenberg, in his great work on Christology, emphasizes that the resurrection of Jesus has the theological meaning of a final, decisive, end-time vindication of Jesus, his life and his destiny, by the Father.[46] The Anglo-Catholic position on eucharistic sacrifice seems to miss the essential theological point of the finality of the cross and resurrection.

Aulen also rejects the eucharistic idea that we 'offer Christ', as an idea alien to the New Testament and a distortion of its teaching, even given the sophisticated qualifications and caveats stressing the priority of Christ's own self-offering. The very fact that such caveats need to be made shows that things have got out of balance in the Anglo-Catholic eucharistic scheme of things. He comments that when Anglo-Catholic thought speaks of the whole Christ offering the whole Christ on the eucharistic altar, it falls into quite serious confusion: 'That the presence of Christ in the eucharist also makes his sacrifice present is not the same as saying that the church "offers" the body and blood of Christ. The latter statement would be true and verified,' argues Aulen, 'only on the supposition that we completely identify Christ and the church. Now it is true that nothing more important can be said of the church than that it is the body of Christ, which implies that Christ identifies himself with his church. But the profound truth of this statement does not permit us to turn this statement around and say that the church is Christ. If this last statement were valid, and if we thus identified the action of the church with Christ's own action, we could without difficulty say that the church offers Christ. The offering of the church would then be identical with Christ's own sacrifice. But if the sacrifice made by Christ once for all is primary in relation to the church, this identification becomes impossible. The sacrifice of Christ,' he concludes, 'is and remains his own sacrifice, eternally valid, present in the eucharist, but entirely his own, not the church's sacrifice.'[47]

Aulen's criticism challenges the mode of identification between the church and Christ. Christ takes his people into union with himself and makes the church his bride and his body. But this relationship is established on the basis of royal grace, fully maintaining the distinction between the giver of grace and the recipients. The recipients are not in the position to offer the gift which was given on their behalf. It is argued in reply that this Anglo-Catholic view merely rehearses visibly the truth of justification by faith. Ramsey, along with Bicknell, quotes the hymn:

> 'Look, Father, look on his anointed face,
> and only look on us as found in him.'

to reinforce his claim that his theology of offering Christ eucharistically is utterly congruent with classic Biblical notions of salvation in Christ. The church spreads forth the perfect sacrifice before the Father as the beneficiaries of that sacrifice, just as Paul teaches the church to rely not on her own merits and works but on the atoning work of Christ.

The same hymn contains the lines:

> 'And so between our sins and their reward,
> we set the passion of thy Son our Lord.'

The completed sacrifice, coupled with the ongoing pleading, is presented to the Father by the church through the ministry of the priest. In essence the pleading by the Son and by the church is united, and distinguishable in terms of the object of the sacrifice. The Son pleads, offers, his sacrifice only for his church; the church offers it for her own benefit. This is a major distinction, the difference once again between the benefactor and the beneficiary, between the giver of the sacrifice and the recipients of its pardoning grace, between expiatory sacrifice and response to that. However the recipient beneficiary, the church, may respond to Christ's sacrifice in a self-sacrificing way, the real difference between the two sacrifices must be preserved with great care.

This is because howevermuch our minds and hearts, renewed in Christ, overflow with self-sacrifice and costly love, we are never sufficiently pure to be incorporated into Christ's saving work as a saving element. Our renewal is the result of his atoning work and response to it. Our self-offering is patchy and frail, never sufficient to ground our salvation, not even when its motivation is that of God's love within us. Our good works are the fruit of our salvation. Therefore even to co-ordinate our sacrifice with Christ's sails close to semi-Pelagianism, the view that we are accepted by God because of our good works performed with God's help. Importing our own, albeit Christ-motivated, efforts into the theology of the eucharist detracts from the church's total focus on the unique glory of the sacrifice of Christ.

Bicknell formulates a key question about the commemoration, *anamnesis*, of the eucharist. He says, 'Who is reminded and of what he is reminded,' in the accounts of the Lord's institution of the eucharist, 'depend solely upon the context.'[48] Who is reminding whom of what in the eucharist? Is the eucharistic rite directed 'upwards' to the Father? The Anglo-Catholic clearly envisages this orientation, although not in the sacrament of baptism nor other sacramental acts in church life which flow from God to mankind. This notion of re-presenting the saving sacrifice in unison with Christ's pleading sees the movement directed to the Father in the Son. The Father is reminded of the sacrifice of the Son by the church, which in turn is never outside Christ. The Father responds to this *anamnesis* by feeding the church with the living bread and wine, now become the body and blood of the Lord.

Michael Green quotes Knox as asking the theological question, whether God really needs reminding of the sacrifice of his Son,[49] let alone whether the efficacy of this cataclysmic spiritual event requires continuing pleading as if somehow to reactivate it on behalf of the church. On the other hand, the work of the great New Testament scholar Joachim Jeremias can bolster the notion of *anamnesis* as asking God to remember the sacrifice of Christ, although in an eschatological way,[50] and Anglo-Catholic scholars continue to reaffirm their position with reference to a long liturgical tradition,[51] in addition to scripture.

This theological problem can be heightened when it is coupled with the Anglo-Catholic tendency to regard the eucharist as something to be done, a holy ritual to be celebrated, the performance itself becoming the centre of attention. In other words, liturgical ritual with all its beauty and sophistication can turn in on itself in a narcissistic self-admiration and fail to point to God in all his merciful love in Christ. In the extraordinarily powerful synagogue celebration of the Day of Atonement, a crescendo of praise wells up in the threefold *Qadosh*, or 'Holy Holy Holy is the Lord God of Hosts', taken directly from the prophet Isaiah's encounter with the Lord in the Temple. Many churches place this in their eucharistic worship and rightly so, since it concentrates attention, in thoroughly Hebraic fashion, on God's absolute worth and away from ourselves. Any eucharistic theological style which tends to reflect attention back onto the contribution of the beneficiaries of grace, in terms of offering and obedient ritual act, is suspect to evangelical eyes, with the grave danger of priestly 'naturalization of grace'.

Christ's incarnation, the church and the sacraments hang together' inseparably in the Anglo-Catholic theology. The church was founded by the incarnate Christ, God and man, and it is supremely fitting that grace be communicated through physical means ministered by human hands. God's saving action penetrates the world sacramentally, after the pattern of the incarnation. The church is Christ's body on earth, and has official structures. The succession of bishops is the presupposition of the communication of grace in the sacraments and the guarantee of true doctrine.

Participation is another key idea of this ecclesiology, following from the incarnation of Christ as human. Because of the incarnation divinity has participated in real humanity, in all its historical character. The church participates in Christ and the priesthood focuses this sharply in the sacrament, the eucharist of the body and blood of Christ. Christ includes the church, the church participates in Christ. Christ was incarnate and the church is his bodily presence on the earth and in history, incarnation and church interpret each other. To grasp this is to gain the key of explanation of the way this major school of spirtuality and theology sees things. Appealing back beyond the Reformation divide of the western church it listens especially to Alexandrian theology, to Athanasius and Cyril, concentrating on the person of the divine word incarnate as the heart of the living reality of the church. When applied to the church the sacramental principle becomes central: the church is an earthly society but truly a heavenly one to the eye of faith. Owen Chadwick cites George Herbert's hymn[52] to illustrate this sacramental way of interpreting the world:

> 'The man that looks on glass,
> On it may stay his eye,
> Or if he pleaseth through it pass
> And then the heaven espy.'

This sacramental 'world view' reaches its climax with the eucharist when heaven and earth combine and our offering is Christed, Christened, in the archetypal offering of the Christ. A high degree of the patristic platonism colours the interpretation. The divine Logos centres the vast panorama of creation; everything comes from that centre and tends back to it. The visible universe can disclose its spiritual heart to the spiritually minded, to the eye of faith.

The incarnation sums up this high church synthesis of the Word and nature, and gives the church its formative dynamic life in history. Grace perfects nature. Christ's sacrifice grounds the church's sacrifice and perfects it. The church finds an appropriate organ for eucharistic offering in the ordained priesthood. This ecclesiology operates through levels of being reflected in lower levels and representational levels, all held together in the synthesis of divine Word made human flesh.

Evangelical thought acknowledges this vision as aesthetically pleasing and philosophically coherent, but asks whether it follows the burden of the New Testament. Does the New Testament focus on a sacramental church ordered by a priestly ministry? The lack of mention in the New Testament of the ministry as priestly to Anglo-Catholicism is 'not surprising since the early church developed within Judaism and the sacrificial system of the Temple continued until the destruction of the Temple in AD 70.'[53] Nevertheless there is an apostolic continuation, or 'expansion' as Mascall has it,[54] of ministerial, representative priesthood in and over the rest of the church whose primary task, apart from perpetuating its own line, is to minister at the eucharistic sacrifice. A form of priesthood, associated with sacrifice and miracle, however derivative from Christ, gains new birth after its accidental abolition from the faith of the New Testament. The question must be asked whether this is equivalent to the reversal of the general theological tenor of the apostolic faith, let alone of its historical description and terminology for ministry? Is a primarily cultic priesthood really compatible with the gospel?

I think that at the root of the problems an evangelical faces with the sophisticated eucharistic priestly view of the church lies the interpretation of the atonement. All broadly orthodox churchpeople will agree that we participate in Christ. But the eucharist celebrates the theological reason why we can and do so participate. The cross of Jesus and his vindicating resurrection are the only basis for this participation and it is this which should therefore be our focus at the eucharist. 'Look Father look on his anointed face / And only look on us as found in him,' as the hymn has it, but how can the holy God look on us as found in him? How can the church be deemed fit to participate in the crucified and risen Lord? Only because of the sacrifice and resurrection declaration of victory on our behalf. The very idea of the church offering Christ, even in some weak and qualified sense, runs counter to this profound understanding of the force and sufficiency of the death and resurrection of Christ for the church, separate from the church, creative of the church, enabling the church to share in the life of God.

Evangelical atonement theology cannot stop short at the statement of participation, as if the atonement is at-one-ment rather than the ground for the possibility of at-one-ment, for the possibility of participation in Christ. Hence to include the church's self-offering on the altar as incorporated within Christ's offering quite fails, for the evangelical across the denominational boundaries, to do justice to the uniquely regenerative act of Christ's saving work. The reason why evangelical thought finds it hard to accept a sacramental view of the world and the church is its more radical understanding of sin affecting creation, of discontinuity, of the need for very deep redemption brought into the heart by the Spirit of Christ.

Whereas the Anglo-Catholic regards the evangelical theology as guilty of splitting the Son from the Father on the cross in the transactional view of the atonement, the evangelical sees just this fault in the Anglo-Catholic doctrine of the eternal pleading of the sacrifice in heaven. The former stresses the once for all point of salvation, the latter the ongoing ecclesial process of life in Christ's sacrificial work now being offered to the Father and taking up the church in its movement.

As opposed to the exclusivist Roman and Orthodox episcopal systems, the Anglo-Catholic theory of episcopal church order has been shown, by Newbigin especially, to place the church below the ministry, to legitimate episcopalian schism in the name of catholicity, and to reject visible union with other worldwide churches while at the same time acknowledging that they are indwelt by the Holy Spirit. In a way this ecclesiology seems trapped by a rigid theory of the past into failing to recognize that God is God of the living and not the dead, is the God of hope, the God of the future and of community. The notion that the church exists in a place primarily in her bishop, then derivatively in his delegates, the priests, seems an extraordinary clerical distortion, even inversion, of the New Testament vision of the community of the Holy Spirit. It must be said that Anglo-Catholic thought always envisages the ministerial action as the church's action through duly appointed organs, not as formally separate from the community.[55]

Yet Anglo-Catholic ecclesiology, currently normative in Anglicanism at present, has its incarnational centre, and has the great merit of reminding the church of her status and her high calling to be the visible body of Christ, bearing in her body the marks of the crucified Lord in sacrificial love to the world. A purely pietist approach to the Christian life will not suffice, although sacramentalism can transmute private evangelical piety to ecclesiastical ritual. The church of Christ is one visible body with a definite pattern of sacramental ministry established under God, by way of Christ's intention crystallized in historical evolution.

Before liberation theology became fashionable, this strand of the Church of England was notable for its service in the inner cities and identified with the poor, resulting from their commitment to the incarnational pattern of ministry. Although even in this great ministry Anglo-Catholicism was almost wholly priestly, the clergy virtually being identified as the church and in an heroic vein. The Oxford Movement insisted on the independence of the church over against the government, and this ecclesiological stance has often enabled the Anglo-Catholic to criticize social and economic conditions more freely than others within the Anglican family. Anglo-Catholic priests have often lived out the eucharistic offering socially, even challenging structures, as in their South African ministry.

This brings us to our agenda set out at the end of the previous chapter. The most attractive accounts of Anglo-Catholic ecclesiology, like Ramsey's, stress Christ at the centre of the sacramental body, the ministry subserving as well as guaranteeing the visible organism. Barth's Christological centre is vital. But the insistence on adding their episcopal definition as more than just a secondary matter, leaves the great problem of uniting the two principles, one Christological-transcendental, the other legal-historical. Somehow a fullness of being the church requires the historic episcopate. Moberly taught that a Nonconformist might well be more deeply yielded to the Holy Spirit of Christ than many episcopalians, and yet be less fully a member of the church of Christ. Anglo-Catholic theology has never resolved this tension between the spiritual and the structural aspects of the church.

In terms of the models discussed earlier, the Christological 'centre-circumference' model fails to fit the Anglo-Catholic 'foundation-superstructure' model of the threefold ministry. The Anglo-Catholic attempt to link the outward organizational structures of the church to the inner spiritual principle of sacrifice may not convince us in the way it works out, but the attempt to make this link is very important and evangelicals would do well to take up the challenge to theologize about the structures of the church rather than regard them as an historical accident, as a principle of the gospel. Schism is an offence to Christ, for Anglo-Catholicism.

Authority, for the Anglo-Catholic, is apostolic and catholic and rests in the episcopal trustees of the faith who serve to teach and minister grace through the sacraments after the commission given to and through the apostles. Authority in the church is a living reality, not just a matter of consulting texts from the past. In theory the line of bishops embodies the apostolic teaching, they are a speaking authority, ministerial to the gospel of Jesus. The way, the truth and the life together form a rounded idea of church authority, the pastoral coinciding with the doctrinal and ethical in the life of the church. The first four centuries of the church before it was divided do constititute normative teaching and practice. But Newman's critique of this position has not been answered. Today, the traditional Anglo-Catholic finds much distress because of this commitment: the ancient church did not ordain women. This basic tradition lay behind the tragic lament of Gareth Bennet's *Crockford's Preface*. Today's church is breaking with the ancient tradition, and risks losing catholicity also by breaking with the Roman and Orthodox Churches over this.

Anglo-Catholicism, for all its theoretical vulnerability at several levels, retains a powerful and serious religious appeal in an age of superficiality and indisciplined spirituality. The ethos of sacrifice moves from the eucharist into the priestly life. Also it is important to note the visual as a key category in this ecclesiology. Grace comes through the visual, the beautiful. The eucharist re-enacts the incarnational synthesis of divine and creaturely. The consecrated host attracts our adoration amidst the scent of incense rising to heaven. The priest, standing for Christ, mediates forgiveness and blessing. The transfiguration, at which heaven met with earth and the glory of Jesus shone forth, encapsulates Anglo-Catholic worship. We gaze upon Christ and put ourselves on the altar of sacrifice as we go out again into the confusion of the world. When the history of Anglican worship for this generation is written, it may well be reckoned that Sunday by Sunday Anglo-Catholic eucharistic worship proved a far stronger diet than light-hearted family services, so often the fare for evangelical Anglicans, who need to learn much from Ramsey's tradition.

END NOTES TO CHAPTER 2

1. *What is the Church?* SCM, London, 1969 p. 42.
2. *Bishops. But What Kind?* ed. P. Moore, SPCK, London, 1982 p. 125.
3. Titus 1:5.
4. Acts 14:23.
5. *The Gospel and the Catholic Church*, Longmans, London, 1936.
6. 2 Cor. 5:14.
7. ibid. pp. 63–4.
8. Acts 8:26 Essay p. 88.
9. Ramsey op. cit. p. 65.
10. ibid. p. 64.
11. ibid. p. 218.
12. Ephesians 2:14.
13. Ramsey op. cit. p. 154.
14. Essay p. 265.
15. Ramsey op. cit. p. 179.
16. *Doctrines of the Creed* Nisbet, London, 1938 p. 339.
17. ibid. p. 341.
18. Quoted in *From Gore to Temple* Longmans, London, 1960 p. 125.
19. *Stepping Stones* ed. C. Baxter, Hodder and Stoughton, 1987 p. 60.
20. Quoted in *Gore to Temple* p. 126.
21. Richardson An *Introduction to the theology of the New Testament* p. 287.
22. Ignatius *To the Smyrnaeans* VIII quoted in J. Stevenson *A New Eusebius* SPCK, London, 1957 p. 48.
23. A. Richardson *An Introduction to the theology of the NT* pp. 312–3.
24. op. cit. p. 111.
25. ibid. pp. 266–7.
26. See e.g. J. Stevenson op. cit. p. 13 for an extract from Clement on this subject.
27. Richardson op. cit. p. 316.
28. ibid. pp. 316–7.
29. Moberly op. cit. p. 299.
30. *A Theological Introduction to The Thirty Nine Articles* Longmans Green, London, 1925 p. 519.
31. Moberly op. cit. p. 242.
32. Bicknell op. cit. p. 519.
33. Bicknell op. cit. p. 520.
34. *Shape of the Liturgy* Dacre Press, London, 1945 p. 25.
35. Swete *Ascended Christ* Macmillan, London, 1910 p. 48.
36. ibid. p. 519.
37. Faith and Order Group (FOAG) of the Board of Mission and Unity, Report, *The Priesthood of the Ordained Ministry*, General Synod of the Church of England, London, 1986.
38. ibid. p. 91.
39. ibid. pp. 93–4.
40. ibid. p. 99.
41. op. cit. p. 202.

42. op. cit. p. 203.
43. F. F. Bruce *The Epistle to the Hebrews* Marshall Morgan & Scott, London, 1965 p. 164.
44. op. cit. p. lvii.
45. Aulen *Eucharist and Sacrifice* Oliver and Boyd, London, 1958 p. 911.
46. *Jesus God and Man* SCM, London, 1968.
47. op. cit. 181–2.
48. op. cit. 516.
49. *Freed to Serve* Hodder and Stoughton, London, 1983 p. 139.
50. *The Eucharistic Words of Jesus* SCM, London, 1966 p. 253: 'The proclamation of the death of Jesus is not therefore intended to call to the remembrance of the community the event of the Passion; rather this proclamation expresses the vicarious death of Jesus as the beginning of the salvation time and prays for the coming of the consummation. As often as the death of the Lord is proclaimed at the Lord's supper, and the maranatha (come Lord) rises upwards, God is reminded of the unfulfilled climax of the work of salvation, "until (the goal is reached that) he comes". Paul has therefore understood the anamnesis as the eschatological remembrance of God that is to be realised in the parousia.'
51. K. Stevenson *Eucharist and Offering* Pueblo Publishing Co, New York, 1986.
52. *The Mind of the Oxford Movement*, A & C Black, London, 1960 p. 18.
53. FOAG p. 28.
54. *Theology and the Gospel of Christ* SPCK, London, 1977 p. 213.
55. See e.g. Moberly *Ministerial Priesthood* pp. 241–2.

3

THE ARCIC SYNTHESIS: ROME, CANTERBURY AND AUTHORITY

Anglo-Catholicism is controlled by the 'foundation-superstructure' model of the church, with the spiritual 'centre-circumference' idea, eucharistically interpreted, linked on to the early apostolic-episcopal foundation. R. C. Moberly criticizes the Protestant position for ignoring the apostolic structure of the visible church; but on the other hand he criticizes the Roman church for exalting the institutional structure over the spiritual life of the church. The currently flourishing Anglican Roman Catholic International Commission (ARCIC) seeks to go back behind the polemic of the great split at the Reformation in order to re-establish agreed theological positions which will lead to a uniting of the churches. ARCIC has produced two reports, the first on eucharist, ministry and authority, *The Final Report*[1]; the second *Salvation and the Church*[2]; we shall refer to them as ARCIC 1 and ARCIC 2 respectively. This ecclesiology exploits the type of thought used by Newman and the model of development.

Roman Catholicism has undergone considerable change since Moberly's day, decisively expressed by the work of the Second Vatican Council, 1962–5. This softened rigid stances on many areas of doctrine and order and in particular preferred a pastorally sacramental model of the church to the institutional, hierarchically sacramental model. The style and tone of Vatican 2, at least, expresses this change and describes the church in biblical terms, notably as the 'people of God'. Anglo-Catholic and Roman Catholic theology have therefore been converging rapidly and it was only natural that this family of Anglican theology should present the Anglican face in dialogue with

Rome and could secure substantial agreement in the major matters of the faith. This chapter continues the themes of Anglo-Catholic ecclesiology into ARCIC 1 on eucharist, ministry and authority. We shall outline the basic positions adopted on the nature of the church, the sacraments, the priestly ministry, the primacy, and doctrinal authority, offering appraisals theme by theme.

Newman and Barth are crucial companions in evaluating this ARCIC synthesis. Both had a major impact on the Vatican 2, Newman as perhaps the decisive methodological influence and Barth, through his influence on some key contemporary Roman theologians, as part of the momentum for a greater biblical and Christological orientation in theology.

1. Koinonia and the nature of the church

ARCIC has done superbly creative work, aiming to overcome the polemics of the past while sticking to key theological and biblical norms. The introductory material in the ARCIC Report has not been much noticed, and yet it is fundamental to the argumentation and content of all the individual reports throughout the document. The guiding norm selected is that of *koinonia* fellowship, or communion, and this New Testament idea provides the base idea for understanding the nature of the church. ARCIC set its face against starting in the realms of the official, hierarchical, and formal, preferring instead spiritual fellowship, or sharing, *koinonia,* in Christ, as the key definition of the church. We shall see that this concept serves as a wide base for ARCIC 1's ecclesiology, including the theological method used throughout.

'Union with God in Christ Jesus through the Spirit is the heart of Christian *koinonia*. Among the various ways in which the term *koinonia* is used in different New Testament contexts, we concentrate on that which signifies a relation between persons resulting from their participation in one and the same reality (cf. 1 John 1:3). The Son of God has taken to himself our human nature, and he has sent upon us his Spirit, who makes us so truly members of the body of Christ that we too are able to call God "Abba, Father" (Rom. 8:15; Gal. 4:5). Moreover sharing in the same Holy Spirit, whereby we become members of the same body of Christ and adopted children of the same Father, we are bound to one another in a completely new relationship. *Koinonia* with one another is entailed by our *koinonia* with God in Christ. This is the mystery of the Church.'[3] The sublime teaching of the New Testament could hardly be more clearly put. All Christian people in all denominations, certainly the orthodox main body of believers, would agree wholeheartedly with this statement, from the most formal episcopal churches to the apparently much less formal House Church movement. Fellowship with God through the redeeming Son in the Holy Spirit, this is the fundamental *koinonia* of the church and from this participation in Christ flows the fellowship which constitutes the church.

This core definition is thoroughly in tune with the ecclesiology of Barth and evangelical theology generally. We might even say that initially the keynote concept of ARCIC ecclesiology represents what Sykes called the centre-circumference model, Christ being so very firmly at the centre and, perhaps even more significantly, the Holy Spirit rather than the sacramental system, being the primary medium of our contact with Christ, the true life of the church. ARCIC 1 starts Christocentrically in defining the church as spiritual communion.

Sacraments and ministry, for which another New Testament word *episcope*, oversight, is used, receive their definition in terms of *koinonia*: the eucharist is the effectual sign of *koinonia* and *episcope* serves to foster fellowship with Christ and one with another in the church family. Primacy or papacy similarly exists to promote the overall *koinonia*. The *koinonia* of the church requires visible expression. She is to signal the saving work of Christ to the world and is to be the instrument used for realizing God's plan of salvation by her life and witness.[4] ARClC 2[5] adds the description 'steward' to sign and instrument, because the church is entrusted with the gospel of redemption to proclaim and live out. The church is *koinonia* in her being but equally sacrament in terms of her doing, since she is sign and means, effectual sign, of God's saving grace in Christ.

As steward of the gospel, the church 'is servant and not master of what it has received,' says ARCIC 2, continuing in perhaps even more evangelical vein, 'Indeed, its power to affect the hearer comes not from our unaided efforts but entirely from the Holy Spirit, who is the source of the Church's life and who enables it to be truly the steward of God's design.'[8] The church also is always in need of renewal and purification in this world and is not yet fully the kingdom of God but rather a foretaste of it until the consummation at the end time.[7] Therefore we can say that the ARCIC ecclesiology abandons triumphalism and pride in the institution. The church depends constantly on the Holy Spirit for her life and mission. This initial ground plan ecclesiology of ARCIC squares with Barth's views on the nature of the church; she is wholly dependent upon, and points to, God; she is the instrument of God in the world. She is both holy and yet in need of repentance. Barth also has much teaching on the sacramental character of the church: she is the means chosen to mediate the gospel in her proclamation, not herself divine but the channel, effective in the power of the Spirit. In a sense she stands in the place of John the Baptist, not the light but appointed to witness to the light. ARCIC 1 plainly implies that the *koinonia* of the church is spiritual and invisible since it 'requires visible expression'.[8]

If ARCIC takes *koinonia* as its base model of the church, it regards the concept as in need of development since it 'is not a static concept—it demands movement forward, perfecting. We need to accept its implications.'[9] These implications develop the *koinonia* ecclesiology in a certain direction which may not, perhaps, seem quite so congruent with the New Testament as *koinonia* itself. Inevitably for an ecumenical work, ARCIC 1 strives to hold together very different interpretations of the faith, although it must be noted here that these differing interpretations are both thoroughly orthodox, both acknowledge the Christian scriptures as normative and meaningful, both acknowledge Christ and the Holy Spirit as central. ARCIC is an exercise in orthodox, trinitarian, ecumenical theology.

As an ecumenical exercise it uses what we can call a dialectical method of discussion, that is to say the reasoning very often affirms one side of the debate then affirms the other, swinging between the two poles. Medieval theology often took the form of running one point up against its apparent opposite, 'yes and no' or '*sic et non*', in order to come to a synthesis. ARCIC methodology uses a similar dialectical approach. Having made the firm statement of spiritual *koinonia* ARCIC 1 goes on to say that the church's visible form signifies this inner communion with Christ and one another. But we learn that the *koinonia* must involve mutual recognition of sacraments and form of ministry, 'together with the common acceptance of a universal primacy, at one with the episcopal college in the service of the *koinonia*'.[10] Already the introduction gives the superstructure which ARCIC 1 finds it necessary to place over the *koinonia*: the evangelical emphasis is made, but quickly receives the catholic impress. Rather than a 'yes and no' method what we really have is a 'yes and yes' approach! We shall look at how the ARCIC view of the church, ministry and sacraments develops, after its radically biblical start.

2. The sacraments

A. BAPTISM

ARCIC speaks both of the Holy Spirit and of the sacraments without ever truly clarifying their relationship, particularly over baptism which does not receive separate attention. 'By his word,' ARCIC 1 tells us, 'God calls us into a new relationship with himself as our Father and with one another as his children—a relationship inaugurated by baptism into Christ through the Holy Spirit, nurtured and deepened through the eucharist, and expressed in a confession of one faith and a common life of loving service.'[11] The Christian hears the word, is called into relationship with the Father, a relationship which is initiated 'by baptism into Christ through the Holy Spirit.' Both the water sacrament and the Holy Spirit effect the initiation in this statement. ARCIC 2 tells us that 'baptism is the unrepeatable sacrament of justification and incorporation into Christ (1 Cor. 6:11, 12, 12-13; Gal 3:27);'[12] but also agrees with Augustine that baptism is the 'sacrament of faith' in which we die and rise with Christ. The second report also stresses the personal response to grace which is itself enabled by the Holy Spirit.[13] The Holy Spirit makes the fruits of Christ's sacrifice actual within the church through word and sacrament.[14] The total picture amounts to strong evangelical support for the personal spiritual response to the word of grace as well as equally powerful statements of baptism as the effective means of grafting the individual into Christ spiritually.

It may be unfair to expect ARCIC to produce a definition of baptism with reference either to the catholic notion of baptismal regeneration according to which grace passes into the beneficiary, usually an infant, by the very performance of the rite; or, on the other hand, with reference to the protestant notion of receiving grace by faith, grace which is signified by the sign and symbol of the sacrament. 'In the New Testament it is clear that the community is established by a baptism inseparable from faith and conversion . . .'[15] It is not a question of 'either-or' but 'both-and': both the commitment of personal faith in Christ present in the Holy Spirit, and also the duly appointed effectual sacramental conveying of the benefits of the atoning work of Christ. Sacraments also, along with the word of Christ, give us assurance of our salvation.[16]

The sparse material on baptism and conversion, the coming to faith, may be said to imply some form of regeneration as a result of baptism by the operation of the Holy Spirit, and yet the stress on personal faith means that any such interpretation rules out mechanical sacramentalism and leaves room for teaching the baptized that repentance and true faith in Christ must be the only saving response to the sacrament of initiation. The family resemblance most naturally called to mind is with the Anglo-Catholic theology: the inner spiritual life of the church has a definitely established apostolic visible form and baptism is the visible way into Christ and his church. Both the Holy Spirit and the sacrament are necessary to salvation; one without the other is a distortion of the faith and a disobedience. This is exactly in line with Moberly and Ramsey and perhaps Moberly's stress on the instrumental character of the church visible and her ministrations squares best with the tenor of both ARCIC documents. The sacraments are effective not by virtue of the church's own powers but solely because the Spirit acts through the church's appropriate organs or structures to incorporate new members to herself.

This teaching works well when the candidates for baptism are adult believers and most Christians would find few objections, but when infants are the candidates then hard questions arise as to the presence of the faith, the conversion, the mediation of grace and personal response. Unfortunately ARCIC does not tackle this issue of the rationale of infant baptism where one half of the equation is missing. The general tenor of the report would not encourage indiscriminate baptism in that the *koinonia* of the whole family of faith must be a vital context of the rite. On the other hand it would seem hard to interpret the texts as supporting the view that recipients of baptism could possibly be outside the sphere of grace. The result reads like an Anglo-Catholic type of synthesis, but one which, like Ramsey's, the evangelical can almost live with because the spiritual heart of the church, the risen Christ, is the causative and creative power at work and the church is only ministerial to him, and because ARCIC speaks so much about the need for baptism to go with conversion.

Parallel to Moberly's doctrine of ministerial priesthood, ARCIC teaches that the ordained priest is commissioned as the normal agent in the church to perform baptism and is given authority to pronounce absolution of sins in the name of Christ.[17] Absolution receives only a glancing mention in both reports, but again the most natural reading takes the line of 'ministerial priesthood'. The priest visibly ministers Christ's word of pardon in such a way that the two should not be separated: the priest's words and the word of Christ merge sacramentally together and presumably are to be appropriated by faith. The theology of the eucharist, worked out much more deliberately and clearly, does insist on the aspects both of personal faith and of objective grace. Given that this maxim applies equally to baptism, and also to absolution, then sacramental performance alone will never be sufficient in and of itself and will always also require the dimension of personal trust.

B. EUCHARIST

ARCIC explains the eucharist as the means by which all the baptized are brought into communion with the source of *koinonia*. The eucharist has an immensely prominent position in ARCIC. It seems the primary way in which Christ sustains the church, 'Christ through the Holy Spirit in the eucharist builds up the life of the Church, strengthens its fellowship arid furthers its mission.'[18] The nature of the eucharist is initially spelt out in terms of eucharistic sacrifice and the presence of Christ.

(i) Eucharistic sacrifice

The eucharist is the sacrament of nurturing and feeding the faithful in Christ, of bringing the benefits of his passion to the ongoing church. If baptism represents 'the once-for-all' dimension of the faith, the *point* of justification and final acceptance, then the eucharist represents the *process* of sanctification through the crucified and risen Lord.[19] 'The eucharist is the repeated sacrament by which the life of Christ's body is constituted and renewed, when the death of Christ is proclaimed until he comes again (1 Cor. 11:26).'[20] But the church at the eucharist also looks forward to Jesus' final appearing at the eschaton, while secure in the knowledge that she already enjoys a foretaste of the kingdom of God in Christ. All the main New Testament emphases seem to find a place in the overall vision of the eucharist in ARCIC.

A chief concern is to work out how the sacrifice of Jesus on Calvary relates to the eucharist now celebrated by the church. ARCIC wholeheartedly affirms that the death of Christ was a unique and unrepeatable sacrifice for the sins of the world, a fact which must not be obscured in any eucharistic doctrine.[21] But how is the link between the memorial and what is remembered to be interpreted, in a way which goes beyond proclaiming the death of the Lord as a mere memorial, as symbolic of a dead hero? Rather, eucharistic celebration must be seen as given to the church as a means through which the atoning work of Christ on the cross is made effective. At this point the notion of *anamnesis,* discussed in the preceding chapter, comes into play to bring into the present effectively the saving work of redemption. 'In the eucharistic prayer the church continues to make a perpetual memorial of Christ's death, and his members, united with God and one another, give thanks for all his mercies, entreat the benefits of his passion on behalf of the whole Church, participate in these benefits and enter into the movement of his self-offering.'[22]

ARCIC makes plain that it holds the one perfect and sufficient sacrifice of Christ, and that the eucharist sacramentally enters into Christ's self-offering. The church here and now participates in the offering of Christ made there and then, but extending beyond place and time. This participation by the church in Christ and his unique self-offering can happen by grace alone, not by any independent ritual or ethical act of self-giving by the church. The church's self-offering is united to Christ's, and this privilege exists because of Christ's original action. This 'once-for-all' act includes both Christ's sacrifice and its acceptance by God: 'There is therefore, one historical unrepeatable sacrifice, offered once for all by Christ and accepted once for all by the Father.'[23] It affirms the one historical sacrifice of Christ which grounds the sacramental sacrifice, mysteriously incorporating the church now into Christ's saving offering then. This sacramental sacrifice, oriented to the Father in the movement of Christ's self-giving, occurs in the priestly eucharistic prayer.

(ii) Real presence of Christ

The second aspect considered, after the aspect of the sacrificial movement towards God in Christ, is the movement of God in Christ towards the church. Christ makes himself present and effective in various ways in the eucharist. He invites his people to his table through his representative priest who also presides in Christ's name at the altar. Christ also gives himself to his church in the elements of bread and wine, mysteriously become his body and blood. The transcendent Lord, at the right hand of the Father, 'offers to his Church, in the eucharistic signs, the special gift of himself.'[24] Whereas the teaching on the eucharistic sacrifice has God as its focus, the offering of Christ and ourselves pleaded before the Father, the teaching on the real presence has the reverse orientation of the Lord's gift to us of himself. The sacrifice on our behalf, with our participatory offering united to this, is for us; the real presence of Christ in the elements, is to us. The priestly words of consecration first spoken by Jesus 'Take, eat, this is my body,' actually effect a real objective change in the elements, they mysteriously do become the body and blood of Christ. ARCIC clearly states the decisive change resulting from the consecration by the priest: 'Before the eucharistic prayer, to the question "What is that?", the believer answers: "It is bread". After the eucharistic prayer, to the same question he answers: "It is truly the body of Christ, the Bread of Life".'[25]

The fact of a change in the elements may not be in dispute for ARCIC, but the manner of the change is not defined. A coy footnote informs us that the traditional Roman Catholic doctrine of transubstantiation should no longer be regarded as explaining how the change occurs, but rather as affirming that it occurs,[26] whereby Christ's body and blood become really present and given. In the 'Elucidation', the section responding to questions and criticisms, ARCIC 1 goes on to say '*Becoming* does not here imply material change,'[27] the becoming does not imply a re-incarnation of Christ nor a presence in a manner corresponding to the laws of nature. The change, brought about by the Holy Spirit on the bread and wine, brings about an objective 'sacramental presence'. The purpose of the eucharistic change is the transformation of human beings into an increasing identification with the body of Christ.

The real change in the elements does not depend on the faith of the recipient,[28] but on the other hand, the sacramental offering when met by faith brings about an encounter with Christ: the objective presence of Christ indwells the believer. The implication is that faithful reception by the believer is needed for the objective presence of Christ in the element to be internalized subjectively. ARCIC 1 describes the dimension of objective presence in the elements in catholic terms, the dimension of receiving by faith in more evangelical terms. These twin aspects are the dimensions of gift and reception. These are 'complementary movements within an indissoluble unity: Christ giving his body and blood, and the communicants feeding upon them in their hearts by faith.'[29] The manner of reception being a 'feeding in their hearts by faith' is a significant acceptance of the reformed position, suggesting a different type of eucharistic nourishment by the bread and wine: a spiritual feeding on the Lord as he is personally present.

(iii) The reserved sacrament

ARCIC admits real difficulty in holding its synthesis of catholic and reformed together when it discusses the issue of the reserved sacrament. ARCIC has affirmed the objectively real presence in the separate elements and the necessity of receiving by faith. Where does this leave the catholic practice of reserving the sacrament in a tabernacle in church and encouraging the faithful to worship Christ's presence in the consecrated bread? This puts asunder what has been so carefully joined together, and ARCIC, while stressing that faithful reception must be the goal of the eucharist, reluctantly allows adoration of the host without actual reception and feeding, but insists that our worship should most truly be to the Father in Christ and not, presumably therefore addressed to the consecrated host. ARCIC 1 settles for substantial agreement, and an agreement to disagree over reservation, permitting the adoration of Christ present in the consecrated bread, but only as on the margins of acceptable eucharistic practice. ARCIC argues against adoration of the reserved host as a main centre of eucharistic worship, and it argues dialectically according to its chosen method of 'yes and yes'! The heavily emphasized doctrine of a genuine change in the elements is twinned with the necessity to feed by faith, discouraging the worship of Christ in the consecrated bread without reception.

(iv) Appraisal

ARCIC 1 combines a doctrine of eucharistic sacrifice with that of real presence in the elements received by faith. On the one hand the church, focused in the person of the ordained priest, sacramentally presents Christ's sacrifice to the Father. On the other hand Christ faces the people and feeds them with his body and blood actually made present by the prayer of consecration. The elements, mysteriously changed into the very body and blood of Christ, are offered in sacramental sacrifice to the Father, so making present the once-for-all sacrifice of Calvary. The death of the Lord is focused and made present by the Holy Spirit through the eucharistic prayer. The atoning sacrifice for the church faces the Father, taking up the surrender of the church in the movement of Christ's self-offering. At the same time Christ's body and blood face the church as her spiritual food and drink; but now 'the body and blood' of Christ no longer seem to mean the broken, sacrificed body and blood so much as the living Christ, actually present in the bread and wine, feeding his people.

Eucharistic sacrifice

ARCIC does not explain the relationship between eucharistic sacrifice and real presence, nor does it really attempt to integrate them. The prayer of consecration provides the primary dynamic: the elements are changed into the body and blood and these are offered to the Father as the eucharistic sacrifice, then to the people who receive the changed elements in faith as spiritual food. Bicknell could commentate: 'We pray that our earthly oblations of bread and wine may by the power of the Holy Spirt be united with the heavenly oblation of our Lord. God, so to say, shows His acceptance of our offerings by giving them back to us charged with the fruits of our Lord's passion, to be the spiritual food of His body and blood.'[30] Given that the 'movement of Christ's self-offering' corresponds with 'the heavenly oblation', both directed towards the Father, Bicknell's teaching parallels ARCIC although ARCIC maintains the connection with the sacrifice of Calvary more definitely than the Anglo-Catholic Bicknell. ARCIC 2 went on to affirm that the church is declared righteous on the basis of the sacrifice of Calvary, underlining its commitment to the cross as the atoning work of Jesus, accepted by the Father on our behalf.

Evangelical theology prefers this focus on the sacrifice of Calvary to the Anglo-Catholic stress on the ongoing heavenly offering, reflected here below at eucharistic celebrations. ARCIC teaches the movement of Christ's sacrificial self-offering to God as brought into the present by the dynamically memorial effect of the priest saying the eucharistic prayer. *Anamnesis*, memorial, of Calvary brings us into the movement of Christ's priestly self-offering towards the Father. Buchanan, commenting from a liberal evangelical perspective, interprets ARCIC's doctrine of eucharistic sacrifice in terms of the person of Christ bringing his finished work to the church, which responds by self-dedication.[31] Entry into the movement of Christ's self-offering he equates with responding to the eucharistic action, after the manner of Romans 12 and the ASB's post communion prayer, 'We offer you our souls and bodies to be a living sacrifice . . . .' But ARCIC clearly states that the *eucharistic prayer*[32] constitutes the memorial and the entry into the movement of Christ's self-offering. Again, 'In the celebration of the memorial, Christ in the Holy Spirit unites his people with himself in a sacramental way so that the church enters into the movement of his self-offering.'[33] The entry into the movement of the offering is not consequent upon or responsive to the eucharistic action, it is the eucharistic action, for ARCIC.

Ramsey's use of Augustine's phrase, 'the whole Christ offers the whole Christ' usefully describes the shape of the eucharistic sacrifice for ARCIC. Christ, including his work and his church, is offered to the Father sacramentally by the priest in the name of Christ and on behalf of his church. This idea of eucharistic sacrifice constantly involves the church's participation in Christ. Christ offers himself and his Calvary sacrifice, with his church and by his church, which participates in consecration to Christ. Evangelical theology, above all anxious to preserve the completed act of vicarious atonement by Christ as the focus, finds the coordination of Christ with us a difficult eucharistic centrepiece, however carefully the two coordinates are distinguished into primary and secondary. It also finds the stress on the movement of offering awkward, in that it does not speak of the completedness of Calvary. The discontinuity between the atonement and what Christ regenerated by it, the uniqueness of the great moral act of salvation, needs sharper emphasis. It is this which *creates* the continuity and participation, therefore language of coordination and offering at the heart of eucharistic sacrificial doctrine grates on evangelical ears.

The saving death of Christ is betokened by the sacramental elements of bread and wine, and they must be considered when appraising ARCIC's position on eucharistic sacrifice. The body and blood of the Lord are present in the elements, for ARCIC, not just 'to us' but objectively in themselves and prior to reception by the faithful. They will exist in relation to the Father as well as to the church and will reflect the self-offering before the Father in an earthly form. Here is a genuinely transactional sacramental event, between Christ and the Father and between

Christ and the church. Francis Clark points out that the decision as to the real objective presence of Christ in the elements does have a major effect on the meaning of eucharistic offering, or pleading, of the sacrifice of Christ: 'It must be remarked once more, however, that the notion of the Eucharistic sacrifice as the "pleading" of Christ's redemptive sacrifice is ambiguous: it takes on a different meaning according to whether the doctrine of the real objective presence of Christ in the consecrated elements is admitted or denied.'[34] The offering of the sacrifice sacramentally involves the real Christ in the elements for ARCIC, but this is not spelt out. Clark continues by adding that another key contextual difference in defining eucharistic sacrifice is whether the offering is conceived as performed by the consecration of the Eucharist by the priest, or only by the reception of the Eucharist by the worshipper in holy communion.[35] ARCIC elucidates this clearly: the words of consecration change the elements, and the priest, representing, the church, makes the offering.

Johann Adam Möhler, the great Roman Catholic apologist and theologian, close in thought to his contemporary Newman, set out his doctrine of the mass in his *Symbolik* of 1832. It is strikingly parallel with the ARCIC interpretation. In particular he makes the point that

> 'the real presence of Christ in the Eucharist forms the basis of our whole conception of the mass. Without that presence, the solemnity of the Lord's Supper is a mere reminiscence of the sacrifice of Christ . . . On the other hand, with faith in the real existence of Christ in the Eucharist, the past becomes present,—all that Christ hath merited for us, and whereby he hath so merited it, is henceforth never separated from his person; He is present as that which He absolutely is, and in the whole extent of His actions, to wit as the real victim.'[36]

Möhler, anticipating ARCIC, is also very keen to explain to his Protestant readers that the Roman Catholic eucharist does not abolish the actual sacrifice of Golgotha nor demean it as less than complete and in need of a supplement; rather 'by keeping the oblation of Christ on the cross, or rather his whole ministry and sufferings, eternally present, presupposes the same, and in its whole purport maintains the same; and, instead of supplying the bloody sacrifice of the cross with some heterogeneous element, it brings that sacrifice in its true integrity and original vitality to bear the most individual application and appropriation throughout all ages.'[37] Möhler, subtly expressing the essence of Roman Catholic thought, comes astonishingly close to ARCIC, affirming the primary, historic, bloody universal sacrificial death of Jesus and the secondary, sacramental, particular, applicatory eucharistic sacrifice. He teaches that the church has nothing to offer but the sacrifice of Christ and that he is the source of our worship.

ARCIC's theology of the twofold movement, towards God in the eucharistic sacrifice and towards man in the feeding on Christ present in the elements, could hardly be better expressed than in Möhler's vivid statement: '. . . the Redeemer present enables us to be entirely His own children, or to become so in an ever-increasing degree. The present Saviour, in a voice audible to the spiritually-minded, incessantly addresses His Father above: "be graciously pleased to behold in me the believing and repentant people;" and then He crieth to His brethren below: "come to me all ye that labour and are heavy laden, and I will refresh you: each one that returneth to me with all his heart shall find mercy, forgiveness of sins, and every grace".'[38] The double movement, of Christ's inclusive self-offering to the Father, and of feeding the people, without any claim to repeat the destructive death occurring on Calvary or to add to it, but rather to represent its dynamic effect, anticipates precisely the ARCIC doctrine.

Möhler continues his exposition by insisting that it is really Christ who is active, with the church participating in him:

> 'Hence, in the liturgy of the Latin as well as of the Greek, Church, it is rightly Christ, who, in the holy action, offers himself up to God as a sacrifice; He is at once the victim and the high priest. But we, recognizing in the Eucharistic Christ that same Christ who, out of love for us delivered Himself unto death, even the death on the cross, exclaim at the elevation of the Host . . . "O Jesus! for Thee I live, for Thee I die! O Jesus! Thine I am, living or dead!".'[39]

ARCIC encourages reception of the eucharistic elements rather than worshipping Christ in them, but does not exclude it and logically it is difficult to see why Möhler's worshipful ecstasy is incorrect if the bread and wine are, after consecration, the present Christ in some special form, however undefined: if we do not adore Christ in this guaranteed local presence after consecration, surely the very stones should cry out?

Real presence

Although it may sound initially a crude and unsophisticated point, the question should be asked as to the appropriateness of the sign to the reality. The sign is the twofold sign of bread and wine, body and blood. The presence of Christ in the consecrated must reside in both, not materially, but not spiritually only. ARCIC speaks of the bread as changed, and we must presume the wine likewise is mysteriously changed. Their very separation, however, poses a problem for the doctrine of the real presence of the glorified Christ in the elements prior to, and independently of, reception by the congregation. The crude problem results from the theory itself, a theory which insists on the change in both bread and wine at consecration and which is not satisfied with the really spiritual presence of Christ coming through the whole action of the eucharist including faithful reception. Interestingly ARCIC does not speak of the wine becoming the very blood of Christ, although this must be the implication of its doctrine.

ARCIC is agnostic over the way the elements become the body and blood. The presence resulting is not a material presence, but a real one, distinct from Christ's spiritual presence generally in his people. This position was subjected to keen analysis and criticism at the turn of the century by the liberal Anglican philosophical theologian Hastings Rashdall. Rashdall's analysis may help to clarify some of the issues involved with a real presence doctrine, and in particular with attempts to offer a softened or vaguer version.[40]

Rashdall points out that the doctrine of transubstantiation was originally formulated to avoid the grossly materialistic superstitions which had evolved in the middle ages. Although few today accept the idea that the 'substance' of a thing can be separated from its 'accidents', (its essence from its qualities) yet, says Rashdall, 'The more clear-sighted Anglican upholders of the doctrine of the Real Presence . . . have seen that this philosophical doctrine represents the only way in which it can properly be maintained that the presence of the body and blood of Christ is in the strict sense of the word *real*,–the presence of the real thing, the very same thing that is also pronounced by this theology to be at the same time in heaven.'[41] There is, for Rashdall, no distinction between the transubstantiation concept and the real presence doctrine save that the latter does not assert the annihilation of the bread and wine in its substance. Transubstantiation, reasserted as normative by the Papal Encyclical *Mysterium Fidei* as recently as 1965, resolves the problem by saying that whereas the substance changes, the accidents or the outer form, remains. This doctrine is far from being crude and stupid, and it expresses exactly the kind of distinction upheld by the doctrine of real presence in the elements: the sacrament appears to be the natural bread and wine but in deepest reality is the genuine body and blood of the Lord. This is the view adopted in a soft version by ARCIC 1[42]: after the prayer of consecration we are dealing with the body and blood of the Lord.

Rashdall says that his Anglican Tractarian brethren are content to say that they do not know how the change takes place, and of course this is precisely the view of ARCIC theology. 'But,' he continues, 'they forget that what they are committed to is the presence of Christ's body and blood, not of His Spirit, of His influence, of the spiritual help and strength which flows from the life that he once lived on the earth that He now lives with God.'[43] This point has some force: real presence in the physical elements after the prayer of consecration as a result of supernatural change before reception is a precise claim about an objective reality. It makes little sense then to be vague about how this reality comes about and to reject transubstantiation on those grounds as ARCIC does.[44] For, as Rashdall continues:

> 'How the presence of literal body and blood can mean anything but Transubstantiation or Consubstantiation[45] it is difficult to see. There can surely, in strictness of speech, be no such thing as the spiritual presence of a material thing, if presence is to mean anything more than a presence to the minds of those who think it. And if it is the presence of Christ Himself—of the spiritual Being—that they mean, they are bound to explain how a spirit can properly be said to have any local presence at all. Spirits do not occupy space. We may indeed, if we please, say that a spirit *is* where it acts. In this no doubt we may quite reasonably talk about a real presence of Christ in the Holy Eucharist. But in that sense the real presence is after all a purely spiritual presence—a presence in and for the mind of the faithful receiver. And no doubt nothing can be more real—if by that is meant simply true, actual, or efficacious—than a spiritual presence, as is eloquently set forth in Jeremy Taylor's admirable treatize on "the Real Presence".'[46]

But in that sense we cannot deny the presence of Christ in prayer, in reading the scriptures, in the ongoing Christian life. Rashdall says that when the upholder of the real presence is confronted by this he generally reduces his assertion to some vaguer idea of a special presence in the eucharist, different in kind or degree from that in the other channels. Rashdall does not find this notion of a special presence a very illuminating one. 'We cannot lay down any hard and fast rules,' he says, 'and say that all Christians must as a matter of fact realize the presence of Christ in the eucharist in some quite different way or sense from that in which they realize His presence in private prayer or in reading the gospels.' He reads no special promise connected to the institution of the Lord's Supper in the New Testament; he finds a special command but not a promise of a special presence. If our Lord said 'this is my body,' He also said 'Where two or three are gathered together in My name, there I am in the midst of you.'

Rashdall's analysis shows the great difficulty in producing a modified or 'soft' view of the real presence, as ARCIC attempts to do. Rashdall seems to compel a straight choice between a theology of transubstantiation, wrongly maligned as crude, and that of the spiritual presence of Christ to the faithful. Macquarrie,[47] the contemporary Anglican systematician, appeals to the New Testament to disagree and press his view that a doctrine of the real presence in the elements is necessary, citing Paul's message to the Corinthians that some were dying because they were eating and drinking without discerning the body (1 Cor. 11:20); Kasemann is cited as an interpreter who holds that Paul held a view of the real presence.[48] The debate over this text hinges on whether judgement comes from the Lord to these wayward Corinthians, or intrinsically from the elements.

Faithful reception

ARCIC teaches the need for faithful reception *as well as* real change in the elements, simply insisting on both but not explaining how this marriage really works. Catholic theology never abolished the requirement of faith in the recipients of the consecrated bread, but like ARCIC has always held to the prior change in the elements independent of the eating and drinking. Macquarrie, in his consistently dialectical way, teaches that the eucharist must be seen as having two poles of emphasis: the existential and the ontological[49] and ARCIC argues similarly for both the objective and the subjective, faith and real presence.

Reserved sacrament

ARCIC's dialectical technique of 'yes and yes' ecumenical theology runs in to a straight contradiction over the issue of the reserved sacrament, which is not consumed but worshipped. If the elements are actually changed objectively, then the consecrated host is worthy of adoration, since the glorified Christ is present there independently of reception. ARCIC also says 'yes' to the need to receive the consecrated elements by faith. The question raised by adoration of the reserved sacrament shows that the stitching tears open, even within the agreed statement. The reader of ARCIC gets the impression that the drive of the eucharistic theology is towards the faithful reception of Christ, the feeding with spiritual food, the transformation of the church, rather than the transformation of the bread and wine. But this dynamic thrust is checked by the eucharistic sacrifice and real presence doctrines which add complex metaphysical considerations and provide a different centre of gravity. The issue of reservation reveals this tension. The Holy Spirit, the medium of Christ to the church in New Testament doctrine, acts personally on *people* rather than *things*, even bread and wine.

As a statement on the eucharist ARCIC, although it retains a doctrine of eucharistic sacrifice and real presence in the elements independently of reception, is preferable in the eyes of evangelicals to most Anglo-Catholic statements on the subject, notably to the FOAG Report,[50] with its emphasis on the heavenly offering rather than on Calvary, for its eucharistic focus.

3. The priestly ministry in ARCIC

A. THE ARCIC ARGUMENT FOR A PRIESTLY ORDAINED MINISTRY

The treatment of the ministry follows quite closely Moberly's influential work *Ministerial Priesthood* discussed briefly in the previous chapter. The priestly ordained ministry is God given, but crystallized through the processes of historical development under the providential hand of God. The FOAG report on the priesthood also corresponds closely to this rationale. The argument hinges on the link between the ministry and the eucharist.

ARCIC 1 begins by repeating that the ordained ministry exists to serve the *koinonia* of the church and especially to foster *koinonia* with Christ after the pattern of the cross.[51] The church is apostolic in two ways: firstly because she reflects the apostolic teaching resulting from the apostles special relationship with Jesus; secondly because she performs the functions first carried out by the apostles in preaching the gospel to all the world. These ministerial functions were handed on to the ordained ministry. A tradition of authorization and commissioning built up which now exists as ordination, a tradition which we can call apostolic. Although we cannot trace an absolutely unbroken historical path of the threefold order of bishops, priests and deacons, this pattern emerged early and its shape is vaguely discernible in the New Testament.

ARCIC parallels the development of the New Testament canon with that of the threefold ministry in the age after the apostles.[52] The ministry is apostolic in that it teaches the apostolic faith, and also in that it flows from the apostolic commission from Christ to the apostles and on to the earliest bishops and presbyters. ARCIC insists that the ordained ministry is apostolic in this double way, in a 'correspondence' structure as regards the content of the faith and in a 'coherence' structure as regards the authority to commission and to minister in the name of the church as a whole.

As Moberly argued, the church's priestly nature needs to be focused in the priesthood of the ordained ministry despite the fact that the New Testament does not use this term of the ministry, reserving it for the people of God as a whole. The pattern of the whole and the focus of that whole emerges as important to the ARCIC system of interpretation of the ministry. The whole *koinonia* of the church, and the *koinonia* of the church with Christ, needs to be overseen and guided by the ministry in many ways, several of which would be agreed by most Christian denominations such as preaching, teaching, coordinating and discerning policy for the advancement of the church. The minister proclaims the pardoning word of Christ to the people, teaches the word, pastors them and guides them in the steps of Christ. He represents Christ to the people. In Moberly's terms, the minister is the instrument of Christ for these purposes in and for the whole priestly people of God.

Oversight, *episcope*, is the task and commission of the bishop in the apostolic succession and the presbyterate or priesthood 'are joined with the bishop in the oversight of the church.'[53] ARCIC adopts the catholic view of episcopacy as the primary agency of the oversight of the whole *koinonia*, the presbyterate or priesthood being secondary overseers, exercising a ministry derived from the bishop's general apostolic *episcope*. The one who has oversight should be the one who presides at the eucharist, the central act of worship which nourishes the life of the church from the source of her *koinonia*, the sacrifice of Christ. The ordained ministers appropriately celebrated the eucharist on behalf of the whole church, and so 'Christians came to see', in the course of time and under providence, the priestly role of Christ reflected in these ministers. This was the rationale for the ordained ministry having a priestly nature, notwithstanding the deafening silence of the New Testament on Christian leadership being priestly.

The minister stands in the place of Jesus at the last supper as he celebrates the *anamnesis* of the atoning sacrifice at each eucharist. For ARCIC, priesthood of the ministry arises from the sacrificial character of the eucharist and the sacramental relation of the minister with the great high priest, Christ.[54] The eucharist is the quintessential moment of all Christian ministry, and the properly ordained ministers focus the priesthood of the whole people of God in presiding at the eucharist. ARCIC therefore speaks of the priest as like the centre of an hour-glass, standing for the double movement already described in eucharistic theology. He represents Christ to the church, and focuses the priesthood of the church, 'representative of the whole church in the fulfilment of its priestly vocation of self-offering to God as a living sacrifice.'[55] Priesthood itself is thoroughly sacramental of Christ to his church and of the church's own nature. The priest sacramentally shows forth the twofold movement of the eucharist, towards God and towards man.

While describing the priesthood of the whole people of God as vital, 'setting the ordained ministry in that context' and therefore implying a fundamental unity of priestly ministry and priestly people, yet ARCIC effects a quite radical differentiation between the lay and ordained priesthoods. In a very important statement ARCIC divorces the ordained ministerial priesthood from the priesthood of all believers because the priestly ministry 'is not an extension of the common Christian priesthood but belongs to another realm of the gifts of the Spirit.'[56] ARCIC elucidates this in terms of a triangular model. At the top is the priesthood of Christ, a New Testament idea. From this comes the priesthood of all believers, also found in the Bible. The priesthood of the ordained ministry is 'set in the context of the common priesthood' but derives from the special sacramental relationship with Christ as High Priest.[57]

B. AN APPRAISAL OF THE ARGUMENT

The upshot of this argument is that the common priesthood and the ministerial priesthood 'are two distinct realities which relate, each in its own way, to the high priesthood of Christ, the unique priesthood of the new covenant, which is their source and model.'[58] Therefore ARCIC seems to turn back on its original rationale of the ministry as the servant of the general *koinonia* of the whole church and in the end result defines the ordained ministry in terms of a separate spiritual caste, a different realm of the gifts of the spirit. The apparent base in spiritual *koinonia* gets forgotten in this switch of emphasis.

At this point the earlier background discussion of Newman and Barth may help us to pin-point some of the slipperiness found in ARCIC and its method of apparently affirming contrary views of ministry. Newman stressed the development by the ecclesial tradition of the relatively unformed, primitive New Testament documents in the constant guidance of the Holy Spirit. For him the written word had to be interpreted in the context of the living community of faith, a community whose very shape and structure were also under the Spirit's control. The development of the canon, of the threefold order of authoritative ministry, and of the priestly ministry was a natural organic evolution. There could be no question of the developments in the Spirit filled body of Christ offending the apostolic base of the church either in terms of teaching or ministerial structure.

The New Testament was bound to need filling out, expanding into full bloom and colour, as a rose at the early spring contains latent the glories of high summer. When ARCIC affirms the priesthood of the ordained ministry in terms never used by the New Testament, the Newman line of theology with its biological growth model of the church, and indeed the Anglo-Catholic line with its foundation-superstructure model, finds no problem at all. Their methodology rules out any conflict between the root of the plant and its stem. The Bible is the church's book and can only be read in the light of the ongoing developments of the living church. The biblico-patristic method of interpretation rules out any such conflict, as does Newman's expanded version of spirit-breathed ecclesial interpretation.

For classical evangelical theology the perspective is different. The canon is the primary authority for the faith, and the words and concepts of scripture are to be interpreted historically in the contemporary horizon and then related to today. This is the sense of historical exegesis that evangelical theology accepts, the examination of the context of the time of writing and the application of the normal grammatical sense in interpreting the texts. The era of the apostles, their writings and the writings coming from their immediate spheres of influence under their supervision, these are normative. Barth broadly follows in this method of accepting the written word as the normative agenda for the church, under which the church stands. Barth's particular view of the dynamic way in which scripture functions is not wholly in the classical evangelical mould, but his assertion of the primacy of the written word as a possible critical norm over the church's historical developments certainly expresses this theological stance.

Given the normative status of the scriptures and the commitment to historical, grammatical interpretation in the light of the context of the time of writing, evangelical theology will be very hesitant to accept any usage of New Testament terminology and conceptuality which seems to conflict with the original theological tenor of the texts as a whole. In this it is at odds with both the style of Newman and of the biblico-patristic method of the Anglo-Catholic school. ARCIC produces a theology of priesthood from two New Testament ideas by subtle theologizing. It commits itself to the definition of the church as a Christocentric spiritual *koinonia* and wholeheartedly accepts the New Testament idea of the priesthood of all believers. ARCIC starts with the premise of the whole church as basic. It accepts the fact that the New Testament specifically does not use priestly language of the ordained ministry. But, plying a roundabout route via the high priesthood of Christ—a notion not taken up in the eucharist report, ARCIC theologizes a priestly ministry back into the church. This priesthood specifically does not derive from the common priesthood of all believers but from the unique priesthood of Christ, although the discussion is surrounded by mention of the priesthood of the whole. 'In this as in other cases the early Church found it necessary for its understanding and exposition of the faith to employ terminology in ways in which it was not used in the New Testament.'[59]

It is no mere crass fundamentalism that baulks at this subtle manoeuvring. Of course, theologians have used terms from the New Testament in ways not used in the text. But what if that usage actually *contradicts* the general tenor of the text as a whole? Priestly terms are not used of the ordained ministry in the New Testament, as ARCIC agrees. The debate revolves around the theological import of this remarkable and deafening silence. If Jesus absorbed all the atoning functions ascribed in the Old Testament to the priestly ministrations of the Temple, if worship was to be in Spirit and in truth, if the synagogue eldership was the pattern laid down for establishing a ministry in the churches by the apostolic mission, then is it valid to reintroduce a priesthood which was apostolically excised?

ARCIC replies that it is merely engaged in *analogy*. 'The word priesthood is used by way of analogy when it is applied to the people of God and to the ordained ministry. These are two distinct realities which relate, each in its own way, to the high priesthood of Christ. . . .', and this in such a way that the ordained ministry 'is not an extension of the common Christian priesthood but belongs to another realm of the gifts of the spirit.'[60] This reading of the New Testament as a source of analogies for the history of theology is classically typical of Newman's style and apologetic. ARCIC makes use of the technique again as a hinge point in its discussion of authority in the church and the papacy. The precise question exegetically is whether such an analogy is not exactly excluded by both the high priesthood of Christ and the priestly character of the whole church? Does the re-introduction of the priestly ministry, cultically focused on the eucharist and its sacramental sacrifice, not reverse, or at best cloud, the faith concentrated in the mediation of the Son and his presence in the Spirit?

To show that this profound hesitation lies deep in the Anglican evangelical mind let us hear the words of the Bishop of Durham at the time when Moberly's virtually identical theory was being introduced: 'It has been reasoned, indeed, that he (a minister) may in a guarded and secondary sense be called, officially, a *sacerdos*, as he is in some respects the representative of the congregation to God and of God to the congregation. But,' the bishop goes on, 'such reasoning and usage is absent from the New Testament, in which the pastoral aspect of the ministry is (to say the least) very far more conspicuous than the representative.'[61] Moberly's work was a controversial reply to that of Bishop Lightfoot, also of Durham, whose view as an outstanding exegete and classical Anglican was precisely that of Moule.

ARCIC 1 favours Moberley against Lightfoot, preferring the Newman line of theologizing to that of the Anglican exegetical tradition. The New Testament itself has ceased to be a sufficient critical norm and needs to be coordinated with living tradition, assuming that parts of ecclesiastical history are providentially guided. Against this subtle method of theologizing from historical development Barth's evangelical thunder would undoubtedly have been turned!

4. Primacy

A. THE WAY TO PAPAL PRIMACY

ARCIC wrestles with the issue of authority in the church and in particular examines the papacy, a key problem in the ecumenical dialogue. The commission was determined to begin, once again, with the base of *koinonia* and proceed from there in this as in other questions. The result is an ascending pattern of authority, rising from the laity, to the clergy, the episcopate, the archi-episcopate and finally reaching the crown with a primate of the whole worldwide church. The kinds of authority in question relate to faith and pastoral government in the church.

The Spirit-filled *koinonia* constitutes the whole priestly church. The *episcope* or over-sight is at once within the whole, and yet differentiated from that unity, existing in union with, and also distinct from, that whole. On the one hand, the *koinonia* of the whole is the spiritually bonded society in Christ, on the other hand, the ordained ministry is a different realm of the gifts of the Spirit, part of the whole but going beyond it and complementing it.

The ordained ministry, as we have seen, sacramentally focuses the ministry of the whole spiritual organism. It represents the people to God and Christ to the people. As regards teaching, the clerical line acts as a filtering and forming agency in harmony with the people, giving expression or formulation to insights and suggestions prompted by the Spirit in the church as a whole. 'All who live within the *koinonia* may become sensitive to the leading of the Spirit . . . Ordained ministers are 'commissioned to discern these insights and give authoritative expression to them . . . .'[62] As well as coming from above, from a different realm of the gifts of the spirit, ARCIC tries to keep on the track of the other route from below, from the spiritual *koinonia* of the whole body including the laity. This whole united body and any part of it can have insights into the truth of God. But the proper instrument of that body to focus and decide on these insights is the ordained ministry. The ministerial priesthood gives form to the intuition, and possible chaos, of the spiritual whole.

As a human person is one living organism, and yet has a mind to control and reflect on the whole self to analyze and direct it, so the vital life of the whole church is directed and shaped by the ordained line. Like the mind of the person, there can be no divorcing the one from the other: they are inwardly linked together and would be inconceivable apart. The general body of the church has a spiritual feeling for the truth, called in ARCIC the *sensus fidelium*: 'The *sensus fidelium* is a vital element in the comprehension of God's truth.'[63] The church's structures of oversight interact with the *sensus fidelium* so that error can be avoided and truth discerned. The *sensus fidelium* finds its focus and articulation through the episcopal office shared by the clergy. The faithful have a feeling for what is true, and this finds critical expression and interpretation through the ordained ministry.

Just as the clergy are part of, yet different from, the general community of the faithful, so the process of union and differentiation continues upwards. The clergy as a whole form a group and from them emerge bishops over them, who in turn form a group, or a council, to be led by archbishops. The pyramid is crowned by the primate as leader of his council of archbishops, and also as the leader of the whole church. *Episcope*, oversight, has its final focus in him over the whole worldwide *koinonia* of the faithful and their ministry. The steps upward follow the pattern of the whole *koinonia* and the focus for that whole. ARCIC uses the poles of lay and ordained, *koinonia* and *episcope*, conciliarity and primacy, the group and the individual who focuses and represents the group.

For example, the local bishops themselves need to have their views and insights tested by councils of bishops who can make authoritative decisions using scripture and tradition in the light of modern developments and problems. Unity of the *koinonia* needs to be fostered and discipline maintained within it. The ordained line therefore arises from the whole and exists to govern and further its development. The process of distilling wisdom from the *sensus fidelium* reaches its final court of appeal at the very topmost point. In ARCIC language 'conciliarity' relates to 'primacy' all the way up to the top in a creative tension; that is the whole group relates to the leader of the group differentiated from the whole. Just as the laity relate to the clergy, so the clergy to the bishops, bishops to archbishops, and archbishops to primate. This creative tension we can call the dialectical pattern of ARCIC ecclesiology.

ARCIC uses this dialectical method in developing the structures of the church, moving from the common spiritual whole to the vital particular organ of the ordained ministry, where the living voice of authority is found both in terms of government and of teaching. Starting with the distinction between lay and ordained (that different realm of the gifts of the Spirit) within the *koinonia*, ARCIC moves upwards in zig-zag stages to the tip of the pyramid. It is important to note that as well as using the dialectical steps up from stage to stage of authority, ARCIC clearly holds that there is a special relationship between the very top and the base, the final particular point of the pyramid and the organic whole, the primacy and the people with its *sensus fidelium*. The primate, presiding over the whole *koinonia*, can speak with authority in the name of the church.[64] This primacy is one means of the church gaining an authoritative declaration of the truth; the other means, conciliar, is the decision of a universal council of bishops, but the primacy has a priority of authority. The result is that the primate is a bishop with authority going beyond diocesan borders.

An important ARCIC concept, vitally related to this process of laying down authoritative statements, is the role of the people, the *sensus fidelium*, and their 'reception' of the statements. This too becomes a matter of creative tension, it is an important indicator, in relation to the clerical voice, of whether the statement is in fact a formulation of Christian teaching, is authentic. But again this must be carefully put into relationship with the oppposite factor. On the one hand, reception by the faithful does not create the authoritative status of an official pronouncement, on the other hand, its acceptance is significant. The Commission 'therefore avoids two extreme positions. On the one hand it rejects the view that a definition has no authority until it is accepted by the whole Church or even derives its authority solely from that acceptance. Equally the Commission denies that a council is so evidently self-sufficient that its definitions owe nothing to reception'.[65] ARCIC again uses its method of holding two poles in tension: the 'conciliar' community principle over against the principle of 'primacy' acting as the final decision maker.

The official structures of authority, therefore, are threefold: the *koinonia* or whole community, the ministerial *episcope* at its several levels, and the ultimate primate. The dialectic works from the whole to the focus for that whole, and this principle operates upwards, level by level, to its topmost point. ARCIC concludes that the church needs the ministry of an overall primate in order to foster the unity of the whole worldwide fellowship. This figure is needed as the ultimate focus of the unity of the whole, pastorally and doctrinally.

B. THE APPROPRIATE ROMAN PRIMACY

Having set out this case arguing that a single primate is needed in the structures of the church, ARCIC then asks the question whether there is any candidate or claimant for the post, and answers its question with the Roman Papacy. Here is precisely the only bishop claiming a universal primacy of authority in the church. The Roman Papacy has therefore a *prima facie* claim to be considered.

ARCIC explores the various bases for the Papal claim to universal authority in the church. It rejects the view that the Bishop of Rome's role as Peter, or 'Petrine' ministry, can stand on the evidence of New Testament texts. Peter clearly was a leading and decisive figure in the earliest church, and his particular function is defined by ARCIC as 'helping the church to overcome threats to its unity.'[66] But ARCIC notes that the New Testament knows nothing of a transmission of Peter's office of leadership, nor indeed 'is the transmission of apostolic authority in general very clear.'[67] Therefore we move away from strictly biblical rationale and go to early church history, because the city of Rome was where Paul, certainly, and Peter, probably, were martyred, and Rome came to possess a special status among the churches of the early centuries.

At this point ARCIC appeals to the development of the interpretation of the New Testament in church history, the same move we noted in its rationale for a priestly ordained ministry. 'Fathers and doctors of the Church gradually came to interpret the New Testament data as pointing in the same direction,'[68] that is, some Latin theologians linked the texts in the New Testament with the validation of the Papacy as the continuing role of Peter as head of the apostolic college. The texts in their original context cease to function as the decisive norm for interpretation, giving way to a section of the early church's exegesis, however mistaken that interpretation is now acknowledged to be. Although their exegesis was mistaken, the point being upheld by such theologians must now be recognized as very important, and their association of Roman primacy with the Petrine texts may be refashioned and rehabilitated in a more sophisticated way. This way lies through the use of analogy.

Analogy brings the role of Peter in the New Testament to relevance now. Peter played the part of leader of the first apostles, as the defender of unity, of *koinonia*. This service is now needed in the church, there is a gap to be filled and the 'Petrine ministry', that task undertaken by bishops of Rome, should fill it. There is an analogy between the role of Peter, as it came to be understood in the course of time, and the Papal ministry. Today especially as the ecumenical advance goes on just this kind of visible primate is needed, and should appropriately be the bishop of Rome.[69] The argument is that although the claim is not justifiable from taking the New Testament in its own context, yet taken in the changing historical context a Petrine primacy was not illegitimate and meets a genuine church need. The development of this Roman primacy can now be seen as providentially ordered by the Spirit in the process of church history.

The Bible offers us some kind of an analogy of the ministry of Roman primacy and the role of Peter. The development of this link down the centuries of church thought can now be regarded as providentially ordered by the Spirit to meet a gradually evolving need of the church. This universal primate usually works within the context of councils of bishops, but has universal jurisdiction throughout the church. He also has a special spiritual gift helping to preserve him from error, although the Anglicans on ARCIC could not agree to the term 'infallible'.

C. AN APPRAISAL OF ARCIC'S ARGUMENT FOR PRIMACY

ARCIC uses Newman's model of organic development, coupled to the key ideas of union and differentiation, and the focusing of the whole in the particular. We have seen already this method being used in the theology of the eucharist and priesthood. This conceptuality, characteristic of Hegelian thought, has found its way into ARCIC as a means of theologizing in an historically developmental fashion. For this philosophical tradition, historical process develops truth and thought, reconciling opposites into new syntheses, through human consciousness. 'Spirit', or 'mind', runs through the process of the developing meaning of history. For ARCIC, the history of church thought and structures embodies divine guidance, coming through theology and clerical validation.

A strikingly parallel rationale to that of ARCIC comes once more from the writings of Möhler, himself influenced by German idealism, who argues:

> 'They who require incontrovertible proofs for the existence of the Primacy, require what is unreasonable, the law of a true development not admitting it. And vice-versa, the trouble which some have given themselves to discover, before the same epoch, the full idea of a Pope, or the notion that they have discovered it, must be considered as vain, and their conclusions untenable. As throughout the inferior organization of the Church, so in this point the want must be felt before the supply could be found. It is evident that during the first three centuries, and even at the close of them, the primacy is not visible save in the first lineaments; it operates as yet informally; and when the question arises, "Where and how did it practically manifest itself?" we must confess that it never appears alone, but always in conjunction with other bishops; though it is true that a peculiar character is already seen to attach to the Roman See.'[70]

Like ARCIC, Möhler also thought that without the logical completion of the episcopal structure then something was missing: 'If the organization of the Church be arrested at the point of the episcopate, the ascending series will be suddenly broken off, and the energy that moulds the whole so debilitated as not to be able to perfect the work after the proposed type.'[71] Once again we find ARCIC echoing the modern Roman Catholic method of Newman and Möhler, using the developmental, organic model of ecclesiology to justify church structures as divinely ordained.

Crucial to this mode of theologizing is the role of the Spirit in the historical progress of the church. At the end of chapter 1 we drew up an agenda of issues for modern ecclesiology, one of which was the question of divine presence in the church and her history. This is a key question for ARCIC because it claims that the Holy Spirit, acting through history, validates the Roman primacy. The subtle rationale for the need of a primacy, and the Roman primacy in particular, carries the weight of the Holy Spirit and not simply the commendation of an eirenic group of theologians. In a passage pregnant with self-fulfilling prophecy, ARCIC says that 'from time to time Anglican theologians have affirmed that, in changed circumstances, it might be possible for the Churches of the Anglican Communion to recognize the development of the Roman primacy as a gift of divine providence – in other words, as an effect of the guidance of the Holy Spirit in the Church.'[71]

The Spirit knits up conflicting interpretations, through changes in historical contexts, to produce a reconciliation or synthesis, an idea of primacy which goes well beyond a mutual acceptance by the churches of a presidential figure with an honorary courtesy title of the chairmanship of the highest council of bishops. ARCIC's primacy speaks and acts with divinely appointed jurisdiction and authority, *de iure divino*, not simply with the authority of a courtesy chairmanship, *de iure humano*. The changed context of present ecumenical friendliness has the power to reshape the meaning of past developments and to remodel and rehabilitate past interpretations of texts, even when these interpretations are acknowledged to have been misplaced as a matter of pure exegesis. This type of theology closely corresponds to Newman's, deriving its power from the process of interpretation, the growth of an idea. It also resembles Newman's thought in its use of a subtle argument from analogy with the past combined with the needs of the present: in a vague way the alleged role of Peter then comes to be accepted as primacy today.

At a very simple level of exegesis it must be asked whether the ministry of Peter in the New Testament provides the analogy sought. Can he really be best summed up as the steady promoter of unity? Peter, the brave proclaimer of the gospel, the rock or springboard for the initial explosive spreading of the message, seems the more obvious description of what we read. Peter needed to be confronted by Paul and persuaded against excluding Gentile believers who did not keep the whole Jewish Law, hardly the role of the archetypal builder of *koinonia*. ARCIC exegesis at this point looks artificial, even in using Peter as some kind of analogy for today. ARCIC reads into the text what it wants to find. Determined exegesis suffers because of the dominance of the present context and need. The text becomes illustrative and not the primary source for our understanding.

ARCIC might have concluded, with equal validity, that the analogy to be derived for a focus of unity should be one of joint headship, perhaps comprising a team of Peter, Paul and John who could stand for Rome, Reformation and Eastern Orthodoxy. Unity could be visibly focused and realistically fostered by such a senior bench of representative church leaders. This would make a final conciliarity or complementarity the chief symbol of church leadership and power, instead of attributing that to an individual personal primacy, in line with the Anglican Orthodox agreed statement. This would enable ARCIC to conclude on the principle with which it began, that of *koinonia* at the apex of a flat-topped pyramid. Anglicans have agreed with the Orthodox that the senior bishop among bishops 'does not have the right to intervene arbitrarily in the affairs of a diocese other than his own,'[73] which reflects the ethos of Anglicanism far more than does the ARCIC doctrine of primacy.

The contemporary Lutheran theologian, Wolfhart Pannenberg, has developed a doctrine of history and truth whereby the arrival of the future into the present can change the meaning of past events. The resurrection of Jesus, his great example, in this way constituted Jesus as the divine Son 'retroactively'. Earlier understandings are taken forward into new interpretations as the Spirit links these with fresh insights from the future. New understandings of past events can confer fresh identity or definition onto those events.[74] He illustrates this idea from historical figures whose meaning or value in their own day has been drastically revised with the passage of time. Great painters or composers have gained recognition only after their death, and on the other hand apparently significant politicians may suffer harsh judgement as the passage of time alters the interpretation of their contribution. The final truth about someone can therefore be said to lie in the future history of their interpretation. Meaning reads back to decide what a person or event really is. ARCIC uses a similar line of reasoning. Fresh contexts and insights provide new interpretations of past events, in this case of the Papacy, even a reversal of interpretation. The new context of today makes possible acceptance that divine providence always was behind the papal evolution, the only concrete incarnation of primatial ministry. Today's revaluation and reappraisal is that the papacy always was, however hiddenly, the plan of God.

The convoluted reasoning constitutes the very weakest point of ARCIC. To produce the Holy Spirit to validate what amounts to a plain reversal of interpretation verges on the bizarre and lacks justification. The reading of the history of Christianity might equally well conclude with H. B. Swete, a cautious scholar, that, 'For the time being, it must be recognized that the vision of a united Christendom has been wrecked by the Papacy. The Papacy is ultimately responsible both for the breaking away of the Orthodox Church from the communion of the West and for the revolution that shattered the unity of the West itself.'[75] ARCIC *assumes* not only that one universal primate can help promote unity, is needed to do so and has done so from Rome. Swete thinks that this office has promoted enormous *disunity* in the past.

In effect, ARCIC concludes that spiritual truth and reality always have been with the Papacy, but that only now, in the changed context, are other non-Roman churches recognizing it as the providential design it always must have been. Interestingly, the whole Anglican church is bidden to make the very change of mind and to take the same route trodden over a century ago by one of her most notable sons, Newman in 1845, and using his very mode of reasoning. This primacy cannot be regarded as a matter of the church deciding to order its structure as seems fitting, a convention or honoured custom. This special ministry carries a particular gift of the Spirit. Here the inwardly spiritual and the outwardly historical merge in the organic 'body and soul' model. ARCIC envisages the development of the primacy and identifies the features of its proper occupant as best fitting the Roman portrait, much as did Newman.

D. A SOFT PRIMACY?

ARCIC 1 argues the need for a visible personal focus of the unity of the *koinonia*, for a primate to complement the highest council of the episcopal line in the church. A primate is a central identifiable point of reference. He will usually exercise authority only in the context of the college of bishops, but may at times take decisive action independently to uphold the faith and order of the whole church, should the need arise. The Primacy stands over against the whole church as well as emerging from it.

In this he serves the *koinonia* of all and acts as the agent specially gifted to discern and sift the promptings of the Spirit in the church, especially in complementarity with the episcopate and also with the faithful. The development of these two forms of complementarity, with the clerical line and with the whole body of the faithful, exemplifies once more the technique of differentiation within union; ARCIC is not clear about an *infallible* Pope and agrees to differ on that. Also it insists that the primacy excludes no other church bodies outside the scope of the primacy; although this seems a pastoral rather than a theological statement, if we take seriously the theological constructions concerning the need for primacy and the spiritual promptings encouraging its recognition now. Here the official Roman Catholic position is cited that Eastern Orthodoxy is regarded as a true church, although in dispute over Roman primacy; also that other churches somehow participate in the church of God, although not in the truest and fullest way because of the lack of recognition of the Roman Pontiff and the consequent loss of a fullness of unity.

Just as the Anglo-Catholic regards the Free Church as a partially severed branch of the tree of faith, so the Roman Catholic ecclesiology regards the churches outside her jurisdiction. Life does flow into the the severed limb, but imperfectly and in a wounded way. The break needs a perfect healing by a fuller ingrafting into the main trunk. Nevertheless, the church does 'subsist' in other churches and the Holy Spirit is found at work there. The papacy is of the essence of the healthy church, certainly of her fullness of being. This keystone of the arch of *episcope* can prevent episcopal schism. The primacy functions as the queen in the beehive: the source of self-definition and energy, without whom the whole body is in danger of disintegration and chaos. The logic of ARCIC can only be that failure to grow into this divinely appointed centre of *koinonia* and *episcope* must grieve the Holy Spirit, must mean church life deprived of a vital dimension.

Primacy is the sacrament of unity and also the means of fostering unity, the ordained instrument for this task. ARCIC denies that it suggests 'unchurching' those groups not in communion with the see of Rome, just as the High Anglicans disclaim any denial of Nonconformity. But the logic of the ARCIC theological argument conflicts with its reassurances. If there really is a divinely provided focus of unity, and if some churches are outside its ambit, then those churches are deficient not only in terms of something secondary and conventional, but in terms of obedience to the Holy Spirit. Primacy is not just of the 'well being' of the church but of her very essence, certainly of her fullness of being.

ARCIC has made a decision that primacy, and the Roman Papacy, does and will foster unity. This decision receives little or no justification. No argumentation is brought forward against the interpretation that the Papacy is inherently divisive, an interpretation made by Swete above in his claim that the Papacy broke with the East and then was responsible for the Reformation and the expulsion of the Protestants. That primacy fosters the unity of those submitting to its authority cannot be doubted and likewise the sheer size of the Roman Catholic Church is plain. But do these two truths point to a pastoral success of the Papacy, or to a formidably organized clericalist structure, ruled with a rod of iron, brooking no disagreement? Those who disagree are put out of fellowship by this primate, who therefore functions to institutionalize division also. If this is the reality of Roman primacy, whatever the definition of ARCIC, then the job specification and the applicant do not match up.

But ARCIC has redefined the primacy towards a more pastoral model, and has sought to protect the rights and privileges of Canterbury from the Roman tendency to impose its own patterns on native church life. Yet the ARCIC theological method, using the living voice of history and the current context to shift meaning and interpretation, destabilizes what it defines, and this must worry non-Roman Catholics. If the change in the current context can work in the direction of a liberalized Papacy today, then another twist of historical context can effect the opposite shift tomorrow. 1870 saw a decisive change toward a more officially powerful and infallible Papacy, a change which led to the breaking away of the Old Catholics of Germany. Vatican 2 has witnessed an official move stressing the Pope as a member of the college of bishops. The present incumbent is known for his more conservative style and exercise of Papal ministry with a traditionally Latin authoritarianism. The problem with an appeal to the present context and the living voice of today, is that today changes with the arrival of tomorrow. What is to prevent the primacy in the future doing precisely what was done in 1870, should the Spirit providentially so prompt the incumbent of the day, should the contemporary context 'require' it, should the church 'come to understand' things differently – again? ARCIC uses the organic growth idea, rather than that of 'foundation-superstructure'.

Even if we lay aside such concerns and accept the ARCIC redefinition, we still have to face the dilemma posed by Swete. He says: 'It may be taken as certain that unity will never be restored on the basis of Papal supremacy. Nor does experience favour any Papal attempt to form a fresh centre of Unity . . . Such an endeavour to give logical completeness to the organization of the Church can only end either in speedy failure or in the creation of a spiritual autocracy.'[76] Swete argues two possibilities for a new Papal scheme, either a rigid one or a soft and ineffectual one.

The Anglican office of the Archbishop of Canterbury may perhaps be said to exemplify a soft version of primacy, a soft focus of unity. In a very general way Canterbury acts as a centre for the loose-knit Anglican communion. But there are considerable differences in the churches of this communion and the primate of the Church of England has no power to intervene in another country. It is possible for a church to be out of communion with Canterbury, such as the Church of England in South Africa, but in communion with a diocese which is in communion with Canterbury, as Sydney has recognized the CESA in some measure. Logically, to make the situation neat, Canterbury might withdraw fellowship from the diocese recognizing a rejected church, but if the only grounds for such exclusion were that Sydney, for example, recognized another church, then the focus for unity and fellowship, *koinonia*, would have turned into a spiritual autocracy, and become a self-defining norm. Perhaps the choice is between an effective but harsh primacy, or a soft but ineffectual one. In fact, ARCIC proposes a primacy much more powerful than that of Canterbury.

5. Doctrinal authority in ARCIC

A. THE FORMATION OF AUTHORITATIVE DOCTRINE

The issue of authority in terms of doctrine as well as jursidiction is a most important aspect of this ecumenical agreement. A church will act according to its understandings of what is true and the mode of establishing correct doctrine underlies much else. The ARCIC method of defining the church operates in this area also: differentiation and relation, or union in distinction, a dialectical approach holding factors in complementarity and tension, this is the way forward.

The two fundamental factors to be held together are scripture and church teaching. ARCIC affirms both as vital to the process of developing Christian understanding of the faith in the contemporary context. All such restatement must be consonant with the apostolic witness recorded in the scriptures; for in this witness the preaching and teaching of ministers, and statements of local and universal councils, have to find their ground and consistency.'[77] The ministry of the *episcope* includes the interpretation of the scriptures and the discerning of truth and error. This process works its way up through the hierarchical structure to the very top. At the top of the pyramid the primate is specially authorized and gifted to declare the faith to the church. This will be in conjunction with the senior bishops, yet also in distinction from them as the unique ministry of primacy demands on occasion.[78] The Holy Spirit works through the oversight of the ministry and especially through its sharpest focus, the primate, to bring the church to the fulness of truth. ARCIC depicts apostolic scripture in the context of the living apostolic church as the guiding teaching authority.

Great councils of the church have produced specially authoritative pronouncements, 'When the Church meets in ecumenical council its decisions on fundamental matters of faith exclude what is erroneous.'[79] The Holy Spirit will protect great ecumenical councils from error only on fundamental matters of faith, which are 'faithful to Scripture and consistent with Tradition',[80] and a *fortiori* the primate will be protected from making erroneous statements on questions of central concern. On the other hand, 'neither general councils nor universal primates are invariably preserved from error even in official pronouncements,'[81] but only if the content touches matters of central import and accords with scripture. These pronouncements are to clarify and not to add to the faith revealed in the apostolic writings.

ARCIC insists that the reception of such formal statements of doctrine by the faithful is a vital part of the whole process. The *sensus fidelium*, the spiritual instinct of the whole people, has to be satisfied. But this instinct is not a final test, rather the two poles are assumed always to work in harmony, the dialectic of the clerical line and the lay instinct never really produces conflict. The movement seems to form a cone or spiral, up from the base of the whole to the focus of oversight, and back to the receptive base. The primate has the final word, and he has a special rapport with the *sensus fidelium*. The finally valid proclamation of a doctrinal or ethical statement by the hierarchy is 'binding' on the church.[82]

The Holy Spirit works in the process of reception by the faithful, their response to the clerical 'discernment', and an overall satisfaction indicates that the right decision has been reached. This sense of agreement signifies that all is well, but does not validate a doctrine. The question as to how we have access to this general assent is not tackled, but the general tenor of ARCIC suggests that the conversation simply continues and unease would somehow feed back to the clerical line of interpretation. No structured *lay* forum or synod is mentioned as a way of articulating the instinctive spiritual insight of the people. It is left to the clerical line, and particularly the primate, to do this. Certainly there is an important relationship between the totality and the single primate, a direct relationship, not only as mediated through the intervening tiers of the clerical hierarchy.

'Binding' teaching emerges from the whole living church pondering scripture and received tradition. The Holy Spirit gives the church layers of interpretative ministry, culminating in the primacy, with the raw innate *sensus fidelium* at the base. Conciliarity and primacy balance each other; laity and clergy constitute another balance, although in each of these relationships the 'focus' function has a precedence over the generality. Perhaps the whole picture may be likened to our legal system again. The English Common Law is a living tradition. It looks back to earlier judgements, its precedents, but tries to marry the binding principles arising from these past decisions with the new conditions arising today. There is a sense in which the law changes, yet its principles do not, or such is the hope and theory. For ARCIC the 'combination of permanence in the revealed truth and continuous exploration of its meaning is what is meant by Christian tradition. Some of the results of this reflection, which bear upon essential matters of faith, have come to be recognized as the authentic expression of Christian doctrine and therefore part of the "deposit of faith".'[83] The principles officially validated by the *episcope* and finally the primate achieve this status of binding doctrinal interpretation.

B. FAMILY RESEMBLANCE

The ARCIC view of authority in teaching on matters of faith

does not wholly square with the evangelical view nor the traditional Anglo-Catholic, but falls most easily into the modern developmental Roman Catholic understanding, indebted to Newman, Möhler and idealist interpretation.

Evangelical theory of authority rests on a scriptural base which stresses the horizon of the author of the text as a vital control, as well as attempting to link this with the modern horizon of meaning. The text is authoritative. How this is defended will be a subject for the next chapter, but for the moment Barth's stress on the central norm of the canon of scripture as the key to church teaching authority will supply the broad summary of the evangelical position.

Barth warns against 'the little word "and"' in this question. A theology can start by emphasizing scripture as the foundation, but can move on to obscure its central control by claiming that scripture needs to be supplemented by tradition. This in effect coordinates scripture 'and' tradition, the voice of the church, as the *joint* authority. It is this coordination that Barth resists: he rejects the idea that scripture alone is dumb or unclear.

Barth detects this tendency to the left and to the right, among the liberals and the Roman Catholics. Liberal theology conforms scripture to the opinions of current thought; Roman Catholicism conforms it to her own historic ritual and philosophy. The notion of the line of clerical interpretation having a special, spiritually guaranteed, mode of discernment seems to introduce this kind of coordination of scripture with the spiritual experience or insight of the hierarchy. Evangelical theology insists that the written word is open to laity and clergy alike, needing no special charism of the spirit for its interpretation.

Moreover, the concrete examples of doctrine being thought out in ARCIC do not encourage the evangelical. Priesthood is attributed to the whole people of God, the category of 'the laity' is not known in the New Testament. Yet, while on the one hand this undeniable burden of the apostolic writings is acknowledged, on the other hand its significance seems deliberately to be ignored as ministerial priesthood is subtly smuggled back in! As a result of sophisticated dialectics ARCIC produces a priestly ministry which is of a different realm of the gifts of the Spirit. Evangelical unease lies in the fear that central New Testament principles, while being given formal acknowledgement, are really neutralized by the description of how those principles were developed through the centuries. The New Testament becomes the historical seed bed of later structures, without itself applying doctrinal control over such developments.

On the other hand, ARCIC 2 with its clear adherence to the primacy of grace and to a forensic view of justification goes far to reassure those unsettled by ARCIC 1 on authority. But the issue of authority in teaching is vitally important to the evangelical, for whom truth is a live issue, as well as meaning. Evangelical ecclesiology wishes to make the structural proposals of ARCIC 1 subservient to the more basic salvation principles of ARCIC 2. One could use these principles of ARCIC 2 to criticize the ecclesiology of ARCIC 1.

The classical Anglo-Catholic view rests on the established block of teaching it perceives in the patristic view of the Bible. There are for this theological family fixed norms of doctrine. ARCIC uses the more modern, open-ended, evolutionary mode of theologizing, not cutting off tradition after the fourth century. The living *sensus fidelium* as a source of wisdom, for example, can become a way of ignoring or trimming authoritive, established, teaching. On the question of the ordination of women, this is exactly what the traditional Anglo-Catholic thinks is happening. The *sensus fidelium* can in fact reflect simply the current *mores* and anthropology of contemporary secular society.

R. A. Knox, later to become a leading Roman Catholic but here writing as an old fashioned Anglo-Catholic, attacked the notion of the living *sensus fidelium* as a source of, or validation for, correct teaching:

> 'The whole theory of the *consensus fidelium* has had a great vogue in the Church of England in recent years, owing to a difficulty often felt as to the ultimate seat of ecclesiastical authority. For, when we ask the question, "How is it possible to determine which of the Councils were orthodox, and which were not?", the Roman Catholic has a very simple ready-made answer, "Those which are recognized by the See of Peter." But the Anglican, not quite liking to refer the questioner to the XXXIX Articles of Religion, is forced to say, "Those which were subsequently ratified by acceptance on the part of the faithful." It is not relevant to our point here to consider the very difficult objection, "Yes, but how do you know whether the Nestorians or their opponents were the faithful?" However this may be, to whatever extent, or with whatever right, the faithful as

> a democratic body may claim to ratify the decrees of the Church, it is quite certain that as a matter of history they never claimed to originate them on the strength of their own "spiritual experience".'[84]

Knox prefers the 'foundation-superstructure' model here.

Knox requires norms by which the experience of the faithful and their innate sense for the faith, can be measured. Here the old fashioned Anglo-Catholic shares a methodological stance with the evangelical in favour of settled norms as the yardstick over evolving corporate or individual religious experience. Lash's description of the shift brought by Newman applies equally well to ARCIC: 'Criteriologically there is indeed a shift of emphasis, from the normative function of antiquity to the living voice of today.'[85]

ARCIC has developed a theological method closely resembling Newman's organic picture of the living interpretative church. The prophetical office is the spiritual reflective dimension, the episcopal office is the official validating function discerning the truth or error of the prophetical ideas, with the Papacy as the ultimate arbiter. Scripture is part of this interpretative, hermeneutical process.

The way ARCIC argues the Papacy into existence as a spiritual need, providentially filled by the Roman Pontificate, demonstrates this method in action. It works from the corporate experience of the church and conditions its exegesis of scripture accordingly. The Petrine texts are interpreted as rather forced analogies for a modern focal ministry. This kind of interpretation can undergird all kinds of dogmas. An example of the very same technique can be seen in Lash's defence of of the bodily assumption of Mary into heaven, declared official dogma by the Pope in 1950. Against Harry Williams, who cannot find a shred of historical evidence for this, Lash says, 'There is historical evidence, however slender, of Mary's obedience and trust, from Nazareth to Calvary. And this seems to me just the kind of evidence that we would need in order to be able to see in her the "image" of the faithfulness of Israel and thus, in the light of our faith in her son's resurrection, to trust that she, too, was brought by the grace of God to die into his glory.'[86]

Here is exactly the same method of reasoning backwards, in the light of what the church came to believe, to uphold a doctrinal truth. The New Testament is used not so much to ground a doctrine but as a starting point for a highly speculative theological and historical construct. Spiritual convictions of the present, without historical or doctrinal root in the scriptures, are read backwards to gain some justification for a current dogma.

ARCIC makes claims for the primacy beyond those of the purely human and historical. The Holy Spirit has unfolded this design and revealed its truth in today's new context. This gives the primacy doctrine a status equivalent to that of revelation, reserved for the scriptures by the Anglican tradition. Although this deduction is not drawn by ARCIC, it follows logically from its argumentation. Owen Chadwick, in the classic work on Newman, we recall, made the same point: 'Newman's theory . . . is dependent upon the contention that definition by the Church is "equivalent" to revelation.'[87] In this example, the process of the living church's reflection has received the baptism of the Holy Spirit, has become an inspired doctrine. In a sense the canon has been opened, especially since the primacy acts to decide upon true or false interpretations of the canonical scriptures. A doctrine declared by the official channels of the church to be true and binding and to be brought forth by the Spirit and given form by the primacy and episcopacy, cannot be distinguished in status from a biblically given doctrine. ARCIC seems to have developed a new form, of the revealed word, a living form, as opposed the written form.

This resembles what Vatican 2 teaches, speaking of a twofold source of certainty, scripture and the living tradition of the church, 'For both of them, flowing from the same divine wellspring, in a certain way merge into a unity and tend toward the same end.'[88] Tradition comes from the apostles and develops in the church by the Holy Spirit,[89] and the two forms of the apostolic word interpenetrate to maintain the church in the unity of the truth. ARCIC belongs to this family of ecclesiology and has the same authority structure.

Barth criticized Möhler's very similar view of interpretation and authority, holding that it brought forth another medium for revelation, equivalent to the very word of God to the church. Indeed Barth argues that the development of a focal primacy is essential for this kind of developmental theory, since otherwise the living process will have no certain mouthpiece to articulate and clarify the new developments prompted by the Spirit. Barth warned that the primacy will always tend to predominate over the conciliarity for this reason, the living whole needs to have some clear identifiable source of interpretation and articulation.[90] Barth regards this system as evolving its own form of revelation, an alternative word of God, the voice of the primate speaking in the Spirit. Newman and Möhler, so influential for Vatican 2, and now for ARCIC, argue that there can be no conflict between the scriptures and living church tradition, because the two must relate together in a constant harmony under the same inspiring Spirit. Both flow from the same wellspring and unite as distinct forms of the same thing.

In a recent book elucidating Roman Catholicism, Strange takes this line of refusing to allow the canonical scripture to test the authoritative declarations of the church. He likens the constant harmony to an actor who incarnates the text of the play and represents it, filling it with life and putting it across with fresh interpretative power.[91] Even accepting this analogy, the argument breaks down since the actor or director can never be always an infallible presenter of the text. Can he not distort or even contradict it? But the analogy itself is not appropriate, because the performer subserves the work and stands under its authority, he is not on the same level of creativity in terms of the content, although in terms of delivery his art is creative. The fact that he can make a mistake, or give an inauthentic performance, reveals his need to serve the play. Indeed the very notion of a 'mistake' in this context reveals this.

Strange's view, and it is the modern Roman Catholic line, rebuts the principle of canonical supremacy by merging the living church with the normative prophetic and apostolic witness. Such a failure to distinguish the two will inevitably result in some forced treatments of the text to fit the contemporary needs and tendencies. It also means the evolution of binding doctrine, not gained from the text so much as read into it.

This family of theology, stemming from Newman and Möhler,[92] shows signs of the idealist philosophical strain which formed an important, if unacknowledged, influence on those great minds. For the idealist, historical fact illustrates meaning and truth is in an historical process. Meaning seems prior to being, and indeed creates being and truth from the ongoing process of history. This historical evolution is always indwelt by the Spirit and human minds can focus or formulate the spiritually evolving truth. This framework has parallels with the ARCIC view of the development of doctrine in the living, Spirit-filled church, brought to formulation by the *episcope* and particularly the primacy.

Retrospective meaning creates fact, symbolizing interpretation swamps historical exegesis. The canonical text seems capable of producing, by illustration and symbolic interpretation, all kinds of doctrines not obvious to the reader but which, in the light of living tradition and corporate spiritual experience, may be taken to be spiritually ordained and true in the present context. Church history, selectively read, becomes another agent of revelation if the methods and claims of ARCIC 1 are taken to a logical conclusion.

These rather severe evangelical criticisms relate to ARCIC 1 on method and authority. ARCIC 2, however, *Salvation and the Church*, presents teaching which evangelical Anglicans should gratefully applaud.[93]

END NOTES TO CHAPTER 3

1. *The Final Report* CTS/SPCK, London, 1982.
2. *Salvation and the Church* Church House Publishing/CTS, London, 1987.
3. ARCIC 1 para. 5 p. 81.
4. ARCIC 1 para. 7 p. 7.
5. ARCIC 2 para. 27 p. 23.
6. ARCIC 2 para. 27 p. 24.
7. ARCIC 2 para. 30 p. 25.
8. para. 7 p. 7.
9. ARCIC 1 Preface p. 3.
10. ARCIC 1 para. 9 p. 8.
11. ARCIC 1 para. 2 p. 12.
12. ARCIC 2 p. 18.
13. ARCIC 2 para. 9 p. 14.
14. ibid.
15. ARCIC 1 para. 8 p. 8.
16. ARCIC 2 para. 10 p. 14.
17. ARCIC 1 para. 8 p. 33, para. 11 p. 34.
18. ARCIC 1 para. 3 p. 12.
19. ARCIC 1 para 2 p. 12.
20. ARCIC 2 para. 18 p. 18.
21. ARCIC 1 para. 5 p. 13.
22. ARCIC 1 para. 5 p. 14.
23. ARCIC 1 para. 5 p. 20.
24. ibid. para. 7 p. 15.
25. ibid. para. 6 p. 21.
26. ARCIC 1 fn. 2 p. 14.
27. para 6 p. 21.
28. para. 8 p. 15.
29. ibid. para. 7 p. 22.

30. Bicknell op. cit. p. 518.
31. *ARCIC and Lima on Baptism and Eucharist* Grove, 1983,
32. para. 5 p. 14.
33. para. 5 p. 20.
34. *Eucharistic Sacrifice and the Reformation* DLT, London, 1980 p. 264.
35. ibid.
36. *Symbolism* by I. A. Möhler translated by J. B. Robertson 3rd edition London Catholic Publishing and Bookselling Company, undated, pp. 234–5.
37. ibid. p. 238.
38. ibid. p. 234.
39. ibid. p. 234.
40. *Christus in Ecclesia* T&T Clark, Edinburgh, 1904.
41. ibid. p. 41.
42. ARCIC 1 p. 21.
43. op. cit. p. 42.
44. ARCIC 1 p. 14 footnote.
45. Consubstantiation is the doctrine that after consecration the bread and wine coexist with the body and blood of Christ.
46. op. cit. p. 42.
47. *Principles of Christian Theology* revised edition SCM, London, 1977 p. 470.
48. *Essays in New Testament themes* p. 128.
49. *Principles of Christian Theology* p. 480.
50. *The Priesthood of the Ordained Ministry* FOAG Report op. cit.
51. para. 3 p. 30.
52. para. 6 p. 32.
53. para. 9 p. 33.
54. para. 2 p. 41.
55. para. 13 p. 36.
56. ibid.
57. para. 2 p. 41.
58. ibid.
59. para. 2 p. 42.
60. ibid. p. 411.
61. H.C.G. Moule *Outlines of Christian Doctrines* Hodder and Stoughton, London 1890 p. 223.
62. ARCIC 1 p. 54.
63. ibid. p. 73.
64. para. 28 p. 93.
65. para. 3 p. 72.
66. para. 5 p. 83.
67. para. 5 p. 83.
68. para. 7 p. 84.
69. para. 9 p. 85.
70. *Einheit* pp. 236–7.
71. ibid.
72. para. 13 p. 87.
73. *The Dublin Agreed Statement* 1984, SPCK p.17.
74. For a useful introduction to Pannenberg's view, see *Theology and the Kingdom of God* W. Pannenberg, ed. R. Neuhaus, Westminster Press, 1989.

75. *The Holy Catholic Church* Macmillan, Lonodn, 1915 p. 83.
76. ibid.
77. ARCIC 1 para. 15 p. 59.
78. ibid. p. 94.
79. ibid. p. 62.
80. ibid. p. 72.
81. ibid. p. 94.
82. p. 62.
83. ibid. p. 70.
84. *Some Loose Stones* Longmans Green, London, 1914 p. 193.
85. *Newman on Development* op. cit. p. 132.
86. 'Easter Meaning' in *Heythrop Journal* vol. xxv no. 1 Jan 84 p. 15.
87. *From Bossuet to Newman* CUP, Cambridge, 1957 p. 160.
88. *Constitution on Revelation* 9.
89. ibid. 8.
90. *Church Dogmatics* 1/2 p. 560.
91. R. Strange *The Catholic Faith* OUP, Oxford, 1986 p, 66.
92. In *Church Dogmatics* 1/2 p, 560f, Barth brackets Möhler's teaching on doctrine with that of Schleiermacher, the former using a corporate version of the latter's view that doctrine was 'religious affections set forth in speech.'
93. A second agreed statement has been published by ARCIC 2, *Church as Communion*, Church House Publishing/CTS, London 1991, too late for detailed analysis here. It adds nothing substantially new, however, to the ecclesiology of ARCIC 1. Its elaboration of the category of communion accords with many of the conclusions reached in my final chapter.

4

EVANGELICAL ANGLICAN ECCLESIOLOGY

Defining 'evangelical Anglican'

This treatment intends to articulate the classical reformed Anglican position inherited from the time of the Reformation, set out by early English reformers, notably Cranmer, and Elizabethans such as Jewel, Field, Hooker and Whitgift. It is becoming increasingly hard to pin down today precisely what the term 'evangelical' does mean. It can indicate a certain zeal for the Lord; a particular attitude to the Bible; a tradition of 'low church' ritual in liturgy. In terms of 'church ministry and sacraments', however, the classical reformed heritage remains the presupposed foundation for evangelical Anglicans. The lack of a definitive exposition, such as those of Moberly and Ramsey for Anglo-Catholicism, will mean this chapter, having to draw on many sources, will be longer than the others.

1. The covenant people of God

A. THE COVENANT: A PAULINE THEOLOGY

The biblical notion of 'covenant' relationship between the God of Israel and his people controls this ecclesiology. Paul in Romans and Galatians refers to Abraham as the particular person singled out by the Lord to be the founder of a great family of faith and trust who are taught to look to their Lord for everything. The term 'covenant' today smacks of legal contracts and tricky disputes over rights of way on land! But biblically it signifies relationship. God has freely given the gift of his presence to a people who then become 'his people'. The Lord of creation commits himself to a small tribe, asking for the response of dedication and worship.

Today, covenant language is heard in a personal sense in the marriage service: the ring is given, to 'remind you of the vow and covenant which you have made this day'. Marriage mutually commits the partners together, and the further we go back in history the more we find it envisaged as a protective relationship by the husband, the stronger party, for the wife whom the husband promises to cherish. The wife for her part, in the old form of words, promises to obey. The covenant relationship is such that the two really are now deemed as a single entity, their coming together forms a new unit. Paul uses the analogy of husband and wife in their intimate union as illustrating the closeness of Christ and his people.[1] For the Hebrew mind this is covenant language: the two are as deeply united as possible while retaining their identities. The marriage analogy recurs in the biblical narrative to describe God's relation with Israel: Hosea the prophet teaches and lives through the trauma of his faithless wife, who seems bent on ignoring her husband, in order to illustrate the Lord's care and commitment, his covenant love, towards wayward Israel.

Reformed ecclesiology, following Paul's interpretation especially, teaches that God has been building a people for himself for centuries by means of freely relating himself to his people, whom he asks to respond in trust and obedience. The Abrahamic covenant begins the historic process. Abraham, long before Moses, received the call of God, was chosen by grace to be the historical root of the Israel of God. Just as Peter and Paul served as crucial formative figures in the days of the New Testament church, Abraham was a similarly key historical foundation person in building the people of God. Abraham hears, trusts and obeys the living God. He commits his progeny to this faithful obedience, signing himself and his son with the covenant sign of circumcision. The birth of this son Isaac to the aged Sarah was not a question of human possibility but of promise, miracle and pure gift.

Abraham becomes the archetype of the whole future people of God as well as its historical particular source. The pattern of God working from the particular individual to the whole people seems significant. Abraham, chosen out of pagan people, becomes father to a great people, like the multitude of stars in heaven or sand grains on the shore. He serves as father in the sense of starting a blood line; but for Paul his deepest significance lies in his acceptance of his call in trustful faith, not unlike the role of Mary centuries later.

The reformed ecclesiology might be described as Pauline in that Romans and Galatians develop this theme of the people of God who live by the key principle of trust in the God of grace. Trust and faith in God defines the sons of Abraham. Abraham received the covenant, the relationship of promise given out of the love and mercy of God. Covenant promise, to be believed in and trusted by the recipients or beneficiaries, lies near the heart of the structure of the reformed faith. Paul uses this to demonstrate the priority of God's grace evoking human faith, the true mark of the people of God, to be worked out ethically. The covenant relationship with God, for Paul, is pure grace. It is communicated in comprehensibly spoken promise, received in faith and obedience. This simple, personal shape forms the umbrella framework, the canopy overarching the Mosaic substructure of law and life, according to the Pauline interpretation so central to reformed ecclesiology.

Through Abraham, God had formed a visible historical community of faithful people, bearing the covenant mark of circumcision, separated off from the surrounding pagan nations and so 'holy' in the sight of God. The Abrahamic people journeyed at the call of the Lord, listening to his voice as their guide. Experiencing slavery in Egypt and release through the mighty acts of God and the ministry of Moses, this people renews her covenant with the Lord and gains the Passover covenant meal, as well as the priestly cult ritual system. In essence the definition of the visible church in the Thirty Nine Articles is here already: 'The visible church of Christ is a congregation of faithful men, in which the pure Word of God is preached, and the sacraments duly ministered . . .'[2] Even the lack of the Messiah Jesus at that point in history, the obvious deficiency in the Abrahamic anticipation of the church, does not really affect the shape of how the community knows the Lord. Paul takes the history of the wandering people of God as quite in line with the present church even taking events as hiddenly invested with the presence of Christ.[3] The lesson to be learned about the need for obedient faith, according to Paul, remains the same now as then. The basic nature of the church is a visible community of faith, guided by the word of the Lord, sealed with the covenant signs.

This basic Pauline interpretation of the people of God emphasizes divine grace and responsive faith from a definite historical community and regards as transient and secondary the arrangements of the Temple cult with its priesthood, the requirements of the Law. These arrangements were, as history was to show, divinely ordained but temporary sub-structures within the overarching relationship of grace and faith, as was the monarchical political system. Such structures of the community of faith were not of her very essence and in due time fell away to be fulfilled by and absorbed into the atoning ministry of the crucified and risen Lord, the final priest-king. The essence of the Israel of God for Paul was the historical community, the one people of God, faithfully obedient, attentive to the word, precious in the eyes of the Lord. The essential, most basic fact is that of the covenant *people*: events can alter the structures of worship and leadership as seems most appropriate, under God, but these do not constitute the people. An interesting biblical example of this can be seen in the terrible sacking of the city of God, Jerusalem, and of the Temple, which meant the end of the sacrificial system for decades. Jeremiah (chapter 24) brings the word to the devastated people that those who go into exile, not those who continue to dwell in the ancient land and city, are the true continuity of the Israel of God.

The Israel of God is primarily a covenant people of faith: the cultic and political arrangements are very important, since the Lord ordains them, but subserving the people of faith. 'No one can deny,' says Newbigin commenting on Paul's interpretation, 'that the crucial word in this whole argument is the word "faith". The text on which the whole is founded is . . . "he who by faith is righteous shall live".'[4] There is no other claim to be God's people than on the basis of grace given and accepted in trustful faith.

Paul, in his anguished description of the Jewish people who refused to believe in Jesus as Messiah, defines the covenant people of God: 'They are Israelites, and to them belong the sonship, the glory, the covenants, the giving of the law, the worship and the promises; to them belong the patriarchs, and of their race, according to the flesh, is Christ.'[5] They lack only the fulfilment of their long-held covenant faith, faith in the Messiah and the Messianic Spirit prophesied in Joel. 'From the true promise that God had entered into a covenant with Abraham and his seed, they drew the false conclusion that, if they kept their side of the covenant, they had a status before God as of right . . .'[6] The ancient Israel needs to exercise faith, in the pattern of their father Abraham, in the grace of Christ.

Evangelical Anglican ecclesiology bases itself on this interpretation of the people of God, her ministry and sacramental pattern, appealing to the Thirty Nine Articles of Religion, both in their general tenor and in their teaching on specific points of ecclesiology.[7] Griffith Thomas, the evangelical counterpart to Bicknell on the Articles, draws from this the point that Anglican ecclesiology commits itself to the community, 'The visible Church is a community. It is a congregation, not an aggregation . . .'[8] Article 17 states a doctrine of divine election to salvation, not commenting on any doctrine of the negative decree, stressing prevenient grace behind the congregation of the faithful. This fits in with the generally Augustinian tenor of the Articles as a whole, and ecclesiologically gives the Church of England quite a reformed base: the church is the community of the faithful issuing from the hand of the gracious and merciful Lord, a listening and obedient people.

B. ADOPTION INTO SONSHIP: THE NEW COVENANT HEAD

The theology of covenant as the overall framework for our understanding of the church and salvation has been interestingly restated by the Anglican New Testament scholar N. T. Wright in several articles. In his contribution to the symposium on justification, *The Great Acquittal*, he argued that biblical teaching on the subject amounts to holding that 'Justification is no legal fiction, but God's righteous declaration that the believer is within the covenant.'[9] Paul teaches, explains Wright, that because of the work of Christ 'God pronounces in the present the future verdict of "righteous" over all who believe. Irrespective of moral or racial background, believers are declared to belong for all eternity to the true people of Abraham, the family of the renewed covenant, the people whose sins are forgiven. And from this perspective, Romans 9–11 falls into place: God is redefining Abraham's family as the worldwide covenant community . . .'[10] Wright regards this as a revision of the traditional reformed view, which would add that this adoption happens on the basis of the cross of Christ. Wright's work, standing in the reformed Anglican family of interpretation, seeks to integrate the doctrines of salvation, on which evangelicals have concentrated, with those of the church and sacraments on which they tend to be weak.

James Packer, the influential Anglican writer in the reformed and specifically Puritan mould, had already made a similar point when he pleaded for a recovery of the category of adoption as perhaps the primary one for salvation, embracing even that of justification. 'Sonship to God then,' he writes, 'is a gift of grace. It is not a natural but an *adoptive* sonship: and so the New Testament explicitly pictures it.'[11] Along with many such texts from other authors, he cites Paul: 'God sent forth his Son, born of woman, born under the law, to redeem those under the law, that we might receive the adoption of sons.'[12]

The New Testament stress on the church's free adoption into the family of God, unites the doctrines of salvation and church: we are the family of God our Father, not only deemed in the right and pardoned from our sin but intimately loved by God and secure in his family. The parable of the prodigal son may illustrate the nature of this relationship in that the father's child was never cast out from the family, that despite his behaviour he remains 'family'. Surely this is the ecclesiological complement to the evangelical insistence on justification by grace rather than by earned acceptance. As adopted sons and daughters the church has no need to fear. She is adopted and accepted, she has this real relationship to God as Father.

Christ provides the whole dynamic for this possibility. Jesus, himself the embodiment of the covenant of God with man, is the quintessential Israelite. Born of woman, born under the law, he fulfils the law and reconstitutes the covenant people, making possible the anticipations of the earlier prophets who spoke of a new covenant, a new heart, a new intimacy between God and his people, going beyond and completing the relationship under the covenant before Calvary, Easter and Pentecost. This has been re-expressed in different forms by several recent Anglicans in the reformed tradition. Thomas Smail's *The Forgotten Father*,[13] focuses on the Sonship of Christ and our relationship of security and love with the Father, our adoptive sonship. Evangelical ecclesiology claims to be Pauline in its trinitarian shape here: 'For you did not,' Paul tells the Roman church, 'receive the spirit of slavery to fall back into fear, but you have received the spirit of sonship. When we cry "Abba, Father!" it is the Spirit himself bearing witness with our spirit that we are children of God, and if children then heirs, heirs of God and fellow heirs with Christ, provided we suffer with him in order that we may be glorified with him.'[14] The motif of sonship as opposed to slavery or servanthood stresses the difference between genuine 'personal' relationship as opposed to external, master-servant relationship of employment,[15] or between a mature personal relationship and that of the heir who was under age and who in Roman law was therefore 'no better than a slave'.[16] 'To those who are Christ's, the holy God is a loving Father; they belong to His family; they may approach Him without fear, and always be sure of His fatherly concern and care. This,' concludes Packer, 'is the heart of the New Testament message.'[17]

The pattern of covenant, or 'family', ecclesiology flows from the Christological doctrine of the Son, the pioneer and perfecter of our faith, who fulfilled and perfected the human relationship with God as son to the heavenly Father. Jesus is our new 'covenant head' and representative. Bishop H. C. G. Moule, tells us that 'The Epistle to the Hebrews, the great treasury of covenant doctrine, leads us, along with the rest of the New Testament, to the conclusion that the covenant blessings were so won by the perfect work of the Lord Christ as to be lodged in Him for His Church, and to become actually theirs on their becoming His.'[18] Interestingly, he interprets the heavenly intercession of the ascended Lord in the context primarily of the covenant: 'The essence of the matter is His union with His people, and His perpetual presence, in that union, with the Father, as the once slain Lamb.'[19] The high priestly ministry of Christ, exercised from the royal throne, is likewise the mediatorial 'high priestly work no longer of offering but of intercession related to it'.[20]

This distinctively reformed idea of Jesus as the church's covenant head arguably stands in the tradition of Irenaeus of Lyons, who developed the notion that Jesus re-ran the course of human life, cutting against the grain of sin, undoing the disasters of the old Adam and realizing the proper potential of an obedient mankind, culminating at the absolute act of obedience at Golgotha. Jesus 'recapitulated' and healed the career of wayward mankind creating a new Adam with an even higher destiny than his forerunner.[21]

This fits well with the Christology of Galatians which tells of Jesus being born into the Jewish tradition, under the law, in order to redeem humanity. The Irenaean picture is often criticized for failing to take sufficient account of the atonement, to make it only the climax of a victoriously obedient life, but reformed theology wishes to make the additional point given by Galatians, and the extra elaboration in Romans, that 'God has done what the law, weakened by the flesh could not do: sending his own Son in the likeness of sinful flesh, he condemned sin in the flesh, in order that the just requirement of the law might be fulfilled in us, who walk not according the flesh but the Spirit.'[22] Recapitulating wayward humanity also involved the Son in accepting the condemnation of sin in the human race. A moral and forensic aspect is not inconsistent with Irenaeus' incarnational portrayal of Jesus' life and death healing a thoroughly diseased humanity. Reformed Christology insists on the atonement as the hinge needing to be turned to bring sinful humanity into the inner family, covenant, relationship with the Father. The Holy Spirit, the 'paraclete', is promised in the Gospel of John by Jesus who says, 'if I do not go away, the paraclete will not come to you'[23]: Jesus consecrates himself to death, goes away, that the small band of disciples would themselves be consecrated by the sanctifying Holy Spirit, according to John, by the risen Lord, three days later. Jesus' redemptive death and resurrection revitalizes, perfects and fulfils the Israel of God.

Perhaps the most exciting statement of this strand of Christological covenant ecclesiology recently from the evangelical stable comes from Wright in his small Latimer Study, *Evangelical Anglican Identity*. 'If God's purpose in calling Abraham,' he says,

> 'was to reverse the sin of Adam: and if that purpose has been achieved in Jesus Christ: then in Jesus Christ God has not only rescued sinners, but is planning to turn them into his true humanity, humanity at last as it was meant to be. When Jesus rose on the third day he rose with a body which, having passed through death, was no more subject to it (Rom. 6:9f.). Jesus has *reconstituted* humanity in himself. *Sinful* humanity died on the cross (Rom. 8:3): true humanity, continuous with that sinful humanity but now purged by Jesus' death, rose on Easter morning. All those who belong to Jesus the Messiah therefore belong not with the sinful humanity but with the true . . .'[24]

Christian life involves the paradox that sin still clings and has to be beaten, that what we are now in the Spirit will be fully completed at the final endtime. As regards the specific doctrine of the church, 'Israel—as the people of God, but also the people in whom Adam's sin is seen to its full extent because of the law (Rom 5:20)—is reconstituted just as humanity has been. The church rises on Easter morning in place of the Israel that has died on the cross, and all who want to belong to the reconstituted people of God must be joined to the Messiah, by baptism and faith, in his death and resurrection.'[25]

This might perhaps be expressed in terms of the universalization of Israel, her true destiny 'to be the light to lighten the Gentiles': Israel in the person of Jesus includes all the faithful. The people of God, 'the redefined Israel, are still,' for Wright '*the historical people who look back to Abraham as their chronological starting point*, precisely because they look to Jesus as their chronological raison d'être . . . the process of renewal has not meant abandoning the idea of an historical people.'[26] The historical Israel continues as the visible and historical mission of the church, the family of the *kyrios*, the Lord: 'The historical mission of the church . . . depends theologically on just this fact, that in the death and resurrection of Jesus Israel has been reconstituted, has in fact been turned inside out.'[27] Wright stands in the heritage of reformed thought in affirming the historical continuity and renewal of the Abrahamic people of God, as well as the new creation, brought about in Christ. Lesslie Newbigin had earlier written on similar lines in his *Household of God*.[28] The Newman-type ecclesial model of historical development finds its place in evangelical ecclesiology in this covenant people's history down the centuries. The stress falls on the *people* not its structures. With this, or in it, comes the 'centre-circumference' model, the people are called always to true faith, supremely in Christ by the Spirit.

C. THE BODY OF CHRIST

We have reached a point reminiscent of Ramsey's teaching of the church as the 'new race' constituted in Christ, and he provides a fruitful comparison. Ramsey seeks to avoid a purely incarnational catholic interpretation of redemption and states the vital importance of the death and resurrection of Jesus for the church, so joining hands with evangelical theology. The difference lies in the way Christ is perceived to relate to the church. The Reformation is sometimes said to have been a Christological correction to the medieval church. This seems questionable since the medieval doctrine of Christ exalted the incarnate Son as much as did the reformed formulations, indeed both restated the Chalcedonian definition of 451, the teaching of two natures, divine and human, in the one person. A more precise summary of the theological reason for the Reformation lies in the area of how Christ relates to the church, and in particular in the recovery of the realization of the New Testament teaching on the Holy Spirit bringing Christ to the heart of the trusting believer. Theologically the Reformation concerned the teaching of Christ dying and rising on our behalf, so making possible a fresh relationship with the Father and becoming directly present by the Holy Spirit. The place of the church's prayer life should be stressed in this context, both corporately and individually: evangelical ecclesiology regards this as crucial to the body of Christ, to the royal priesthood, a huge privilege arising from the Spirit of the Son being sent into our hearts, fostered by the sacramental aspect of church life.

Ramsey wholeheartedly agrees with this recovery of the apostolic understanding of the personal presence of Christ in the church, and today Roman Catholic theology in the main likewise agrees. At the same time there remains a distinct difference of emphasis in the way Christ is perceived to relate to the church and to define her. Whereas the catholic Anglican tradition stresses the fact that the *church is in Christ*, the evangelical stresses *Christ in the church* by the Spirit. The church is not so much a form of Christ as the people of Christ, in covenant with him. Evangelical ecclesiology, perhaps because of its strong hold on the doctrine of the personal Spirit, stresses the notion of Emmanuel, 'God with us'. Anglo-Catholic ecclesiology, as emerges most clearly in the eucharistic teaching on self-offering, understands the church as the body of Christ as well as his bride. While preserving the distinction between Christ and the church, the best and most characteristic Anglo-Catholic thought insists on a closer identification than does most evangelical ecclesiology. Reformed thought more comfortably speaks of Christ 'the head of the Body' than Christ as the body. Another way of putting this point, which involves a whole ethos and spiritual feel as well as strict theology, is to say that the model of the incarnation, that of the indwelling Word suffusing and transfiguring the human historical church, best captures the catholic vision.

Interestingly, the well known distinction between the two basic types of orthodox Christology in the early period of theology mirrors this ecclesiological difference of emphasis. The Alexandrian school, of which Athanasius was prominent, produced the 'word-flesh' model of incarnation emphasizing the integration of the divine word into the humanity of Jesus. The school of Antioch on the other hand is generally agreed to have taken a rather different perspective, stressing the duality of the divine and human in the person of Christ, both to preserve the true humanity and to protect the deity from change. Luther's doctrine of Christ tends to be characterized as Alexandrian, Calvin's as Antiochene, and it is the influence of Calvin that is decisive for reformed theology. Transposing this across to ecclesiology we see how the notion of covenant and relation reflects the more Antiochene ethos of God with us. A more Alexandrian ecclesiology will envisage the church's human historical form suffused with grace. Divine grace indwells the historical visible church in all aspects and the church therefore can aptly be called the permanent visible sacrament of God, the body of Christ in the world.

Ramsey considers the reformed vision of the relation of Christ and his church rather a cold one: 'Calvinism is second to no form of Christianity in its emphasis on order and discipline. It misses, however, a great deal of the inner spirit of Churchmanship. While Luther ignores outward order he has a warm sense of the Church's mystical meaning in his view of Christ and the Christians. "Ye are the body" rings through his writings. For Calvin, however, the Church is rather utilitarian. It is not perceived as the glow of Christ's incarnate presence; it is the policeman sent to protect the Christian life by commands and prohibitions. Here is discipline without the sense of union with the death and life of Christ which gives discipline meaning; here is order without the sense of the wondrous historical and apostolic race which gives order its meaning.'[29] This comment has some truth in it as regards the Alexandrian kind of incarnational suffusion of the whole church with Christ; it is unfair when seen against the Antiochene family of Christology, because the reformed interpretation of the body of Christ stresses God with us, with each church member, binding them into one.

The interpretation of Paul's teaching of the church as the body of Christ has proved a major point of debate between catholic and evangelical ecclesiology in the past. The former argued that this language in the New Testament means that the duly organized church really is now the physical presence of Christ on earth and in a sense is an extension of the incarnation, the latter that the language must be seen as a metaphor to explain the intimate union of Christ and his church. Bishop John Robinson, a thinker impossible to 'pigeon-hole' in any one party of theology or churchmanship, argued against the reformed interpretation and held that Paul envisaged the church as the 'Body of Christ' as a literal fact, but even Roman Catholic interpretation now doubts this. Dulles points out that Paul is quite conscious of speaking figuratively when he speaks of Christians as eyes and ears of the whole church body, for example. The analogy, in Dulles's view, 'breaks down at a certain point because in the Church the head and members do not make up a single organism. The members are distinct and complete persons, having their own freedom and responsibility.'[30] Further, if taken literally, the image of the head and the body 'would not do justice to the very intimate union between Christ and the Church,'[31] since in an organic body the head is not in the other organs but external to them. Christ must be held to be in all the members, and they in him. This has been the reformed understanding of the teaching of Christ and his church as his body, which has always been wary of pressing the identification of Christ the sinless Lord and the church, always prone to sin. The body of Christ image, for reformed ecclesiology, needs to be understood in terms of the covenant image: the church forms a single people indwelt by her Lord, but the notion of a corporate personality of the whole church, separable from the individual members and somehow identifiable with the cosmic exalted Christ, is foreign to Anglican evangelical thought.

In his commentary on the Epistle to the Ephesians, Bishop Moule expresses the evangelical view of the utterly close communion between Christ as head and his people as the body: 'He is the ruling and life-giving "Head" of a vast multitude of human beings who absolutely belong to Him, and absolutely live by Him. They are His Body; they exist, collectively, to be His limbs and implements. They are "His Fulness", the *Pleroma* in which this sublime Person actualizes His will. He is their "Ful-filler"; all that is receptive of spiritual life and power in them, it is He who makes it and keeps it full. He is such that He is the source of all grace, and the Hope of all glory for fallen man.'[32] All Christians are united in *koinonia* with Christ, and are therefore his body. This body metaphor is another way of putting the evangelical covenant notion of the church expressed, for example, in Wesley's hymn:

'Alive in Him, my living head,
And clothed with righteousness divine'.

D. INVISIBLE AND VISIBLE CHURCH

The church as the body of Christ, for evangelical theology, means the whole body of Christians who are joined to Christ in the bond of the Holy Spirit. Christ indwells each one and the whole body therefore forms a unity which crosses all the barriers of denomination, culture and nation. The body of Christ is a catholic spiritual *koinonia*, a worldwide fellowship across time and space of all inwardly united to the living, redeeming head of the body. If the covenant idea serves as the structural key for reformed Anglican ecclesiology, this notion of the intimate union of Christians in Christ is its final completion and inner heart. This is not simply a matter of subjective feeling, but is communion through the Holy Spirit with the risen and ascended Christ. Jeremiah's ancient prophecy to Israel comes to fruition with the body of Christ: 'This is the covenant I will make with the house of Israel after those days, says the Lord: I will put my law within them, and I will write it upon their hearts; and I will be their God, and they shall be my people.'[33] The Epistle to the Hebrews cites this prophecy to describe the church's relation to her Lord. This profound reality of the body of Christ gives the evangelical faith its ecumenical range and defines catholicity. The fact that all Christians know God in Christ by the Spirit means that under all disagreements and barriers there is one church. Article 18 of the Thirty Nine Articles endorses this understanding in underlining that salvation is in the name of Christ only, not by membership of particular sects or any other scheme of life. Christ provides the central pivot of salvation and the church throughout the world. This leads us to what has been a distinctive feature of reformed Anglican ecclesiology from the earliest days of the Reformation, the insistence on the distinction between the church visible and invisible or spiritual; the church on earth is always a visible body, but it has a spiritual 'heart', her relationship to the invisible Lord.

God always had been the invisible God, universal and known in faith by the Hebrew people. The church continues to know this God and in basically the same kind of way, but in a still more privileged way because of the indwelling Spirit. When evangelical theology speaks of the invisible church it means to say that Jesus is the Lord of the church and that communion with him establishes the church and adds new members to the whole body. This has regularly been discussed in terms of the inner heart of the church, and also of the inner spiritual life. Litton can agree with a modified version of Newman: 'There is much truth in the observation that "Christianity came into the world as an idea rather than as an institution", if for the word "idea" we substitute the presence of Christ by His Spirit in the hearts of believers.'[34] Christ's spiritual presence is what is invisible, the church never was. The fact that Christ is invisible now, that the church lives between the times of the first coming and the second, does not mean that the faith is purely or mainly 'inward'. Christ is an objective reality outside the church as well as indwelling her. Therefore the invisible aspect goes beyond some 'inner' aspect. The church relates to Christ, the second Adam who became 'life giving spirit'[35]; he is the head of the body, who pours his life into his members.

The concept of the invisible church means that the church knows her Lord spiritually. But spirituality for the Christian faith is hard to pin down: it does not simply mean an invisible plane higher than the earthly. On the contrary, Christian spirituality cannot be separated from involvement in the physical world of the cheque book and the ballot paper. Paul teaches that despite the daily wearing out of the physical bodies of believers, 'inwardly we are being renewed' so that we look forward to receiving what he perceives to be something immensely solid, the opposite to anything abstract or ideal,—an eternal weight of glory,[36] the 'spiritual body' perhaps. The picture seems desperately hard to understand for the Western 'enlightened' mind trained to think in terms of the invisible spirit or idea, over against visible physical matter: for such a mind either something is spiritual or it is physical. Spirit stands opposite matter. The doctrine of the church has to involve talk of the spiritual and the visible, but along the lines of Paul rather than of a spirit-matter dualism gained from Greek and enlightenment culture. The spiritual church is the church, united with the Lord and, leaving aside the unseen 'cloud of witnesses'[37] who are with God on the other side of death, this spiritual church is the physical, tangible and audible family of God. The church's spirituality cannot be regarded as the reverse of her physical historical being. When evangelicalism forgets this and identifies spiritual with invisible, then it lapses into a form of pietism, of which is has all too often been guilty.

Evangelical ecclesiology agrees with Hooker that the distinction between the spiritual and the visible aspects of the church cannot be avoided for Christian thought, and that it prevents confusion. The church spiritual is the church as known by God, who alone knows the hearts of men and women. Hooker, the great Elizabethan Anglican theologian, lays it down that this distinction must be upheld for the sake of clarity. 'For lack of diligent observing the difference, first between the Church of God mystical and visible, then between the visible sound and corrupted, sometimes more, sometimes less; the oversights are neither few nor light that have been committed.'[38] This distinction claims the authority of Paul, for whom membership of the community alone is not sufficient, the need is for a living communion with Christ. Evangelical Anglican stances on the sacraments and ecumenism are best explained with this distinction in mind.

E. PRIMARY AND SECONDARY LEVELS OF AUTHORITY

In terms of the 'order of being' the human historical people of God are Spirit-filled believers if they are the church; in terms of the 'order of knowing' evangelical ecclesiology denies any spiritual 'geiger-counter' exists in the hands of the church to assess those who are sincerely faithful or not. Anglican evangelicals have traditionally followed the wisdom of the theologians of the Elizabethan settlement after the Reformation and adopted an 'order of speaking', which presumes that those who declare and practise their faith outwardly are in fact spiritual people. This 'charitable presumption' has been usefully summarized again recently by Avis as a distinguishing feature of historic Anglican reformed ecclesiology.[39]

This important principle flows from the distinction between the spiritual heart and the outward appearance, which in turn roots back to that between the divine and the human. God truly knows the depths of the heart. Parallel to this is the evangelical Anglican conviction that God has provided clearly and definitely in some areas of church life, but has left others more open and flexible. The aspects in which revelation firmly operates concern salvation in Christ; the areas in which the church has a freedom to act concern the structures and customs of the church. 'Hooker for example clearly distinguishes between things necessary to salvation and things indifferent'.[40] Hooker argued on the right against Rome and on the left against Presbyterians, both groups insisting that their form of church government was laid down as a divinely given blueprint. 'The apologists of the Anglican settlement did not regard polity as of the *esse* of the Church.'[41] The celebration of the sacraments and the teaching of the word were divinely ordained, but how precisely these were carried out was a secondary issue in the hands of the church. Changes in historical circumstance would also lead to flexibility and adjustment in church government.

This evangelical attitude alienates the higher church Anglican. It seems to smack of pietistic individualism, of negligence, of irresponsibility. The church of God must strive to repair the wounds of historical division, according to the appropriate tenets of episcopal order. But the evangelical, deep down, does not regard the issue of formal unity as the heart of the matter. Structures of the visible church are important, but no mandatory blueprint exists to define precisely the shape of structural organization. Here the Anglican evangelical faces the wrath of the Anglo-Catholic to the right, and of the House Church restorationists, with their conviction that the book of Acts provides a precise plan for church order, to the left.

Following Hooker, evangelical Anglican ecclesiology regards the body of Christ as already extending across denominational barriers, the Holy Spirit being no respecter of persons or structures, as Peter, the arch-ecclesiological conservative in Acts, was forced to learn. Even Gentiles could be indwelt by the Spirit and therefore be included in the people of the covenant, without undergoing circumcision. Likewise evangelical faith knows that the covenant community extends beyond the episcopal pale; and that the episcopal organizational structure can take several forms, some of which refuse to acknowlege others and therefore do not promote unity. The visible church, the people of God, the covenant community, for evangelical theology, is not the same thing as a set pattern of organization. Sykes correctly observes that a central principle of the Reformation theological consensus was the idea of secondary issues, matters *'adiaphora'*, on which different situations could properly reach different conclusions.[42]

Such organizational matters were of the church's well-being (*bene esse*), not of her very essence (*esse*). The essentials of the visible people of God were to do with the word and the gospel. Today evangelical ecclesiology gladly points to the formal endorsement of this reformation principle in the Thirty Nine Articles, which plainly define the visible church of Christ as 'a congregation of faithful men, in which the pure Word of God is preached and the Sacraments duly ministered according to Christ's ordinance',[43] omitting any reference to a type of church order. The following article declares the authority of the visible church 'to decree Rites or Ceremonies' to have authority in controversies of faith: but only under the yardstick of 'God's Word written' that is only in a subservient manner which must not offend against biblical principles. Article 34 strikes exactly the same note in affirming a legitimate diversity of traditions and ceremonies, 'for at all times they have been divers, and may be changed according to the diversities of countries, times and men's manners', but always, 'so that nothing be ordained against God's Word.' In short, this view regards the organization, ceremonies and customs of the historical visible church as necessary and authoritative, but operating under the critical norm of the prophets and apostles. Therefore the organizational patterns and customs are not so much a fixed stream of tradition beside the biblical authority as subserving that authority. Episcopacy, for the evangelical Anglican, stands as one form of church order which has evolved in time to suit particular circumstances, and has served the church well in many ways. But to regard it as essential to the very being of the church of Christ exaggerates the case. The history of the covenant people has involved changes of organization, ritual, and custom and no set structure must be exalted into some institutional idol. The true essence of the church can only be the presence of Christ by the Holy Spirit, set forth and taught with reference to authoritative word of God. Organizational questions theologically are secondary or *'adiaphora'*.

Existing patterns of church government command respect, and the gospel principle of unity in Christ strongly urges maintaining fellowship in the present structures.

In this Anglicans stand as distinctive among fellow evangelicals. Oliver O'Donovan states the position neatly: 'speaking of the "catholic church",' he says, 'is a different thing from speaking of the institutional church which can determine its own limits, make conditions of recognized membership, count its adherents and so on. The catholic church cannot do any of these things. It is simply created by the Holy Spirit's work in bringing members of the human race to believe in Christ. And yet this amorphous company needs to find institutional forms. If it is to serve as a sign of the coming Kingdom, then it must have a coherence and order which expresses the character of the kingdom appropriately. A community which was evanescent and transitory could hardly be a sign of the eternal Kingdom. . . . A community which lacked sufficient organization either to meet or act together, for worship or for witness, could not represent the effective freedom of God's rule. In order to be what it is called to be, the catholic church must be embodied in institutional churches which, besides being "visible", do have some organizational definition.'[47] Organizational arrangements are inevitable, even the decision to have none and find oneself at the mercy of the strongest personalities constitutes an institutional arrangement.

The Holy Spirit does not need to work through chaos and anarchical spontaneity; the Spirit is of the Father, and therefore of order in the church. But the *precise* pattern of that order is for the church to work out. When confronted with the theological challenge to visible unity, notably that arising from the text in John's Gospel giving Jesus' prayer that the church may be one,[44] the evangelical will point to the context to argue that no mere organizational unity is intended. John here tells of the profound unity of the Father and the Son as the way the disciples, and future converts 'who believe in me through their word,'[45] will relate to God and to one another. Bishop Moule states the evangelical Anglican ecclesiological priority: 'Poor and unsatisfying are the results where "unity", "corporate life", and the like are the perpetual watchwords, but where they bear a *primary* reference to order, function, and succession in the ministry of the Church. One cannot but ask the question sometimes, when contemplating phenomena of an ardent ecclesiasticism, is *this* the worthy goal of ten thousand efforts, of innumerable assertions of "catholicity"—this spirit and tone, these enterprises and actions, so little akin either to the love or to the simplicity, the openness, of the heavenly gospel? Suppose such "unity" to be attained to the uttermost, beyond even the dreams of Rome. Would it contribute at all to making "the world believe that the Father hath sent the Son, and hath loved us even as He loved Him" (John 17:23)? No, it would not.'[46] Organizational, especially hierarchical, arrangements are temporal products of history for evangelical ecclesiology and are a second order issue, where diversity of custom may be no bad thing.

The church does have proper authority and power to organize herself according to principles of the gospel, and such patterns command loyalty. The secondary level of authority has a proper claim, and is essential if anarchy is not to break out. Organization is necessary, but not sufficient, in time and space. Anglicans have found that the ancient structure of episcopacy has served the church well, and would not wish to abandon it. On the other hand episcopacy, simply because of its existence through history, changes its face: the bishop now of a huge connurbation cannot possibly have the same relation to his diocese as had the bishop of a town in Asia Minor eighteen hundred years ago. Sociological forces have and will alter the character of episcopacy, and it must therefore be subject to the scrutiny of the whole church which will assess alterations needed. It may now be argued that smaller dioceses are needed in England. The issue of women as bishops presses. Organizational matters are vital, but matters for the church, in the light of scripture and tradition, to decide. Episcopacy of the Anglican type has proved a church tradition of much worth, not conflicting with the gospel. The wisdom of tried and tested ecclesiastical tradition does command an authority, according to authentic Anglican evangelicalism, albeit a secondary form of authority, which is the view laid down by Hooker and Field in the Elizabethan settlement. This differs from the view articulated by Ramsey earlier which argued that the shape of the church structure had a precise moulding from the gospel of Christ; the Anglican Fathers argue for a continuity of principle rather than detail.

This approach to derivative authority vested in the church, the whole church rather than just the clerical line, may be also peculiarly English, chiming in with the English parliamentary tradition of the rule of law. This parliamentary doctrine of the British constitution lays down that all people are under the law, answerable to it and protected by it. Until the law is altered by parliament it applies for everyone, and the judiciary must administer it. The traditions and structures of the church, subservient as they are to the word, nevertheless count until they are properly changed by the church. Again the Old Testament provides examples of both changing structures and also of old structures being renewed. Anglican evangelicals hold an ecclesiology which respects the past and yet accommodates ongoing reform in the light both of scriptural principle (rather than blueprint), and application to the current context. This is where evangelical Anglicans seem too liberal to other strands of Anglicanism!

2. The Word and the church

A. GOSPEL, CANON AND CHURCH

The church is the 'reconciled and reconciling' covenant community of the risen Christ. She lives by her vital contact with him through the Holy Spirit, and shares this saving good news, the gospel, with the world. The word is the primary category of ecclesiological authority for evangelical Anglican faith, and this has a rich texture of meaning. The word is the living Word, Jesus Christ who is the content of the gospel, the message by which the church lives and the way of life for the church. The gospel has this content, and the gospel therefore implies the canon of the scriptures as a whole, without which the content would become a matter of subjective experience. Wright explains that evangelical Anglicans are gospel people and Bible people, therefore, and as part of the historical stream of the people of God, also church people.

This new life and new way cannot exist apart from the messianic truth of Christ passed to the church by the prophetic and apostolic voice. Evangelical ecclesiology claims to obey this word as the final source of authority for the church. The written word of the Old and New Testaments, one stream of wisdom reflecting God's dealings with his people in all kinds of literary forms, speaks to the church and the church listens, responds and obeys. Authority flows from the word. Whereas the other strands of Anglicanism can be flexible on this issue and rigid on the question of church organization, evangelicals insist on the normative, constitutive givenness of the word alongside a regulative status for church organizational structure. The people of God have always heard the word of the Lord through the personalities of chosen ministers, from Abraham to Moses, from Samuel to Isaiah, from Amos to John the Baptist. The entry and ministry of the Word himself, made flesh, was then testified and interpreted by the apostolic circle. This, for evangelical ecclesiology, forms the foundation of this one, holy, catholic and apostolic rock.

The covenant people were formed by the approach of the Lord in his word of summons and of promise. Thereafter they were challenged and sustained by his word and his mighty acts fulfilling this word. This ecclesiology insists that the word came to the people from the Lord; it denies that the word primarily resulted from a corporate religious consciousness, to be given articulation by one of its key representatives. The word of the Lord came to the particular prophetic figure, who then undertook the often unpleasant task of delivering it to the reluctant people. The people did not create the word but received it, and kept it, cumulatively, down the centuries. The authority for the community comes from the Lord, and this Lord is the Word who chooses to speak, to explain, to make clear by giving his church the written word through personal interaction. Covenant ecclesiology has the character of dialogue and drama.

The accumulation of the canon of scripture follows this pattern. Scripture is the collection rather than the creation of the people. How often was the word hated, even buried, almost literally in the case of Jeremiah, thrown down a well to silence his message. But events ratified the authenticity of the prophetic word, and the people simply kept these utterances, even when they stood in judgement over them. This very strange phenomenon has received little attention, but it is a truly remarkable fact that the Hebrew tradition accumulated, with utter loyalty to the truth, tracts directed at their own sin and failure. They kept them because they were convinced of their divine origin. James Barr, who criticizes evangelicalism with all the zeal of the convert, correctly isolates this structure of evangelical theology. He says that 'The central feature of the classical fundamentalist (in which term he includes evangelical) doctrine seems to be that the Bible is part of a movement of true doctrine from God to man. It does not emerge from the community; rather it is directed towards the community and transmitted to the community by people like prophets and apostles who are authoritative didactic functionaries.'[48] In terms of our models, the canonical scriptures form the doctrinal base of the church in the evangelical appropriation of the 'foundation-superstructure' idea.

Clearly evangelical and catholic conservatives regard prophets and apostles as more than just 'didactic functionaries'; they live out their message ethically and spiritually for the people. But Barr is right to point out the movement from God to the people through the appointed personal agent. He himself prefers a version of inspiration working the other way round: the theology and text are created by a preceding corporate religious consciousness, 'from below'. Evangelical ecclesiology regards the faith people of God as created by the 'descending' and authoritative word of promise, not the other way round. Revelation is not the distillation of the highest aspirations of human thought. The faith of the people, for the evangelical, can hardly have arisen mysteriously, 'from nothing' amid the pagan ancient Near East to create the Hebrew view of God.

In the beginning was the word which created the faith and evoked the response of faith. To believe that this extraordinarily different faith arose from a people's natural religiosity seems naive: such a view implies an irrational version of *creatio ex nihilo*. The corporate religious consciousness was precisely often the object of sheer contradiction, of harsh judgement, down the Hebrew centuries: this tradition depends on the word coming to it from outside, of so often being made to accept criticism of itself. This appears to have been an important part of Jesus' view of the religious tradition of which he was part, and to which he spoke: 'O Jerusalem, Jerusalem, stoning the prophets . . .'

The word imposes itself on the often recalcitrant community which subsequently saves, records and seeks to obey. The relationship of church to scripture is akin to that of the supporter and the great football team. Supporters do not create the greatness of the team, but they acknowledge it and follow loyally. More technically,

> 'The Scriptures, then, have the prior existence, owe everything to the Master, and do everything for the Church. Then, if the Bible is made to depend on the Church, is it not evident that it is the Bible conceived as a book, and not as revelation? For these two things are most dissimilar, and indeed opposite. The authority that belongs to the Bible belongs to it not as book, but as revelation; what the canonizing process created was not a revelation, but a book. In other words, the process that created the revelation was prior and causal and material, but the process that created the canon, later and sequent and formal. The revelation did not come to be because of the canon; the canon came to be because of the revelation.'[49]

Barth's teaching that the prophets and apostles bring the authority of the Lord to the people sums up this understanding of the visible source of authority in the community: it is really best interpreted as an *audible* authority. It is not so much the sight of the written words inked onto the page as the words spoken and heard. Jesus left no writings. He left the small covenant community impregnated with his words, with the whole impression of himself, and with himself present through the Holy Spirit. Evangelical faith views the the content of the New Testament as authentic apostolic teaching and interpretation, including principles for its development, exemplified when the gospel encountered cultural problems such as Gentile converts who were used to pagan sacrificial food. What was not authentically apostolic, or validated as expressing apostolic teaching, seems to have excluded itself from the canon of the New Testament. The ongoing church did not create the teaching, but accepted it when it imposed its authority by virtue primarily of its content, closely linked to its provenance. The church had to hear the voice of the apostles concerning Jesus. The content of scripture, taken as a whole continuum, gives the church her source of authority.

Jesus himself emerges from the Old Testament, bringing with him the highest possible understanding of the authority of the ancient Law, Prophets and Writings. Jesus embodied and summed up the law and the prophets in his person and work, summing up divine revelation, as the Epistle to the Hebrews tells the church.[50] He becomes the archetypal man of the word, constantly patterning his ministry, in thought, word and deed, on his inherited scripture. The Hebrew canon of the Old Testament accepted by Jesus seems to have been that accepted still by the Jewish people today. Again the principle of listening to the word of the Lord as it defines, itself controls the evangelical understanding of the authority of scripture. Jesus assumed, or seems to have used, the Hebrew canon preserved by the covenant people over the centuries, therefore the church today follows him. To follow the Jewish estimate of the Old Testament canon has Pauline precedent: 'They are Israelites, and to them belong the sonship, the glory, the covenants, the giving of the law, the worship, and the promises; to them belong the patriarchs, and of their race, according to the flesh, is the Christ.'[51]

E. A. Litton puts the evangelical view:

> 'the office of the Church, in relation to Scripture, is defined to be "a keeper and a witness"; a keeper in as much as to its custody the sacred records are committed, to be jealously guarded from addition, mutilation, or deprivation; and a witness inasmuch as it is incumbent on the Church to hand down, from age to age, the chain of evidence which proves these books, and no others, to have been from the first acknowledged. . . . this is a very different thing from assuming power to *make* a book Canonical by simple authoritative decision. The Church, in this matter, discharges an office similar to that of the Samaritan woman

> in John iv, who invited her fellow townsmen to come and see a man who told her all that ever she did: she was the means, or occasion, of their becoming acquainted with the Messiah, but she did not make Him what He was, nor could she produce any saving faith in them: they believed, when they did believe, not because of her saying, but because they had heard Him themselves, and perceived that it was indeed the Christ. The Scripture is never fully received on its proper grounds until a similar personal experience is wrought in its readers.'[52]

Canon and gospel unite for evangelical theology in this dynamic way. The word is a dynamic word of power, the saving word. Revelation in the words of the prophet and apostle concerns redemptive knowlege of the living God, the redemption proclaimed in the gospel of Jesus. Jesus Christ, as heard in the scriptures, speaks authoritatively to the church, impelling her to proclaim her gospel and to check her preaching of it against the revelation. The gospel, the message of salvation in Christ crucified and risen, needs the canon of scripture as its necessary background of history and interpretation. The gospel validates the canon Christologically. The gospel also impelled the New Testament canon along its correct line, as is again demonstrated by Peter's enforced change of mind over the Gentiles.

Authority for evangelical ecclesiology is essentially a personal mode, as is all speech. It compels only by the power of its message. The divine speaker comes in the speech, desiring entry upon lifelong, personal, honest fellowship. For Genesis as for Revelation, God relates to people by speaking: 'Behold, I stand at the door and knock, if anyone hears my voice and opens the door I will come in to him and eat with him and he with me.'[53] Covenant dialogue, obedient trusting in the promises of God, such are the bones of the evangelical ecclesiological skeleton. The living word, comes through the written word by the power of the Holy Spirit, uniting the people ever more closely with the Father.

The authority at the centre of the church is the way, the truth and the life. The personal word of the gospel crystallizes, and is interpreted by, the canonical scriptures: 'I–thou' encounter including 'I–it' content. Evangelical Anglicanism classically therefore insists that the church has to be a teaching church and a proclaiming church. She is therefore a 'dogmatic' church: there is content to the faith which must be kept and proclaimed to each new generation.

B. THE APOSTOLIC TRADITION

The tradition, as opposed to varying traditions of church order for example, is the apostolic tradition, the decisive teaching about Christ for the church. The word of the Lord coming to prophets and later to apostles was originally in spoken form, later written down to enable its enduring passage through time and across geographical boundaries. Prophetic and apostolic witness, teaching, exhortation and proclamation are handed on by the church who keeps their words in order to live them. The church teaches the apostolic gospel of Christ in her own words for each generation; always inviting her people to check the message against the apostolic and prophetic record. Like the old town hall clock, the church tells out her message down the ages, but from time to time any clock needs to be checked against the standard time. The church passes on the tradition which she has received. This is the central tradition, resting on, and restating, the word.

Tradition in this major sense stresses the handing on of the faith. Like Newman, the evangelical reacts against any ideal of tradition which implies handing on an ossified or pickled form of the truth. If the message is to be sent forth to each generation then it must be presented in terms contemporary to the age. Bishop Stephen Neill made the comparison with sermons preached years ago: their content will often be excellent, but they could not be repeated verbatim today, because they need recasting into the current idiom and even the current philosophical ethos. But the past, the history of the tradition in its expression down the centuries, does not thereby become a kind of historical trail of rubbish to be discarded and ignored. The great minds and movements of the Christian faith, which have genuinely expressed the apostolic gospel aright, have given us shoulders on which to stand. These teachers, while rarely without any error, have dug mineshafts which we now continue to exploit. The history of the expression of the apostolic tradition also gives us most useful cases of major mistakes which become markers for the faith to avoid. Mere weight of numbers, to the evangelical mind, has never been sufficient to validate a proposed expression: Athanasius's long and lonely struggle against the *consensus fidelium* of the official church of the day, which taught an Arian Christ, stands as the classic case of the theologian of the word being correct against the majority consensus.

History has shown that it is possible for the church to be

doctrinally orthodox but dead. Handing on dry dogmas alone, without proclaiming and living out the life and reality of Christ, means that the church fails the apostolic tradition. Such situations have often led to movements which swing to the opposite extreme and teach a version of Christianity resting on experience alone at the expense of biblical teaching. Schleiermacher, the great liberal theologian, arose from the context of ultra orthodox protestantism. Bultmann of our own century so stressed the personal impact of the gospel message as to cut it free from the canonical teaching and community history of the prophets and apostles. To the evangelical this commits the crime of focusing on the life to the exclusion of the truth, dehistoricizing the gospel into a series of moments of faith. Bultmann has a gospel word of salvation, but without canonical apostolic content. The positive endeavour of Bultmann's programme lies in his crucially important challenge to express the gospel for today, in current terms. His enterprise fails because it leaves the apostles behind. Pinchas Lapide, a Jewish theologian, comments that the apostles and people of their day would not have had the remotest idea of what Bultmann was saying, so far has he travelled from taking their meaning and context sufficiently seriously.

Apostolicity is of key importance to classical evangelical faith. Anglican evangelicals this century have often failed to expound this aspect of their heritage, perhaps because of their fear of an exaggerated Anglo-Catholic stress on the continuing church's episcopate as the bearer of the apostolic office through time. Abraham Kuyper elucidates this theme clearly in his *The Work of the Holy Spirit*.[54] There we read his account of the First Epistle of John: 'The apostle's reasoning is transparent as glass. Life was manifested in such a way that it could be seen and handled. They who saw and handled were the apostles; and they were also to declare this life unto the elect. By this declaration the required fellowship between the elect and the apostolate is established. And in consequence of this, there is fellowship also for the elect with the Father and the Son.'[55] The gospel message requires fellowship with the circle of the apostles, those specially chosen witnesses.

Kuyper does not mean that this fellowship with the apostles ends with the death of the first generation of Christians, rather it goes on and includes the succeeding ages of the church. He says,

> 'This may not be understood as referring only to the people then living; and, regarding Rome, one's position, Bible in hand, is exceedingly weak if he maintain that this higher significance of the apostolate had reference only to the then living, and not in the same measure to us. Indeed we, upon whom the end of the ages has come, must maintain the vital fellowship with the holy apostolate of our Lord Jesus Christ.'[56]

He continues by arguing that Rome makes the mistake of making her bishops the successors of the apostles, whereas the apostles must be unique since only they saw, heard and handled Jesus, which excludes a continuing order of apostles. But 'from this it follows not that Rome errs in the fundamental thought, viz. that every child of God must excercise communion with the Father and the Son *through the apostolate*; on the contrary this is John's positive claim.'[57] This may have something to teach current Anglican evangelicals. The solution to this lies in the fact of the apostles' ongoing voice, mediated by the scriptures, across the barriers of space and time. 'Hence even now the apostles are preaching the living Christ in the churches. Their persons have departed, but their personal testimony remains. And that personal testimony, which as an apostolic document has come to every soul in every land and in every age, is the testimony which even now is the instrument in the hand of the Holy Spirit to translate souls into fellowship of the Life eternal.'[58]

Kuyper brings out the unique, living apostolic teaching and witness. Unlike Newman, he teaches that this living voice does not evolve, but remains the constant measure of the proclamation by the living church. With Newman, he reminds us that ongoing fellowship with the apostolic community of faith is basic to the living church. The whole living community is apostolic, resounding with the vibrant testimony of the apostles and prophets.

The role of Peter as a key apostle has often been inadequately treated by evangelical Anglicans, again largely because of the perceived shadow of Anglo-Catholic interpretation causing defensive and sometimes distorted interpretation. Bishop Ryle, following much patristic exegesis, interpreted Jesus' words, declaring Peter the rock on which the church would be built, to mean that Peter's confession, 'Thou art the Christ', constituted that rock. Peter's unique foundational function as the first preacher of Jesus the Messiah in the early church is far more natural exegesis.

Thiselton produces an authentically evangelical Anglican model for the dynamic of the apostolic tradition in his essay for the report of the Church of England Doctrine Commission. 'In an attempt to give some place to both the past and the present aspects,' he says, 'an analogy may be suggested. The Bible may be compared to a musical score. What "controls", or sets limits to, the scope of the present performance is the notation of the composition as it was composed at some time in the past. If it is not based on the score, the present performance is not a performance of *this* composition. Nevertheless what the current audience experiences in the present is the actual *performance*, and no two performances will be quite the same. Wooden repetition may turn out to be less faithful to the score than the use of creative imagination. Yet the creativity of the performer still takes place within clear limits. For without faithfulness to the score, the performance would not be a *faithful* interpretation of *that* work.'[59] Thiselton insists on the completed original work as the controlling measure for the subsequent restatement, while also insisting on the need for continuing faithful re-expression for today.

C. INTERPRETATION OF THE WORD

The gospel itself must be the apostolic gospel once delivered to the saints, not another gospel or some watered down variant. In the era of modern pluralism of interpretations, authentic evangelicalism has to take on the scandal of particularity and confess that there is one faith, as well as one Lord, one baptism, one God and Father. Resisting the modern claim that scripture can be interpreted in all manner of ways, leading to all manner of results which will often conflict, the evangelical, implicitly if not explicitly, goes with Barth in replying that the interpretation of revelation, of the prophetic apostolic tradition, is a subtle blending of voices, even of conversations. But the pluriformity exists inside the canonical whole with a coherence which is immediately apparent when compared with other religious systems. Any reality, especially human and historical, embodies diversity if it is alive at all; but the diversity contributes to an intense personal theological unity, focused in Jesus.

The New Testament interprets the Old, while the Old is the

very dictionary of theology for the New. Edwyn Hoskyns' great book *The Riddle of the New Testament*,[60] while written by an Anglican not identified with evangelicalism, resounds with this evangelical principle of interpretation. It implies an insulated holistic continuum of faith, which is precisely what existed, under God, in the form of the people of Israel, as Paul recognized. It implies that not only is the decisive and saving revelation given in the scriptures, but that the scriptures, for all their apparently scrapbook character, are comprehensible and focused within themselves as a whole. It implies the much neglected interpretative principle not only that the Bible as a whole, the testimony of many voices and events, is the yardstick for faith, but also that these many voices are mutually self-interpreting. Rather than leading to final contradiction, this diversity would not even be comprehensible without a presupposed unity. Diversity itself needs to be in reference to mutually defining realities. Equally the unity of scripture, like that of a great canvas, could not exist without the tensions and harmonies of the myriad of colours, textures and perspectives it embodies.

The scriptures are not a monochrome, single book: they are plural and it is just this pluralism within the continuum of the tradition that evangelical ecclesiology draws upon to affirm the 'analogy of faith' against modern relativizing pluralism. 'The fundamental system of Christian doctrine thus elicited from a comparison of scripture with scripture, and of one book with another,' Litton reminds his fellow evangelical Anglicans, 'is what writers on dogmatic theology call the "analogy of faith", in accordance with which doubtful passages are to be explained. It is obvious,' he goes on, 'that this must be gathered from scripture itself, otherwise it would be tradition under another name. It is not, however a mere stringing of texts together on certain subjects, but the doctrine which lies at the foundation of the various passages which relate to a subject; substantially the same amidst the variety of form under which it may be presented. That such a substantial identity may and must exist is an inference from the unity of the primary Author, the Holy Spirit: if human authors, however otherwise differing from each other, derived inspiration from one source, no real contradiction, none at least affecting essential points, can be supposed possible.'[61]

Henry Vander Groot can sum up the way the canon as the

tradition, functions for the evangelical Anglican as a self interpretative symphony of consistent witness. Introducing his small book, he sets out the evangelical framework:

> 'On the basis of the phenomenally given liguistic word, this essay represents a defense of the notions of literal sense and canonical meaning. The literal sense of the biblical storyline is the sense of what Scripture says, which can only be gotten at by way of the method in which Scripture says it. The literal sense is the non-referential, explicative sense of the text of the Bible viewed as a non-fictional, realistic narrative. Moreover, the canon is the idea that there is an authoritative whole and that this authoritative whole is the conventional Christian understanding of the Bible's overall message as a creation-fall-restoration-consummation story, which should be the controlling ingredient in the interpretation of the Bible's various parts.'[62]

This broad biblical presupposition, shared basically by the ancient people of Israel with the church of Christ, lies at the heart of classical Anglican teaching, that the word may not be expounded so as to fail to see the unity of the whole.[63]

3. The ordained ministry

A. THE FUNCTION OF THE PASTORAL MINISTRY

This living tradition of fellowship with the apostles re-expresses and lives out the gospel of Christ down the ages. The ordained ministry exists to promote and guarantee this process, it is the ministry of the living word, of the gospel. Just as the church is defined as the congregation of faithful people where the true word is preached and the sacraments of the gospel celebrated, the ordained ministry is charged to preach and minister the sacraments, to foster the gospel locally in every dimension. The church is not constituted by the ordained ministry, but this ministry serves a crucial role: the continuing teaching of the faith, the handing on of the tradition, in the pastoral and evangelistic life of the people of God. The ministry, the service, of Christ in the whole church means that the whole body is called to play its part; the ordained ministry subserves the ministry of all the people: such is the ecclesiological theory of the evangelical Anglican. Rather than being a focus of the church's ministry, it is the office to promote and *release* a wealth of ministries, all seeking to conform to the mind of Christ as known in the word.

This explains the enormous dignity accorded to the ordained ministry by the Reformers, and the famous comment of Calvin that 'Neither are the light and heat of the sun, nor meat and drink, so necessary to sustain and cherish that precious life as is the apostolical and pastoral office to preserve a church in the earth.'[64] It also explains why the *Tiller Report*,[65] which recommended that the full-time ordained ministry be centred in diocesan groups to be sent out into localities, as occasion demanded, to help the laity, received little enthusiastic support from evangelicalism in the Church of England. The local pastor-teacher of the faith forms an essential part of the apostolic pattern of building the gospel church of Christ. To withdraw this function into a diocesan centre conflicts with the high apostolic view of the ordained minister of the gospel. The locality of the ministry of the word, its accessibility and continuity, is vital for Anglican evangelical thought, fostering and serving the apostolic and prophetic word among the people of God.

Christ, present by the Holy Spirit, known in the witness of the word, sustains the church. Pastoral ministry, charged to interpret the gospel canonically in the contemporary context, exists to build up the church in the word. To distance this ministry in any way from the local people would harm the local community. It would divorce the role of theological wisdom from that of pastoral care and the evangelical interprets the two as inseparable. The way, the truth and the life coincide. The local presbyter has to be as thoroughly wise in the word as possible for the pastoral care to be as Christian as possible. Like the conservative Anglo-Catholic, Roman and Orthodox, the evangelical Anglican believes in a 'teaching church'. The gospel has a content, and Christian action needs its basis in Christian truth.

The ministry is apostolic, like all the church, in that it repeats and echoes the original proclamation of the apostles. Rather than a ministerial priesthood, this tradition regards its ministry as ministerial to the prophetic and apostolic witness. In a secondary or ministerial way, the ordained ministry stands in the tradition of the prophets. It stands with the people, is of the people, but sometimes has to speak even against the people by way of challenge. The ministry does not create the content of its message, but seeks to interpret the word, measured by the whole canon, so that it becomes increasingly the dynamic impulse of the community. The minister serves the defined purpose of being a local trustee and promoter of the message. Called by the word, acknowledged by the community of the crucified and risen Lord, he serves the living Word as originally uttered by the apostles.

Forsyth, in a remarkable chapter on the ministry, calls it a human, *personal* sacrament of the word, by which he means that the ministry is a means of propagating the gospel of salvation in Christ, an objective office to minister this faith sacrificially to people. Forsyth, who uses the Old Testament infrequently, might have pointed to figures such as Jeremiah as 'sacraments' of the word.[66] Such prophets, pastorally committed to the people, brought the word to the people in utter faithfulness, despite the tensions this ministry produced in relationships with the community. Jeremiah brought the word, and it was not a new message in essence, to a complacent and rebellious community; he was part of the community, yet was over against them as well. He refused to leave them even in their moment of judgement. He bore the pain of being absolutely obedient to the true word and bringing the word to the community at great personal cost. He loved the community enough to tell it the truth it did not wish to hear. He even enacted this message and lived it out.

Here we have an analogy of the apostolic 'pastor-teacher' ministry; today's ordained ministry seeks to minister the word among and for the people. Evangelical ministry often attracts the criticism of being far too wordy and didactic; Forsyth's model points to the total personal gospel ministry, not only the oral, but to the whole personality given over to expressing the word in the community, a truly biblical picture of the 'messengers, watchmen and stewards of the Lord'.[67] Forsyth includes in his vision of the continuing objective function of the ministry the theme of the word of the cross and regeneration. This above all is the heart of the ministry of the church, the gospel ministry. The local pastoral ministry is to ensure trinitarian worship, to fire all the ministries of the whole body to convert the unbeliever and extend the kingdom of God, to realize kingdom values in practice. Only in so far as these goals are fulfilled is the local minister a 'sacrament' or focus of the presence of God. The ordained minister is far more an instrument and a steward, for the evangelical Anglican, than a sign and a sacrament.

B. ORDINATION

What then is ordination? 'It is the setting apart, because of God's calling, of those who exercise a ministry of the Word logically prior to other ministries, which enables the church to develop into the pure Body of Christ.'[68] At ordination to the ministry, the presbyterate, the church formally authorizes the minister to fulfil this office because she is convinced that this person is called by God to do so and has the necessary qualities. The spiritual gifts and call are formally recognized by the whole church through the act of commissioning and bestowing of authority by the church's appointed agent, the bishop.

Pastoral care must be informed by gospel truth, hence the model of the 'pastor-teacher', in continuity with that gospel ministry evident in the New Testament. There the existing synagogue structure of local elders, who had pastoral charge and teaching function, seems to have been appropriated by the earliest church congregations. All the local congregations of which we know from the New Testament had such 'elders' or 'presbyters' appointed to them. They were appointed from the body, and their appointment was ratified by an apostolic delegate of some kind, and evangelical ecclesiology takes this as meaning that the apostolicity of their faith was guaranteed. Ordination follows this broad pattern of a calling being tested and ratified by the church locally and more widely as to their apostolic faith. Formal appointment to office is by the apostolic church, both locally and with a wider regional acknowledgement in the person of the bishop.

The fact of the *whole* body of Christ being involved in discerning and ratifying is important for the evangelical ecclesiology. It is, like all ministry of the church, ultimately Christ's ministry, officially recognized by the whole body, not by a priestly line with the power to create a line of ministry. 'The deepest word which can be spoken about Christian ministry in all its forms, is that it is nothing other than the ministry of the risen Lord among and through his people (Romans 15:18).'[69] The ordained minister has a particularly vital function in fostering ministries of the whole church, he holds an office to which Christ has called him. This Christ-centred focus of both the office and the particular calling means that the debate between 'functional and ontological' views of ministry are really sterile. Wright points out that ordination to this office inevitably means great responsibility and that this ministry carries weight not because of the individual's qualities but because of God's calling and the church's trust. In that sense the ordained ministry does carry an objective status, stemming from that office, and so, for Wright, and before him Calvin, 'to stress the *ontological* character of the ordained ministry is to point away from what someone is in himself, and towards the call and historical action of God. That, not the self-confidence of the gifted leader, is the true basis of humble, Christlike ministry.'[70]

C. CONFESSION, ABSOLUTION AND PASTORAL DISCIPLINE

Classical Anglican theology accords priority to the ministry and status of the whole body of Christ as those who, as a church across the centuries and spatial boundaries, communicate the gospel of Christ's pardon for sin. It is in this light that Bishop Westcott comments on John 20:23 'Whosesoever sins ye remit, they are remitted unto them; and whosesoever sins ye retain, they are retained.' Here the risen Jesus addresses the whole church, the assembled disciples, having breathed on them and told them 'to receive Holy Spirit' (v. 22). His words about remitting and retaining sins, says Westcott, concern 'the reality of the power of absolution from sin granted to the Church, and not of a particular organization through which the power is administered';[71] it is the commission of the whole Christian society and not of the Christian ministry alone. The risen Christ presents himself to the church as the sign of victory over death and sin, the mission of the whole church is to apply to humanity this saving gift. This promise differs from that given to Peter (Matthew 16:18), which is distinctly personal, whereas that to the church is perpetual through time. It also differs from that to the church prior to the resurrection (Matthew 18:18), which concerns 'the enactment of ordinances and not the administration of that which is purely spiritual', although that promise, which laid down the conditions for fellowship, leads to the higher one in question, which 'gives a living and abiding power to declare the fact and the conditions of forgiveness.'[72]

Westcott's classical Anglican exegesis finds that the remitting and retaining as the commissioned spiritual community is a corporate idea, 'There is perfect harmony, perfect coincidence between the divine voice through the society and the divine will.'[73] The spiritual community of Christ brings forgiveness and new life to the world. The presbyter declares absolution pastorally inside the church, a prophetic rather than a priestly function, and it arises out of the general pastoral commission. The Epistle of James enjoins confession not only to God but to other believers, the church. 'Absolving', or 'untying', of a troubled conscience by declaring Christ's pardon orally to an individual is a pastoral assurance performed not only by the presbyter but often so. The declaration of the divine pardon is aptly proclaimed by the pastoral leader of the congregation, the minister of the whole word of Christ. 'The pastor, as the commissioned "messenger, watchman, and steward," will not only, as every Christian man and woman may and should, point the burthened soul to the revealed secret of peace in the Word of God, but will announce the certainty of pardon to the true penitent with just that authority which belongs to his divinely instituted office.'[74]

The minister has no special spiritual insight into the soul, nor any different grace to release from any member of the body. This is a prophetic declaratory role, again repetitive and not creative. The risen Lord has achieved the pardon, the minister declares the fact as it applies to the repenting people, and 'though it cannot make the divine truth truer in itself, can, and should, and in proportion to the man's spiritual correspondence to his office will, make it specially certain to the penitent, specially tangible to faith.'[75] As regards the local church's decisions on discipline and order in the congregation, the presbyter clearly plays a vital guiding part with ultimate responsibility, but along with the other leading members of the church and not as an independent dictator: 'tell it to the church' being an important gospel maxim. In this respect Anglicanism in other continents, notably Africa, may have much to teach the Church of England.

D. PRIESTHOOD IN THE ORDAINED MINISTRY

As regards the issue of a priestly role for the minister, the work of Bishop Lightfoot remains the standard text. Priesthood, a term never used for the presbyterate in the New Testament, cannot be any kind of mediating priesthood in the Old Testament sense, but must have its meaning redefined pastorally. The ministerial office, according to the apostolic practice and doctrine, is centrally that of the pastor-teacher. Lightfoot demands quotation as a full-orbed statement of ordained ministry:

> 'The Christian minister is God's ambassador to men: he is charged with the ministry of reconciliation; he unfolds the

> will of heaven; he declares in God's name the terms on which pardon is offered; and he announces in God's name the absolution of the penitent. This last named function has been thought to invest the ministry with a distinctly sacerdotal character. Yet it is very closely connected with the magisterial and pastoral duties of the office, and is only priestly in the same sense in which they are priestly. As empowered to declare the conditions of God's grace, he is empowered also to proclaim the consequences of their acceptance. But throughout his office is representative and not vicarial. He does not interpose between God and man in such a way that direct communion with God is superseded on the one hand, or that his own mediation becomes indispensable on the other.'[76]

Rather than ministerial priesthood, Lightfoot upholds ministerial pastorate, an instrument for the building up of the body of Christ. The ministry is primarily pastoral, never a third party beside the whole body but one of the ministries of the body.

P. T. Forsyth can amplify, with evangelical gospel zeal, what the cool, scholarly Anglican Bishop has said. Forsyth reminds us that the ministry represents God, carrying the word of mercy to the church and the world. The ordained ministry 'is a living sacrament', a higher idea than the Roman view rather than a lower, since it

> 'is a living sacrament which not only shows something, but by word and prayer conveys something, changes much, regenerates all. . . . Preaching the Gospel is far more truly a deed, an act of the personality, than the priest's in the Mass. It effects more in the unseen. And in the case of the minister, as with the Apostle, it is a life deed. The whole of the minister's life is given up to it. Life and Word are identified. His Word engrosses His life, his life is consecrated to His Word. He is a sacrament of grace (would that he oftener knew it!) always meaning by grace not the substance of Christ assimilated in bread and wine, but Christ as the living Word, appropriated in personality, in the Spirit and in power.'[77]

Forsyth goes on to define pastoral work as another mode of this ambassadorial work of the gospel: only a gospel of grace working through a personal subject of grace can begin to entertain the notion of the cure of souls.

As well as the role of representing God to man sketched by

Lightfoot and Forsyth, there is the minister's role in leading worship from the church to God. For Lightfoot, 'Again the Christian minister is the representative of man to God of the congregation primarily, of the individual indirectly as a member of the congregation. The alms, the prayers, the thanksgivings of the community are offered through him. Some representation is as necessary in the Church as it is in a popular government . . . here again then it must be borne in mind that the minister's function is representative without being vicarial. He is a priest, as the mouthpiece, the delegate, of a priestly race. His acts are not his own but the acts of the congregation.'[78] Lightfoot adds that this office of leading worship is not indispensable, and in emergency the general practice will be set aside and 'The higher ordinance of the universal priesthood will overrule all special limitations.'[79] Forsyth likewise calls the leading of worship and prayer to God in the congregation the 'priestly' aspect of the ministry in which office the minister 'is the organ of the common priesthood of the Church.'[80] We must note that this evangelical view of a priestly dimension is definitely not of 'another realm of the gifts of the spirit,' but a wholly representative office of the common priestly people. Forsyth, articulating a central evangelical concern, says that leading of worship and prayer is a secondary dimension of the ministerial representation, 'since man's faith is second to God's grace.'[81] 'Here the minister is not prophetic but priestly. His voice does not now come to the Church but rises from it . . . When he speaks in God's name to men, he properly speaks down to the people from a pulpit; but, speaking in man's name to God, he speaks properly from the floor, and from among the people.'[82] Ideally in leading the praise, confession and intercession of the people, argues Forsyth, the minister should stand facing the same way as the people. In this aspect of the ministry the people have commissioned him to lead their expression to God.

Here we note how the most penetrating British evangelical mind interprets the two movements, manward and Godward, which for Ramsey and ARCIC, unite in the single eucharistic event of the church receiving Christ then offering herself in Christ. Evangelical Anglican faith distinguishes between the primary creative approach of grace, and the secondary dependent response of faith. As regards the ordained ministry, the most holy and awesome office is the apostolic prophetic, the ministry of the divine word which bears within it the way, the truth and the life. 'The Church', for Forsyth, 'is a great priest, the ministry is a great prophet. The Church confesses for the world, intercedes, suffers, is offered for it. It is, under Christ, the world's High Priest. But the ministry speaks even to the Church, and to the world through it. It conveys God in His Grace to living faith. It has the secret and sacrament of the ever regenerating Word.'[83] Therefore the ministry is more sacramental than sacerdotal, which it is only in the secondary sense of leading the worship of people. The ministry is primarily charged with speech, spoken and enacted, in the living tradition of the Apostles. The ministry of the word, from God to the church, constantly building up the church in the Lord so that the *kerygma*, the message of the gospel, may go out and be handed on. But 'it is the succession of believers,' Schweizer reminds us, 'in which the message is handed on from generation to generation in a succession of living witness.'[84] The church, the people of God, is theologically prior to the ministry, and the presbyteral task is to foster and serve this spreading of the gospel by an apostolic church.

Reformed ecclesiology, the classical evangelical tradition, therefore can be seen to have an extremely high view of the ordained ministry. It is a 'medium' according to Bishop Moule, it is ambassadorial according to Lightfoot, it is the personal sacrament of the regenerating Word, for Forsyth; it is vital to the Church's well-being for Calvin. It continues the apostolic tradition of the word, not creating a new word, but re-expressing the word locally under the canonical fixed form of that tradition.

E. APOSTOLICITY

The ministry has also a historic continuity with the apostles, and here evangelical Anglican ecclesiology should make some very important and careful distinctions as to the precise nature of this historical, institutional, connection. At first, after the Ascension of Christ, the ministry, all ministry of all forms, not only the pastor-teacher task, lies with the twelve, 'whose authority, used temperately and in full consultation with the community, was, however, derived not from the community, but from Christ,' as Bishop Moule puts it.

The initial local ministry seems to have been always authorized, however informally and naturally, in some way by reference to the apostolic circle; in effect the task which the apostles undertook locally as pastors, teachers and evangelists, had to be spread around to trusted people in their various localities. The model of the synagogue presbyter, overseer, seems in a very natural way, to have been copied for this purpose. This crucial ministry devolved out of the apostles' ministry. The example of setting aside deacons for the 'serving at tables' a task initially done by apostles, shows how this process of devolution happened to meet the needs of the church as they arose. The picture of the fast-developing apostolic church, according to evangelical exegesis, is of an informally developing pastorate under the general authorizing oversight of the apostles. What was delegated, or devolved, was the ministry of 'fishing and shepherding' locally.

The precise ministry of an apostle, an actual eye witness and disciple of the Lord in the flesh, obviously was not capable of being handed on. What needed to be done by others was duly authorized and put in hand, by the Holy Spirit and by the ratification of the apostolic circle.

The evangelical Anglican view of the ordained ministry and its relation to the apostles received one of its clearest statements by Bishop Moule who distinguished between the twelve as the first churchpeople, on the one hand, and the twelve as the first ministers, on the other hand. As the first messianic members of Israel, they represented the whole church and received promises as such which therefore applied to all the succeeding faithful. On the other hand the twelve are a ministry. The apostolate 'as a ministry,' he wrote, 'is succeeded to not by one order but by all. All are "differentiated" out of it. The deacon (Acts vi) succeeds the Apostle as table server; the presbyter as one of the local rulers and pastors of the flock; the bishop (in the later sense) as presiding presbyter, competent in a special way to ordain or constitute others. But in the apostolate proper, with its immediate divine authority, and its witness bearing, there is not succession. Matthias and Paul were not ordained by the Church to be Apostles, but designated by the Lord Himself, like Peter and John. Paul was (with Barnabas) ordained (Acts xiii) but not to be an Apostle. His Church commission, given by divine direction, was to be (may we say?) a missionary bishop, a travelling constitutor of churches. Thus the whole ministry succeeds the Apostles, but succeeds them so as not properly to claim their prophetic authority.'[85]

The apostles were succeeded by the whole church, together with the variety of ministries they exercised, save that of unique, authoritative witness and normative interpreter of Jesus, the ministry now played by the New Testament. The continuing church as a whole, crucially enabled by her continuing pastoral ministry, brings this word to each locality in every age. Moule held a classically high view of the historic ordained ministry as an essential instrument for the building and sustaining of the church down the centuries with a monumental symbolism of the enduring gospel of Christ.

Such a view, which recognizes the historical succession of ministry as having a theological, as well as a merely practical value, a view which can for example be found also in Forsyth the Congregationalist, in Calvin the Presbyterian, as well as Anglican evangelicalism, conflicts with the radical evangelical 'restorationist' house church interpretation. This strand of evangelicalism stands in line with the radicals of the Reformation and tends to dismiss the history of the church as mainly unspiritual and in need of restoring to the exact pattern of the book of Acts, the earliest age of the new church. Against the House Church restorationist, the Anglican evangelical regards the history of the church and her ministry as never without flaws: the New Testament church itself plainly had enormous problems of many kinds, judging by the epistles addressed to them! There is a great danger in exaggerating the holy state of the earliest church life. Those churches, like ours today, constantly needed to be brought back to the gospel of Christ and its implications. This must always be by way of reformation rather than revolution. The church down the ages has always been the church. Whatever her follies, she has remained the church to be reformed and corrected. The church with her local ministry teaching from her scriptures and administering the scriptural sacraments, this church has remained an entity to be reformed and led back to the apostles' teaching.

An important point to be remembered by evangelicals in particular is the variety of apostolic ministries, besides the presbyteral, in the earliest church and felt to be needed today. The ministry of the evangelist is especially being rediscovered as often essential where the community itself is ineffective in communicating her gospel and bringing neighbours into the flock of the Lord. The *Partners in Mission Report on the Church of England*,[86] concluded that the pressing need in Britain today was for evangelistic outreach to those outside the fold, whereas the church was in fact geared to pastor dwindling congregations. Local churches know this and often use full time missioners, such as those trained by the London City Mission, to complement their leadership team. Newbigin is again correct when he observes, 'A feature of the present situation is that elaborate patterns of leadership have been developed which bear no apparent relationship to the official ecclesiology of the body concerned.'[87] The evangelistic ministry is now finding more recognition in the wider Anglican establishment and is as much a continuation in the ministry of the apostles as the presbyteral, desperately needed in our ever more secular society.

Again it must be insisted that this is also primarily the calling of the whole body, and the appointment of an evangelist does not remove that calling any more than the presence of the full time presbyter removes the calling of all church people to exercise pastoral care. Evangelical ecclesiology in theory allows for the development of new forms of structure and ministry to suit social conditions, just as its view of episcopacy regards this institution to have arisen naturally in the providence of God. Here below, for Newman, to be perfect is to have changed often.

F. TEAMS OF PRESBYTERS AND THE ORDINATION OF WOMEN

Many evangelicals today would have some hesitations about the classical reformed position spelt out in the high view of the ministry articulated by such as Moule, Forsyth and Lightfoot, if it implies a very individual model of the ministry of the word. In fact this is not necessarily so theologically, although the evangelical tradition in practice can be as clerical as any other. Michael Green, an Anglican in the exegetical tradition of Lightfoot, points out that presbyters in the New Testament, 'like their Jewish prototypes, they always appear in the plural . . . they represent a collegiality of leadership.'[88] This is a vital insight which today's church needs to recover. Teams of pastors, teachers, evangelists, carers and others, with varying complementary strengths, rather than the single bearer of that responsibility, may be the truly evangelical apostolic ideal of ministry.

This would also change the context of the disagreement over whether women should be ordained to the position of the presbyterate. At present evangelicals disagree on this. The disagreement hinges not on the maleness of Christ and the apostles directly, so much as the interpretation of the distinction between male and female in creation and in the church. The more conservative side of this debate upholds the ministry of women in every aspect of church life, apart from ultimate final leadership. Men and women were created in the image of God for complementarity, women have played vital roles in the history of the people of God, both in the Old and New Testaments; but final responsibility rests with the male and Paul is held to root this view back to creation itself according to 1 Corinthians 11:1–16, hence it cannot be simply 'culture relative'. The authority pattern found in Paul, which is more properly a cooperative pattern of one being a 'help meet' for the other, is also invoked in 1 Corinthians 14:34–6; and 1 Timothy 2:8–15. This pattern remains in the home, according to Ephesians 5:22ff, and therefore there is no reason to assume it disappears in the church, even though the distinction between male and female does not count as regards salvation or status in Christ. For the conservative evangelical, however minimizing an interpretation be given to the Pauline passages in question, the complementarity pattern cannot be eliminated altogether. This leads to the question of how a woman presbyter could properly function within that pattern.

Evangelicals favouring the ordination of women to the presbyterate as exactly the same as their male counterparts stress the culture of the day: slavery, for example, seems to have been unquestioned in New Testament passages, yet the principles of the gospel worked through to wash slavery away. The same principles should be allowed to apply in the case of women as presbyters. Paul lays it down that in Christ there is neither slave nor free, Jew nor Greek, male nor female. This spiritual reality of equality ought to be reflected in the shape of the church's ministry. Clearly women witnessed about Christ in the New Testament, indeed they were first to testify to the resurrection. Prophetesses appear in the New as well as the Old Testaments, as in Acts 21:9, and women teach the faith to men privately as in the case of Priscilla. Paul's injunction that women ought not to speak in church seems rightly interpreted to concern chatter rather than teaching. God could bring his word through the means of a woman prophetess.

The real point of disagreement concerns the way the complementarity pattern applies, the issue of 'headship'. Should women regularly occupy the position of the final responsibility, or should the man usually shoulder this function?

Green believes that the problem is instantly defused once a broad view of ministry is taken 'of a shared and multiple local leadership such as prevailed in the corporate presbyterate of the early church.' 'Once we recover that,' he says, 'the problem shrinks to very small proportions. Women as well as men may well show that they have been given the charism of leadership. The church will appropriately recognize this by ordination. Women will then take their place alongside men within the local presbyterate.'[89] He immediately adds, however, that he thinks 'that the creation pattern and the New Testament emphasis on the supportive role in ministry to be exercised by women might be best retained if the leadership of such a mixed team were normally, if not invariably, in the hands of a man.'[90] This would satisfy the needs of the church for women's distinctive contribution and at the same time preserve the principle of a male normally bearing final responsibility. This would probably satisfy the conservative side, but not the campaigners for change. It would rule out women as bishops. Green points out, accurately from the evangelical Anglican perspective, that there would be no problem in his pattern about women on a team of leaders celebrating the eucharist; nor would there be about such women absolving and blessing. The real point at issue is that of final leadership and the nature complementarity.

G. CHARISMATIC ECCLESIOLOGY

Note must be taken of the particular ecclesiological attitudes taken by large numbers of charismatic evangelical Anglicans. Anglo-Catholic charismatic ecclesiology remains basically untouched by their insistence on the direct experience of the gifts of the Holy Spirit: the threefold order of the apostolic ministry is the sacramental framework within which their spirituality works. Greater tensions arise for the evangelical Anglican charismatic. Focusing on the supernatural inbreaking of the Holy Spirit, the structures of the historical church can often seem to impede the progress of the kingdom of God and often to deny the gifts of the Spirit.

In terms of the settled ordained ministry the classical reformed Anglican esteems the ratification of the visible church through her official arrangements, a ratification of the call of God to ministry. Article 23 expresses this: 'It is not lawful for any man to take upon him the office of publick preaching, or ministering the Sacraments in the Congregation, before he be lawfully called, and sent to execute the same.'[91] Here the arrangements of the visible church are deemed very important in continuing the pastoral ministry. Classical reformed ecclesiology, reflected in the Thirty Nine Articles, accepts that the church has an authority, by virtue of being the historical church, to order worship and ceremonies. This authority is not by divine inspiration but historical wisdom and tradition, and has to justify itself biblically. Nevertheless church order is well served by it. This has the justification of the broad theme of the unity of the people of God, who have to reform ancient custom with care, respect for the past, and attention to consensus under scripture.

The New Testament teaching on the gifts of the Spirit is highly significant to charismatic. Any church should expect the Spirit to provide, among her members, a whole range of people gifted for ministries of healing, speaking in tongues of ecstatic utterance, casting out demons, preaching, teaching, giving alms, and others as the needs arise. Such are signs of the kingdom, proclaimed by Jesus, fulfilling Isaiah 61:1–2, when he told the congregation at Capernaum: 'The Spirit of the Lord is upon me, for he has anointed me to preach good news to the poor. He has sent me to proclaim release to the captives and recovering of sight to the blind, to set at liberty the oppressed, to proclaim the acceptable year of the Lord' (Luke 4:18–19). The disciples of Jesus should see themselves as standing in these shoes. Jesus sent out missions of his disciples who returned with accounts of casting out demons and of healing. These were signs of the end-time, performed by the disciples of Jesus in his name to usher in the last days, the final instalment of history.

The charismatic evangelical Anglican, therefore, has a far more eschatologically-oriented framework for ecclesiology and a more insistently expectant one. This theology could well make the point that the Reformation neglected its eschatology; the Thirty Nine Articles do not speak of the end-times. Reformed evangelicalism may need to take its own medicine of listening again to the word, of reading the gospels as attentively as Romans and Galatians. The Holy Spirit may be quenched by the classical evangelical stress on preaching by the local minister at the expense of releasing the equally important signs of the kingdom, signs of divine healing, of casting out demons, of signs and wonders. The traditional order of ministry, authorized forms of service and church regulations can often seem to hinder this eschatological work of the Spirit, in the eyes of many charismatics.

The essence of the problem here is the appeal to gifting by the Spirit as opposed to the appeal to the authority given to presbyters by the whole visible church who have ratified the spiritual call to the task. The ministry of the charismatic prophet who was not fixed in one locality seems to have been part of the church's ministry in New Testament church life.

Paul exhorts his listeners to seek gifts of prophecy in the congregation, as well as those of healing and tongues of ecstatic utterance. The charismatic stresses that such a pattern ought to be ours today, but that instead the church has settled back into an evangelical institutionalism which fails to be sufficiently expectant of the supernatural as part of the dynamic life of the eschatological people of God. Such an orientation finds it far more difficult to adopt infant baptism, or to agree to the Anglican relation of state and church. When the pastorate of the local church, or the bishop, acts in such a way considered to quench the spiritual work of the church, the temptation is to hive off and form a breakaway grouping. Moreover the idea of a church containing both saved and unsaved, the notion of charitable presumption, is less palatable to such an emphasis which sees a continual directness about the Spirit's leading and activity in the church.

Such tensions are not uncommon but not necessary. Eduard Schweizer has shown this tension in the earliest apostolic church, the travelling ministry of charismatic prophets being acknowledged alongside settled local eldership; the eschatological and the historical, the new and the regular, can both be seen.[92] The New Testament shows different emphases in this area, but the eldership principle and the gifting principle are in fact complementary. Paul insists on the spirits being tested by the whole church, prophecies and tongues being rational and upbuilding, on prophecies being given in good order. Likewise elders are to be people of spiritual standing in the community, approved and acceptable to the local church. Forsyth puts this well:

> 'The prophet, the preacher had to *win* confidence. The wandering preacher's gift of uttering the word must be met and matched by the hearer's gift of evangelical discernment. . . . Of old the prophet on arrival offered himself to the spiritual judgement of the Church. . . . In the New Testament age the critical right of recognizing prophets when they appeared lay with the Church. And how? By bringing them to the test neither of eloquence, nor impressiveness, nor idealism, nor mere liking, but to the test of the historic gospel, to the evangelical test, as the Apostles had put it into their hands. (What a pity it has been confounded with Orthodoxy!) That is . . . the test must be applied of . . . redemption. Paul said, if prophet,

apostle, or angel preached another than that gospel, he was to be disregarded.'[93]

Both the eldership and the gifts of the Spirit must be treated in the context of the whole church, and not only of an enthusiastic group within that whole. This itself is a deep spiritual principle, inseparably an ecclesiological principle. 'Is Christ divided?' The crucified Lord died to unite all types of person and temperament, and the Holy Spirit is the Spirit of this Lord of his church. It has to be said that the Roman Catholic and Anglo-Catholic traditions have grasped this far more clearly than recent generations of evangelicals. The authority of eldership and custom, and that claimed to be directly from the Spirit, must both and equally relate to Christ crucified and walk in that humility.

It is fascinating to note that ministries which have not been much acknowledged and perhaps squeezed out by the dominance of the settled local presbyter re-emerge in church life. For example Diocesan bishops will usually appoint exorcists, evangelists or missioners, to work throughout their area. Travelling preachers and advisors of many kinds are found, often licensed by bishops, sometimes sponsored by societies. Missionary societies are very obvious examples of apostolic ministry being forwarded in ways outside the locally settled threefold order of ministry. This reflects the many ministries needed by the whole church, and the plural nature of such ministries should be regarded as apostolic, parallel with the multiform ministries raised up by the Spirit—and accepted by the whole body—seen in the New Testament. To bureaucratize such several organizations into a structured branch of regional episcopal–presbyteral ministry may turn the more flexible and wide ranging ministries into a form of the local and pastoral type.[94]

H. BISHOPS

For the evangelical faith the church as a whole is the primary category of ecclesiology. The local ministry has a centrally important place in serving the church by bringing the word of life, in various ways, to the congregation, or rather by enabling the congregation better to 'harken diligently and obey' her Lord. Traditionally the ordained ministry, the presbyterate, stands as the most important second category subserving the church. Continuity in the apostolic faith is fellowship with the apostles, with their gospel, their true and lively word; it is looking with them at Jesus and seeking to follow him as they teach us to. The pattern of church and word, church and apostle or prophet, finds its reflection and living historical continuity in today's church and her ministry of the word.

Anglican church order strongly affirms the presbyterate. It upholds the diaconate in an extraordinarily uncertain way, and this is a subject under urgent consideration. It strongly affirms the office of bishop: the precise interpretation of this office, with all the ramifications for ecumenism, remains a central disagreement between evangelicals and their Anglo-Catholic brethren, whether of the liberal or conservative variety. The evangelical claims to stand in the mainline tradition of Anglicanism, for the majority of its post-Reformation existence, in holding the view that the episcopal form of church government is ancient, with a proven track record, and not to be abandoned. But episcopacy is ministerial to the church and it cannot be said to be a test of a true church. It may be said to be of the church's *'bene esse'* or well-being, but not of its *'esse'* nor its *'plene esse'* or fullness of being.

Whereas the post Tractarian view is that the presbyterate participates, as a delegate, in the apostolic episcopal office, the evangelical Anglican regards the local ministry of the word as more directly and fundamentally apostolic, and as prior theologically and historically to the episcopate. Apostolicity has its living succession particularly in the church's ministry of the word. From this axiom can come the emergence and definition of the bishop, whose apostolicity is no different in kind from that of the local pastor teacher.

Evangelical ecclesiology therefore focuses most strongly on the presbyteral ministry, regarding the episcopal office as a senior sort of the presbyteral, the latter arising out of the former, 'from below'. The episcopal structure evolved when Christianity grew quickly in the age after the apostles died. Lightfoot's *Essay on the Christian Ministry* remains the classic Anglican scholarly account of this. He rebuts the notion that the office of bishop can be said to continue that of apostle: 'the functions of the Apostle and the bishop differed widely. The Apostle, like the prophet or the evangelist, held no *local* office. He was essentially, as his name denotes, a missionary, moving about from place to place, founding and confirming new brotherhoods.'[95] We may note in passing that the apostolic character of missionary societies, not operating under the aegis of the presbyteral-episcopal line, can gain endorsement from classical Anglican exegesis, rather than being a problem category for ecclesiology!

Lightfoot argues for example that Epaphroditus, called 'apostle' in Philippians, is so called because he is a messenger of the church, demonstrated by the fact that he carried their alms to Paul; he was not a true apostle like Peter or John who bear the title 'as the messenger, the delegate of Christ Himself.'[96] Rather than any idea of the episcopate resulting 'from above' as some handing on of the office of apostle, Lightfoot classically presents the evidence as demonstrating the opposite: 'the episcopate was formed not out of the apostolic order by localization but out of the presbyteral by elevation: and the title, which was originally common to all, came at length to be appropriated to the chief among them.'[97]

The bishop's function developed from that of presbyters, the same in pastoral function but with a wider brief to pastor the pastorate and to be their chairman. Hilary, an early Latin theologian, is quoted by Lightfoot as holding 'Every bishop is a presbyter, but every presbyter is not a bishop: for he is bishop who is first among the presbyters.'[98] Jerome, an even greater patristic authority, tells us that bishops must be aware that they are 'superior to presbyters more owing to custom than to any actual ordinance of the Lord.'[99] The episcopate is not therefore the originative line of the church, nor of the ordained ministry, as if church and ministry were delegated from the episcopate. It exists to promote good order, to provide a clear place where the church's authority is exercised, properly in consultation with the whole church. Episcopacy has proved a vital means of providing a structure for the wider regional connection of church life, as Newbigin has argued.[100]

In particular the episcopate is the appointed means of the wider church ordaining the presbyterate. The bishop represents the whole church for this purpose, and acts with that authority, but only after the candidate's call has been tested and ratified by a whole variety of church membership. Just as the presbyter, the bishop stands for the continuity of the apostolic gospel and its ways. Irenaeus, an early church father associated with the more eastern tradition, made much of the role of the bishop as the defender of orthodoxy in the face of the current gnostic versions of the faith, and this is an important facet of the evangelical estimate of this office, which is basically presbyteral in kind.

Avis has reminded us again of the ecclesiological stance of the Anglican Reformers and that polity was for them a secondary matter after the primary and indispensable marks of the visible church: the proclamation of the word and administration of the sacraments. Hooker stresses the episcopal function of ordination but concedes that the church might in some circumstances have to dispense with a corrupt episcopate. 'Cranmer, Jewell and Field hold that bishops have a superiority over priests more by custom than by irrevocable divine command,'[101] following Jerome and affirmed so strongly by Bishop Lightfoot as we have seen already. The Anglican heritage of the Reformation, claimed by evangelicals, regards episcopacy as desirable for the order of the church, but not constitutive of the church: the church would and does remain, without the episcopate, when events have so dictated. Therefore the continental reformed churches were regarded as fully legitimate with fully recognized ministries. All the evangelical doctrinal authors cite lists of representative texts to show that was the true Anglican attitude, that 'no bishop, no church' is a post Tractarian distortion. For example, Bishop Moule shows that even those regarded as higher churchmen less attached to the Reformation doctrines teach 'the distinction between the Being and the Well Being of a church: affirming that those churches to whom this power and faculty is denied lose nothing of the true essence of a church . . .'[102] Episcopacy is part of the ancient evolution of the structures of the church, *de iure humano* rather than *de iure divino*, a natural process rather than one specifically ordained of God, a question of the judgement of the church down the centuries which by now ought not to be called into question.

Episcopacy for the evangelical works at the level of ancient, trusted church practice and custom; primarily at the historical and traditional level of church order. When defined as the necessary link with the apostles, the 'historic episcopate' has been seen as a hindrance to church unity, a device excluding non-episcopal churches, however ancient and orthodox. Evangelicals perceive this 'sectarian' use of episcopacy to be profoundly uncatholic and unapostolic. Hooker, when faced with the claim that the Presbyterian church order was laid down in the New Testament, argued not that episcopacy was the true blueprint, but that there was no precise blueprint given there. The classical Anglican view is that episcopal order is historically uniform, valuable and congruent with the New Testament principles as any other form. This remains the evangelical Anglican view. Today, following the lead of the reformed bishop of the Church of South India, Lesslie Newbigin, evangelical theology might also affirm episcopacy as a means and sign of visible church unity, although never in such a way as to degrade non-episcopal churches or their ministries.

Litton strikes an evangelical note when he insists that synods of bishops alone ought not to presume to govern the church. The laity too must be represented. Evangelical Anglicans likewise insist on the principle of the laity having an important voice in the choice of pastors. Litton points out that in Acts (Acts 1:24–6) Peter brings the issue of the appointment of a successor to Judas Iscariot before the whole company of believers, and also the appointment of deacons (Acts 7:5, 6). Litton also quotes Cyprian: 'The faithful laity ought rather to avoid communion with a delinquent bishop and sacriligious priests, because it possesses the power both of choosing worthy priests and of rejecting unworthy.'[103] The most important of the rights of the laity, for Litton, is concerned with the exercise of discipline, 'which by Christ is vested in the whole Church, and not in the clerical body alone. "Tell it to the church" is His command (Matt 18:17) . . . That the presiding bishop or elders should be the persons to pronounce the sentence may be admitted, but that the decision (to excommunicate) should rest with the community is clearly the sense of scripture.'[104] The whole people of God remains the prior theological category of the church.

This concern for the laity has been a major reason why a considerable body of evangelical Anglican opinion remains content with the current link with the State. The monarch is technically 'the supreme governor' of the Church of England, a lay person sits on the throne which logic alone might indicate belongs to an Archbishop. This emphasizes the lay principle. The present system once more depends on the supposition, the charitable presumption, that the monarch is a 'Godly prince', anointed and crowned by the Archbishop of Canterbury, a practice which would also have to be dismantled should the link be severed.

Episcopal order serves the church as her instrument for ordering herself, maintaining her visible unity of doctrine and fellowship across geographical, ethnic and spatial boundaries. Evangelical ecclesiology therefore urges a wide, charitable and human-historical interpretation of this venerable ministry. It must be interpreted as church-serving rather than church-defining, and must be susceptible to further historical evolution to fit changing social patterns. The development of the suffragan bishop exemplifies this. As a sign of the continuity of the church and the gospel down the centuries the episcopate stands as an impressive testimony worth guarding and cherishing. As a divine blueprint continuing the ministry of the apostles, originating the fullest life of the church, it is a fallacy theologically and historically. In the form of this fallacy it has, at times, been guilty of introducing a legalism among Anglicans, as if the episcopal tradition were the circumcision required by the free church 'Gentiles', a requirement impugning the evidence of the Holy Spirit, the word and the sacraments.

Evangelical Anglicans argue for the broad, charitable episcopal tradition which includes all people of God in ecumenical life. 'Where there is a strongly articulated episcopal system,' says Eduard Schweizer, 'it is vital that the church as a whole should be taken seriously and not disenfranchised. . . . The main emphasis of the episcopal ministry . . . must therefore lie, as in the New Testament, in the local church itself and its ministry.'[105] Anglicanism seeks to meet this need by its balance of elected synod and bishops conveying pastoral authority 'from below' and also 'from above'.

4. The sacraments

A. GENERAL THEOLOGY OF THE SACRAMENTS

Pauline covenant theology controls evangelical Anglican doctrine of the sacraments. There are two sacraments which function as covenant 'signs, seals and pledges' of the work of God, focused narrowly upon the cross of Christ. The sacraments are vital for the church, being ordained by the Lord himself. They stand in continuity with the passover and the circumcision of ancient Israel. The theology depends on the continuity of the covenant being maintained with the climactic new dimension being given in Christ. 'The Sacramentalism of the New Testament', says Bishop Moule,

> 'will not be viewed aright if viewed in isolation from that of the Old. The Gospel sacraments are most sacred parts of a sacred whole, the sacramental Idea pervading Scripture. From the beginning onward the covenantal Idea appears, and everywhere, at its side, the sacramental Institution; "certain sure witnesses and effectual signs of grace and God's good will", "whereby he doth work invisibly in us",

> in the world of thought and will, "and doth not only arouse", as by a vividly presented object of sense, "but also confirm", as by its revealed designed significance, "our faith in Him"; working on the soul by way of divine (nothing less than divine) attestation and ratification . . . certainly rainbow to Noah, Federal Sacrifice (Gen. XV), and Circumcision (Gen. XVII; Rom. IV:10, 11) to Abraham, the Passover Sacrifice and Feast to Israel; all are instances of the one idea—the giving of and external, and usually lasting or recurring, divine sign along with a divine promise.'[106]

Baptism and the eucharist stand in this line of effectual sign, seal and pledge matching the divine promise of Christ crucified and risen.

The clearest way of understanding the evangelical reformed doctrine of sacraments is to realize that they are visible or dramatic forms of the gospel. They tell out the saving acts of God for his people. They are not really another means of grace so much as another form of the presentation of the word of grace, fundamentally the transforming word of the cross, of Christ crucified, of the very heart of the gospel itself. Just as the word comes to the church, so with the sacraments. They are the visible enactments of costly and assured grace given to the people of God. Without the ministry of the word, the sacraments would be dumb and open to all kinds of interpretations. The sacraments are Hebraic in that they depend on a living tradition of the mighty acts of God, they are for the community of faith. The sacraments are therefore signs of the freely given grace of God. The sacraments focus on the act of God in Christ, his death and resurrection and the church's appropriation of that great, moral act of God.

The sacraments, for the reformed Anglican tradition are not simply a 'bare sign' or as Cranmer puts it, 'not as a painted fire', a mere visual aid. They go beyond being 'obsignatory', says Dimock, the determined evangelical Anglican scholar writing at the start of this century, and are 'donatory'. They are in one respect like a sermon reminding the church of divine mercy and love. But the sacraments are also a kind of coming home of the gospel effectually. As well as relating to the doctrines of the gospel they relate to its powerful grace; this gift is made over to mankind

> 'not only by general declarations of His Word, but by visible signs and seals of conveyance—seals which thus

> become effectual signs of the donation of the gift—sure witnesses and effectual signs of grace and God's goodness towards us . . . The doctrine of the Gospel is as the written parchment of conveyance. The Sacraments are the signatures and seals, worthless as ink and wax in themselves, but the means of actual donation in their connection with the Word of the truth of the Gospel.'[107]

The sacraments are more than what a 'bare sign' means today, as perhaps the sign advertising a house for sale. Rather they are like the indispensable legal 'instrument' of conveying, the title deeds which entitle one to the property and without which the conveyance is not complete. Perhaps an even better analogy is the deed of gift in English law, which needs to be made 'under seal' for the promised gift to be binding. Promise and ratification, gospel and sacrament, these form the structure of the evangelical sacramental theology, and appeal to Article 25 of the Anglican Articles of Religion, quoted in part above by Dimock. Even a gift, signed, sealed and delivered, has to be accepted.

This theology of the sacraments depends heavily on Calvin's writings which in turn often claim the support of Augustine. Gospel reality and sacrament coincide for this family of ecclesiology. The reality signified, that is the work of Christ, and the sacramental, dramatic giving and receiving of that reality become indistinguishable. This is only natural in covenanting ritual. The sign and the thing signalled become one. In the Book of Common Prayer marriage service, a service at which a relationship is formally sealed, a covenanting service, the words 'with this ring I thee wed' are used. The ring, the symbol of the relationship of mutual commitment, is used as the instrument of the union. By the giving and receiving of the ring the marriage is 'declared' says the new Alternative Service Book rite. The substance is the actual committed relationship, but this is only properly sealed by the ring given and accepted. Such is sacramental covenanting practice.

The giving of the ring is in fact the giving of the self, the symbol conveys the person to the other person. 'In baptism,' Motyer tells us, 'we are dealing with a Covenant ordinance, a movement of grace which reaches out from God to men; and when we speak of the baptismal sign we mean the donation by God through his ministers of the mark of the New Covenant.'[108] Bernard of Clairvaux, the medieval theologian, is cited by

Hooker, Dimock and Moule in support of this understanding: 'A sacrament is a sacred sign, or sacred mystery. Many things are done for themselves alone; but other things in order to designate something else, and are themselves called signs, as they are. To take an instance from common life: a ring is given for the ring's sake, and there is not significance; it is given to invest an heir in some inheritance, and it is a sign. The recipient can in that case say, "The ring avails nothing, but yet it is the inheritance which I sought."'[109] It is very natural, unavoidable, to talk of the thing signalled in terms of the sign.

The conferring of the sacrament will not 'cause' the relationship to occur between God and the recipient, but marks and seals and secures what the Holy Spirit has already done or will bring to pass. Calvin, the most powerful sacramental teacher of the Reformation according to Dix, the great Anglo-Catholic liturgist, teaches the coincidence of sacrament and reality. The promisor at work in the sacraments is the Lord who can be trusted to keep the promises of grace made present at the sacrament, to be himself in the sacrament since his promises and his presence are not to be split. 'God therefore accomplishes what he promises in the symbols and the signs are not without their effect in showing, so far as need be, that the author of them is true and faithful.'[110] The seeing of the covenant sign of the rainbow by the people of God is no mere visual aid of God sustaining seed time and harvest, but the very process of this faithfulness to creation is seen in the rainbow itself. The promise and the promised reality coincide. The gift of mercy and divine faithfulness presences itself in that majestic sight, only to the eye of faith, to the effect that God is keeping his promise of mercy and will continue to do so. The gift is real, the sign seals and guarantees this gift. So it is with baptism and the holy communion.

Dimock insists strongly on this point. It stresses the objectivity of the sacraments: 'it is to be observed,' he teaches, 'that this relationship of the sign to the thing signified—in the teaching of our reformers—is not affected by the faith or want of faith of the receiver. The *reception* of the thing signified depends on the faith of the receiver, for without faith it cannot be received. But the sacrament is the seal of donation nevertheless . . . Man's faith does not make the grace of God. Man's faith does not make the sacrament to be the seal of God's grace. It is the office of faith . . . not to make but to receive, and to receive by believing—by believing the gift conveyed by the Seal, by believing that which is in itself truly objective and independent of faith.'[111] Here is shown the classical reformed Anglican stress on objective grace, grace needing only to be accepted trustfully, just as the bride needs only to let the groom put the ring onto her finger.

The Holy Spirit, always informed by Christ, remains the bestower of Christ in the church in the the sacraments received by the faithful, as in the word of the gospel trusted and believed. The sacraments seal the objective work of Christ for us; when they are duly received by faith with thanksgiving, the Holy Spirit brings home afresh the work of Christ personally in the heart. The objective salvation of grace and mercy is pledged sacramentally. Acceptance of this life-giving grace comes home in the Spirit by faith, faith in the sacrament of the gospel. 'Feed on him in your heart by faith with thanksgiving' conveys the evangelical view of sacramental reception of grace.

Faith and the Holy Spirit are not by-passed or somehow materialized, but the being baptized and the eating and drinking are faithfully accepting the gospel realities, sacramentally. 'Hence those aquainted only with modern theology,' admonishes Dimock, 'will in few things, perhaps, be more surprised than in observing how our Reformers teach Faith to exercise itself on the remembrance of Baptism, to rest and assure itself on this sign of regeneration, or new birth.'[112] He quotes Bullinger, 'The promise, yea, the truth of sanctification and free remission of sins, is written and engraven in our bodies when we are baptized. For God by His Spirit through the blood of His Son hath newly regenerated and purged again our souls, and even now doth regenerate and purge them.'[113] More than a visual aid, the sacraments are 'certain sure witnesses and effectual signs of grace'; but they are no alternative to knowing God's grace by the Holy Spirit in faith.

The *classical* evangelical view then is a high sacramental one, the gospel and the sacrament being identified, both accepted thankfully by trustful people of God. This continues the dealings of God with his people down the centuries of faith in the promises of the living and active God. The privilege of circumcision was that it sealed the promises of God on Israel, and it required faith in the promises thereby signed and sealed. Romans and Galatians speak of the need for faith in order to be true Israelites. The seal without faith gains nothing, except judgement, according to the Old and New Testaments. Paul in 1 Corinthians 10 tells the story of the covenant people, called out of slavery, and as it were baptized and partaking in the eucharist, going under the cloud and eating the heavenly food, yet meeting judgement for their lack of faith and obedience. The outward seals proved meaningless without that trustful attitude to them. In the same epistle Paul berates those who eat and drink at the eucharist 'not discerning the body', selfishly indulging in hearty excess, for this also attracts the judgement of the Lord. The gift signed, sealed and pledged, can be gratefully taken or not. It is the sacramental giving of the gospel.

B. BAPTISM

There seems to be a cleavage between the classical reformed doctrine of baptism and much current feeling on the subject among evangelical Anglicans. Certainly one detects a failure of nerve among many in the evangelical Anglican position which argues, just as did the Elizabethan Anglican theologians, on the one hand with Rome and on the other hand with Anabaptist radicals. To the right is the doctrine of baptismal regeneration, to the left exclusively believers', therefore adult, baptism. The classical evangelical view is covenantal and objectively gospel focused. The situation of the evangelical churchmen was expressed by Wright in his paper at an evangelical Anglican gathering, the Islington Conference, in 1980: 'Modern evangelicalism is not in a position to be smug about the weakness of others, as though we had kept on the high road while our Catholic and radical brethren wandered about in the fog. We have tended to stand closer to Bultmann than we like to realize, with his emphasis on faith as experience unconnected with history, his existentialist call for decision, his view of justification as the establishment of a personal relationship with God, his wedge between justification and the historical people of God.'[114] The evangelical today has tended to lose touch with the historical covenant theology of the people of God, with its important stress on the outward and visible seals of the objective gospel of Christ. Deploring the lapse into a purely pietistic, subjectivist evangelicalism, Wright appeals for a return to the classic reformed tradition for the modern church; evangelical Anglicans must learn to be not only Bible people and gospel people, but also church people. 'Justification is to be understood in the context of the historical people of God, the one family of Abraham: as the doctrine of covenant membership it cannot be separated from the covenant signs of baptism and the Lord's

Supper.' Wright reminds church people of their identity as the historic community of God.

(i) What does baptism signify?

Article 27 teaches that baptism is a sign of regeneration or new birth, as well as marking off the Christian from the non Christian. Regeneration through the death and resurrection of Christ lies at the heart of the evangelical interpretation of baptism: having been dead in trespasses and sins, God through his act of grace in the death and resurrection of Christ renews the spiritually dead human nature. Baptism sacramentally entombs the individual into Christ's death, for the new rising with Christ. Again Galatians and Romans are central texts. Paul in Galatians tells the church that they are sons of God through faith in Christ Jesus, then adds 'for as many of you as were baptized into Christ have put on Christ.'[115] Being sons of God through faith is sealed by the event of baptism, the two are the same, the sacrament sealing the life of faith in Christ and death to sin. Burial is itself a sealing of death: 'Before baptism the person is dead, for baptism is a *burial*, not an execution. In baptism there is a resurrection in Christ, through the power of God, and the appropriating agency of faith.'[116] The traditional evangelical regards the statement in the BCP 'seeing these persons/this child are now regenerate' in this Pauline sense: sacramentally the individual is incorporated into the regeneration of Christ.

Romans 6 has the remarkable passage about dying and rising in Christ as the ethical imperative of the Christian life: 'Do you not know that all of us who have been baptized into Christ Jesus were baptized into his death? We were buried therefore with him by baptism into death, so that as Christ was raised from the dead . . . we too might walk in newness of life.'[117] Baptism here might even be interpreted as baptism in the Holy Spirit and fire, the baptism which John the Baptist predicted Jesus would provide; perhaps linked also with texts in which Jesus told his disciples he had to undergo a fiery baptism of death. A line of Australian reformed Anglican interpretation has argued this case. But whether or not the Pauline references to baptism in such passages are to sacramental water baptism, or to a spiritual act of dying to sin into Christ, is not important. The point is that the radical event of entering Christ in itself is a death to sin, a new life to righteousness. This new life through death, enabled only by Christ's death and resurrection, is sacramentally sealed in baptism. The great spiritual renewal through the judgement fire of the crucified Christ is a baptism, sacramentally water baptism. This baptism has to be believed and lived out, says Paul continuing the passage's message, 'the death he died he died to sin once for all, but the life he lives he lives to God; so you also must consider yourselves dead to sin and alive to God in Christ Jesus.'[118]

Baptism into Christ's cleansing and renewing death, for decisive eschatological resurrection, sums up the New Testament teaching on what baptism signifies, it includes all the other ideas found in texts such as washing away of sin (Ephesians 5:26), passing through judgement secure in Christ (1 Peter 3:18), rebirth by water and the spirit (John 3:5). Baptism seals on the individual this radical, decisive, messianic reality of grace through costly love, sacramentally burying the individual into Christ crucified and risen, therefore into the messianic community. In the gospels the Spirit comes upon Jesus in his baptism by John, and the water sign remains deeply linked to the sanctifying indwelling Holy Spirit: 'by one spirit we were all baptized into one body' (1 Cor 12:12); the important note of community, the people of the messianic community into which we enter by receiving baptism by that community, links in here. Baptism into Christ is baptism into the community of the Spirit. Again this is part of what Paul means by baptism into Christ's death.

Baptism, in particular, does not *primarily* signify the act of response or decision, by the believer: its main focus lies on objective grace, the act of the crucified Lord. This is what is believed, what is sacramentally received, this is what is signed and sealed in baptism. Baptism is not therefore primarily the opportunity to focus the individual's act of faith, it is not first and foremost signalling a profession of commitment. Rather it heralds Christ's commitment and atonement, the root of salvation: our response is the fruit of that work of grace. Here the radical reformed doctrine of grace undergirds its baptismal theology: faith itself is a result of grace, of regeneration, as Wright has recognized,[119] and to make baptism a sign of human response reverses gospel and covenant principles.

(ii) The instrumentality of baptism

Perhaps adoption, mentioned above as a vital but neglected category of Pauline teaching, can usefully unite the individual and the corporate aspects of the meaning of baptism; Article 27 takes up this theme in describing baptism as a sign of regeneration or new birth 'whereby, as by an an instrument they that receive rightly are grafted into the Church; the promises of forgiveness of sin and of our adoption to be the sons of God by the Holy Ghost are visibly signed and sealed; Faith is confirmed, and Grace increased by virtue of prayer unto God.' As Christians we are adopted as members of the family of God, through Jesus' atoning death. Sharing in his death means, by that very fact, incorporation into the covenant people. But how does baptism accomplish this? In what sense is it 'as an instrument'?

The answer to this is that sacramentally water baptism is entry into the messianic people of God. It is 'as an instrument' in the sense of the legal, perhaps royal, instruments or warrants crowning with outward authority the gift bestowed. As Motyer clearly points out, the instrumentality involved is not mechanical, as if by a 'blunt instrument' an effect was instantaneously caused![120] Rather the instrumentality is of the outward, formal kind, always assuming the moral and spiritual counterpart of saving grace known in faith. This accords not only with the New Testament understanding of covenant signs, but also with the whole of biblical sacramental theology. For Paul, as has been shown, to go under the cloud, or receive the holy symbol of divine baptism, without faith, attracts judgement rather than grace. Early in Romans this is made crystal clear: 'He is not a real Jew who is one outwardly, nor is true circumcision something external and physical. He is a Jew who is one inwardly, and real circumcision is a matter of the heart, spiritual and not literal' (Romans 2:28, 29). The external rite, however divinely ordained, is itself not meant to replace grace appropriated in faith: it is an outward expression of grace offered to faith. Paul does not conclude by becoming an anti-sacramentalist, or an existentialist! 'Then what advantage has the Jew? Or what is the value of circumcision? Much in every way' (Romans 3:1); the Jew has the external seals and the testimony of the living God, constantly calling forth faith, constantly calling for belief in the circumcision, for 'considering yourselves dead to sin and alive to God in Christ Jesus', as the messianic community.

Pierre Marcel[121] has restated this doctrine of covenant grace and seal powerfully from his French Reformed standpoint. He reminds the evangelical, and particularly Barth who opposed infant baptism, that even in the Old Testament outward circumcision was a seal of inner holiness, of 'the circumcision of the heart' which was the purpose of the rite (Deuteronomy 30:6).

But the English reformed tradition had known this doctrine since the Reformation; Dimock is aware of simply restating the tradition in his exposition:

> 'Abraham received the sign of circumcision, as a seal of the righteousness of the faith which he had, being yet uncircumcised. And circumsion, without faith, was as a seal cut off from a deed of gift. But it was unbelief which cut if off. The privilege and responsibility of circumcision was this, that it was a call to, and required, faith in the promises it sealed. When those promises were believed, circumcision became circumcision of the heart, and a Jew became a Jew inwardly, the Israelite became an Israelite indeed, and the adoption of children became a Sonship indeed. . . . The outward and visible, indeed, might be separated from the inward and spiritual, but only by man's unbelief . . .'[122]

Unbelief is distortion of the natural pattern: normally for theology the two coincide, not in terms of a point in time: people are baptized after coming to faith, or before their faith comes to conscious formulation, but theologically and ecclesiologically. The seal is the seal for the royal priesthood, the people of God: this people has to become what it is, has to realize its inheritance, has to take up its gift.

(iii) Candidates for baptism

Motyer states that baptism is the same in meaning for both the adult candidate and the infant. Its meaning is, as discussed above, the objective gospel fact of the grace of God in Christ crucified. This fact is sealed on the candidate whether old or young: the rite is not primarily an opportunity to declare one's faith. Here lies the basic, often forgotten, difference between the Anglican evangelical and the Baptist or House Church evangelical view of the sacrament. Moule quotes Archbishop Ussher of Armagh, 1624–56, as giving an accurate account of baptismal sealing: 'Baptism . . . is a seal of the righteousness of Christ, to be extraordinarily applied; if (the infant) die in its infancy; to be apprehended by faith if it live to years of discretion . . . All the promises of grace were estated upon me, and sealed up to me, on God's part; but then I come to have the profit and benefit of them, when I come to understand what grant God, in Baptism, hath sealed up to me, and actually to lay on it by faith.'[123] For the Anglican this same interpretation applies to the baptism of an adult. The baptized is urged to trust his or her baptism, because sacramentally it is the grace of Christ which is being trusted, something therefore not dependent on the strength of individual faith but radically objective and powerful.

Adult candidates for baptism must show signs of true commitment to Christ which they will have to declare in their baptismal vows to turn to Christ. They will show that they repent of their sins, conforming to the apostolic call to 'repent and be baptized' (Acts 2:38). The church will do the best she can to insure the genuineness of the spiritual state of the candidate, but of this there is no absolute guarantee, the church has no spiritual 'geiger counter' into the heart, which only God knows finally. The church has to go by the external evidence when administering her outward royal warrants of baptism and eucharist. This will be based on the person's confession of faith, exemplified by the baptism of the Ethiopian eunuch by Philip (Acts 8:36), baptism simply being requested by one convinced of the gospel (without witnesses in an isolated oasis, it seems!). Baptism is properly applied given the confession of faith; the fact that later it emerges the candidate was not truly turned to Christ at all does not make the decision to baptize wrong, the church simply goes on the evidence before her, not on some supernatural insight. Even the apostles baptized someone who professed faith, but later turned out not to have it: Simon, who had practised magic, according to Acts 8:13, was thought to have believed and was baptized, later to reveal a sub-Christian motive.

Hooker's distinction between the spiritual and the visible aspects of the church prevents confusion. The spiritual church is the church as known by God, who alone knows the hearts of men and women. The pastors of the church, even when these are the apostles, are not the Holy Spirit himself and their task is to administer the sacraments using human historical evidence available to them. The faith discerned by the church to qualify the candidate for baptism is the professed faith which hopefully reflects the inner heart, but not necessarily. Motyer makes the helpful distinction between 'admitting' faith, faith professed which prompts the church to baptize, and 'appropriating' faith, this is the attitude of the heart which only God knows. The church is concerned with 'admitting' faith in her administration of the sacraments.

When it comes to infant baptism, the evangelical faith does not argue in favour of baptism indiscriminately. The criteria used are those of the covenant pattern. In brief, the children of the people of God, people who profess the faith and are themselves baptized and partakers in the covenant meal, should be sealed by the sign of baptism. They should be brought up within the covenant, learning to pray with parents and the church, appropriating the promises of God sealed on them at baptism, growing into the Christian faith. Their unbelief can make the warrant, the seal of no account. But that is not the expectation of the prayerful family of the church. There is such a thing as an infant Christian, the church is not catholic without all age groups, and there must be no confusion between knowledge on the one hand, and faith of a childlike kind on the other.[124]

Biblically the debate with Baptist and House Church evangelicals turns on the interpretation of the continuity of the covenant theology. Jesus accepted children, and blessed them; which creates the *a priori* argument that they too belong to the kingdom. Peter's speech in Acts, as well as exhorting the Jewish crowd to repent and be baptized, continues 'for the promise is to you and to your children' (Acts 2:39). This is covenant language, and as Marcel and Motyer tell us, is a virtual quotation of Genesis 17:7, the giving of the Abrahamic covenant which was sealed by circumcision. To the Jewish hearers, this reference would have been immediate: the messianic fulfilment had come, and the baptismal seal was parallel to that of circumcision. Colossians 2:10–13, a text very like Romans 6 discussed above, frames teaching in terms of spiritual circumcision and baptism: 'In him also you were circumcised with a circumcision made without hands, by putting off the body of flesh in the circumcision of Christ; and you were buried with him in baptism, in which you were also raised with him through faith in the working of God, who raised him from the dead.' Again the question strikes the reader whether 'baptism' here is best interpreted as the water rite, or as the baptism Jesus and the Baptist spoke of, baptism of fire into the cross and the Holy Spirit. But once more this does not really affect the reformed exposition, since water baptism is sacramentally the moral, spiritual death to sin into Christ crucified amd risen; the reference is to this one reality, and again faith cannot be ousted from the sacramental sealing. The parallel of circumcision and baptism, each a covenant seal used for the reality it signifies, is plain.

Baptism of infants of the Christian family is regarded with positive expectation by the classical Anglican evangelical ecclesiology, not with a nervousness centring on the existential decision of the child in early teens. Surrounded by prayer, the scriptures, and the testimony of the good God, the child of the covenant, like the Israelite of Romans 3, has the advantage of the oracles of God, the promises, and faith which is to be nurtured and incarnated.

Such is the inheritance of the evangelical Anglican, but it seems currently to be grossly neglected, the cinderella sacrament of the Western church.

C. HOLY COMMUNION

(i) The focus of the eucharist

Jesus' saving death and resurrection focuses the eucharist as it does baptism. Evangelical ecclesiolgy concentrates the eucharist narrowly on this. The atoning work of Christ, accomplished at the drama of Good Friday and Easter Sunday, grounds the church's relationship with God and provides the only possibility for her response of faith and love. Hence the rejection of doctrines implying the inclusion of the church's responsive self-offering at the centre of the eucharist. With Paul, the evangelical proclaims the death of the Lord until he comes. This atoning salvation is what the church feeds on, what constantly enables her to come into the presence of God and make her own response and pledge of dedication. The objective finished redemption is the focus of the celebration, this elicits the praise of the redeemed.

The 'once-for-all' character of the sacrifice of Calvary therefore features prominently in evangelical eucharistic theology. Following the argument in the epistle to the Hebrews, it is held that Christ's atoning sacrifice consummated all the Old Testament sacrifices in a unique, unrepeatable high priestly self-offering. This cosmic spiritual act forms the subject for the sacrament of the Lord's Supper; this is proclaimed sacramentally in the way Jesus ordained, after the manner of his celebration of the passover before he died. Jesus interpreted his death in the tradition of the covenant rite of passover, by breaking bread and drinking poured wine, specifically speaking of the new covenant and echoing Isaiah's self-giving suffering servant whose life was poured out for many.

Evangelical interpretation upholds the primacy of atonement at the Communion. It is the fruits of Jesus' sacrifice on which the church feeds. The body and the blood refer to a death, to a life poured out to death so that new life might begin.

The elements of bread and wine refer to the broken body and the spilt blood, they are separated in the fact of death. This point can be found restated time and again in evangelical ecclesiology. For Bishop Moule the 'ruling fact' is

> 'that the Lord's Supper stands in immediate, indissoluble connexion with His *Death;* that is the Bread is the Body not under aspect, but as "given", being given, yielded up for sacrifice "for us"; that the Wine is the Blood not under *any* aspect, but as "shed", being shed, "for us", as the Blood of the covenant.'[125]

Litton argues that 'As far as Christ in His human nature is concerned, what is present in the Eucharist is not Himself but the *fact,* future at the institution, but on the eve of its accomplishment, of the atonement effected by his death on the cross, and the *continued virtue* of that atonement to be appropriated by faith.'[126] The gospel of Christ 'and him crucified', focuses the classic evangelical view of the eucharist. What is primarily commemorated is the decisive act of the atoning death of the risen Lord for the church. It is this for which the church gives thanks. As she feeds on Christ in her heart by faith with thanksgiving, she partakes of his resurrection life, sacramentally.

The whole drama of the eucharist is consciously celebrated in the presence of the risen Christ among his people. But what is actually commemorated is the terrible, yet joyous, fact of life-giving atonement, an act in the past yet transcending time, the unique sacrifice needing no repetition. The central categories are those of sin and grace, pardon and regeneration. Just as for Paul we are baptized in Christ's death that we rise with his new life, so it is in the holy communion.

Tiller makes clear a distinction of evangelical eucharistic doctrine: 'In both baptism and the Lord's Supper the relationship to justification by faith is the same, but there is a difference with regard to sanctification in the Spirit.'[127] He means that the once-for-all declaration of pardon is signified by both sacraments in their different ways as the same fact of salvation. But as regards the process of becoming actually more holy in the Christian life, 'Baptism is a sacrament of birth; the Lord's Supper of nourishment and growth.'[128] The church receives her spiritual nourishment sacramentally at the Lord's Supper.

Receiving, rather than offering, reflects the order of grace and faith. Just as the evangelical Anglican argues against the Baptist that baptism is not primarily signalling the faith and dedication of the candidate, so he argues against his Anglo-Catholic brethren the very same point as the the eucharist. The church's responsive dedication is not the focus of the covenant rite. The sacrament of the eucharist, as of baptism, is about thankfully receiving from God, not presenting the faith and commitment of the church to God. 'We are indeed partakers of Christ's sacrifice, but partakers only in the *benefits* that flow from it, not in the *making* of it. Our self-offering is not part of Christ's self-offering, but a grateful response to his prior act.'[129]

(ii) Feeding in the heart by faith with thanksgiving

'God has sent the Spirit of his Son into our hearts, crying Abba, Father!' wrote Paul to the Galatians (Gal. 4:6), revealing the apostolic teaching on the shape of our knowledge of God, a trinitarian fulfilment of the covenant. This pattern explains the shape of the feeding at the eucharist. The Holy Spirit brings Christ into our hearts, 'in, with and under' the elements of broken bread and red wine. The elements provide the sacramental focus through which Christ brings his regenerating life afresh into our faithful hearts, by his Spirit. The Holy Spirit acts personally upon and in people, through rather than in impersonal elements. The bread and wine are Christ and him crucified, but sacramentally. The risen Lord gives his people the benefits of his saving death, himself, sacramentally in the broken bread and red wine.

In the eating and drinking, the whole church celebrates the eucharist, the sacramental climax of receiving grace. All counter movements, from the church to God, by way of offering of Christ's sacrifice to God afresh, are removed in favour of the 'one way street' of grace, grace with an eternally secure well-spring in Christ and his work. The church's sacrifice is that of thanks and praise for the mighty saving act of the suffering servant. Lightfoot puts the position exactly: 'In the Apostolic writings we find the terms "offering", "sacrifice", applied to certain conditions and actions of the Christian life. These sacrifices or offerings are described as spiritual. They consist of praise, of faith, of almsgiving, of the devotion of the body, of the conversion of unbelievers, and the like.'[130] The BCP, capturing the reformed view, situates talk of the church's responsive sacrifice of dedication *after* the eucharistic eating and drinking, after the sacramental reception of grace, unlike the ASB.

There is no question, for the evangelical Anglican, of Christ being absent until the opportunity for receiving the eucharist, nor of Christ's presence in a superior way in the reception of the elements. Sacramentally, in obedience to the word of the Lord, the evangelical appropriates the grace of Christ afresh. The sealing of the gift of the gospel needs to be met with worship and faith, not with indifference or contempt, which attracts the judgement of the Lord. Here the evangelical is quick to disown the idea that faith creates grace. He simply wishes to insist on the fact that grace, freely won and given, must be accepted. Once again the evangelical doctrine sees itself in tune with a broadly biblical covenant theology, in particular claiming Pauline precedent, as exemplified in 1 Corinthians 10.

One currently debated point is whether children of the covenant, baptized accordingly, should be denied the covenant meal. Theological consistency may be said to require this, and perhaps a return to the initial passover origins might encourage it. Counter arguments press the need for personal faith and understanding, which young children may lack. Confirmation, another controversial area, now tends to be regarded as the moment when the person takes responsibility in the church and is commissioned for service.

(iii) Pastoral leadership and Holy Communion

The minister at the sacraments, of baptism or the eucharist, will be the pastoral leader, or a pastoral leader, of the local community. That he be ordained to the presbyterate is a condition because this signifies the position of pastoral leadership, not because it signifies that the priest has a special capacity to confer grace through the sacraments. The eucharist expresses and sacramentally bestows the grace of the great High Priest who has passed into the heavens; the ministry is not a sacrificing priesthood making offerings to God, even the offering repeated of Calvary. But the interests of good order in the local church mean that duly authorized ministers should lead at the covenant meal.

Evangelicals at this point raise questions of ecclesiology for the whole Church of England. If bishops can license lay readers to preach the word, what is to prevent this form of authorization for ministering at the eucharist? Evangelical ecclesiology guards the ministry of the word very jealously, and theologically the sacrament expresses the gospel, is a form of the saving word. If the word can be given by a properly tested person in the congregation, why not the sacrament? Biblically the administration of the sacraments has a low profile to say the least: Paul seems to think baptizing a not very significant task. This question presses very hard when a priest is absent and a newly ordained stranger to the parish has to come in to preside, when a seasoned lay person with a longstanding record of pastoral leadership, is available. The question also presses hard in view of the lack of an absolute restriction on ministering baptism, when a midwife, for example, can do this in emergency. More radically, there seems little theological rationale for the evangelical to limit the argument, for permitting presidency to licensed lay readers, to men. Why not allow a woman on a leadership team to minister at communion: certainly if she is allowed to preach? The pastoral orientation of the evangelical view of the presbyterate logically opens up possibilities for declericalizing the church and allowing women's ministry a higher profile. Two thousand years of tradition, however, need to be counterbalanced with this argument.

5. Criticism of evangelical Anglican ecclesiology

A. THE STATUS OF CHURCH STRUCTURE

Evangelical Anglicans come under criticism from the right hand and the left, from the Roman and the Baptist wings. Roman and Anglo-Catholicism, as well as Eastern Orthodoxy, regard the evangelical Anglican view of the church as lacking in episcopal apostolicity. The notion that the episcopacy is fundamentally a second order doctrine makes the classical Anglican view less than fully catholic and apostolic, a child of the Reformation rather than one of the historic episcopal bodies. The episcopal structure has ceased to be part of the very being of the church and is merely functional.

The evangelical Anglican, it is argued, having watered down the vital church-defining function of the episcopacy, has no way of recognizing the true church in the world. Ecclesial bodies without bishops are acknowledged as true catholic and apostolic churches, the test being the preached word and the gospel sacraments. To leave the external order of the church defined in terms only of the proclamation of the faith by word and sacrament, bolstered by a succession of the ministry of the word, makes for a chaotic picture and for innumerable legitimate splinterings of the fabric of the church. This is precisely the problem which bore in upon Newman as he surveyed the Church of England with ever more jaundiced gaze, prior to going to Rome. But he saw also that episcopacy itself had not solved the issue of recognition of the true church: episcopal schism was very possible on Anglican terms, Tractarian or Evangelical. But the point comes home all the more sharply in the case of the evangelical Anglican, for whom commitment to God's word, in the widest sense, forms the most basic test of a church. Evangelicals, after Hooker, deny that the New Testament provides a firm blueprint for a fixed church order, while their critics deny that the doctrines of salvation found in Paul constitute a binding blueprint. Evangelical Anglicans rejoice in the conclusions of ARCIC 2 on justification and sanctification, yet are very uneasy over much of ARCIC 1.

Here the Baptist and independent evangelicals, in the shoes of the Radical Reformation, enter the fray to ask the Anglican why, given the appeal to the Pauline principle of faith, grace and the Holy Spirit, there is so little attempt to decide between those with real faith and those who are not true believers. Why is sanctification and holiness of life not examined more closely, and why is justification with free pardon because of the atonement so exclusively dominant as the excuse for slackness of discipline and spiritual progress? The Baptist evangelical and the Roman Catholic here join hands in their close identification of the spiritual with the visible church. The failure of the mainline Reformation tradition to take the visible aspect seriously, as itself spiritual, leads to slackness in churchmanship and in spirituality. The Baptist evangelical tradition, for example, sees sanctification, for which the outer and the inner cannot remain apart, a sadly neglected emphasis among Anglican evangelicals. Also the Baptist evangelical will accuse the Anglican of failing to uphold the truth in keeping loyalty with experimental bishops who deny central tenets of the faith.

B. AUTHORITY

The beleaguered Anglican evangelical has recourse to the 'judicious Hooker' and the principle of levels of authority. The scripturally clear gospel of Christ must be central, with the sacraments deriving from that. Leave to God the things that are God's, to the church the things that are the church's, bearing in mind that the church is more than merely the present moment in her history. Disagreeing with Rome and the Radical Reformation tradition, the Anglican evangelical refuses to make spiritual declarations on things permitting legitimate variation. This allows recognition of the great church in many denominations, however distorted and unclear some may be.

Liberal critics reject the evangelical claim that the New Testament must be the normative norm. Rather than being God's interpretation of Jesus, it is a reflection of the state of early church belief and practice in picture form. Liberal catholicism denies that the canon can function over against the living tradition. Sykes[131] queries the distinction between gospel fundamentals and ecclesiastical accessories, asking, with Newman, who is to say what is secondary. The evangelical goes with Barth here, affirming that the central thrust of the New Testament is clear, that it even gives examples showing how the apostolic church worked out its priorities, in situations of division, by way of utterly fundamental gospel principles.

C. CHRIST AND THE CHURCH

This ecclesiology interprets the visible, historic community in terms of covenant with Christ present to the believer. Is this a sufficient view of the church as a body, a collective whole, 'in Christ'? Evangelical doctrine stresses 'Christ in us' but struggles with the more corporate idea of being in Christ. It focuses on the cosmic act of Christ and sharing in the atonement-resurrection event, rather than on the life of Christ somehow present in all aspects of the church. It is strong on 'act', weaker on 'being'. The higher churchmen and the free church conservative evangelicals maintain more strongly the sense of being the end-time community of the Spirit, with the commitment to the church body that entails. This may be unfair, but perhaps Eduard Schweitzer can help us make the point. He says that in the New Testament we can see two lines of ecclesiology; 'One is characterized quite early by credal formulae in which the Church looks back to the vital elements of the cross and the resurrection. . . . The other is shown by formulations in which the Church looks "upwards" to the Lord. . . . This line is characterized by the incarnation and exaltation.'[132] The evangelical Anglican stands in the former tendency and may need to ensure the latter is not neglected. Ramsey would echo this point. Regaining a hold on adoption into Christ must be an evangelical priority in order to stress Christ in the body as a whole, and the church as no merely *optional* aid to individual spiritual life.

It has been remarked that to focus on the atonement and redemption, as undoubtedly evangelical thought does, is at root man-centred. Concern primarily for the forgiveness of sin by grace causes an inwardness and gloomy focus on self, and an insufficient sense of worship of God for God's intrinsic worth. Or, to put the criticism in another way, to focus on the work of Christ and his benefits so much as to distance the person of Christ, is a danger evangelical doctrine risks. Sin and salvation in Christ form the first concern of evangelical faith; the church exists to bring people to a saving knowledge of God. If this is man-centred, insufficiently religious, then the evangelical is content to say that without the redemption he is not able to focus on God; his natural capacity fails and he remains dependent on grace. Evangelical spirituality knows of no 'spiritual masters' or experts who get beyond this grace. They are obstinately content to glory in the cross, however crude that may seem to more sophisticated and mystical interpretations of the faith.

D. MINISTRY AND SACRAMENTS

Evangelical Anglicanism has had recent difficulty in holding the balance between the leadership of the minister, and 'every member ministry' of the whole church. The presbyterate has been seen in an over-individualistic way and needs to capitalize on the team idea as a model to the church. Ramsey's critique of the reformed doctrine that the ministry seems to have a rather 'policeman' function, harrying the flock with the stick of the word, also has some truth. How is the minister to foster, to stand for, the indwelling permanent presence of the Lord amidst the church? Forsyth's teaching of the ministry standing for redemption and regeneration may be important here. Christ is present in his royal priesthood, the whole body, not just in a punctiliar way coming and going with acts of repentance. Again adoption needs stressing; although the church sins she is still the church.

The fact of being an established church affects the character of the Church of England, and evangelicals tend to be easier about this than Anglo-Catholics, whose movement began with Keble's Assize sermon protesting at state involvement. Evangelical Anglicans, for whom the outward and visible structures are secondary, can aquiesce in the monarch being the 'supreme governor' of the Church of England. The House of Commons in the past has served the evangelical cause well in stopping high church legislation. The pastoral system of the local clergyman gives an accepted place to the minister. This has great advantages, but must water down the *eschatological* feel of the evangelical Anglican ministry and churchmanship. The church is in the world and part of the world, perhaps insufficiently against the world? Anglicans gain a breadth and accessibility with their warm charitable circumference, but lose out on what their free church evangelicals have in the sense of being called very much out of the world as a minority of the elect.

This point carries over into the sacraments, where western individualism needs correction and the sense of being the end-time family of God, in Christ, needs stressing. 'Fundamentally the Supper is not there for the individual. It is given to the Community.'[133] Forsyth also stresses the corporate focus of sacraments, but the western church of all persuasions fails here, and evangelicals need particularly to learn it. Here they have allowed the theological agenda to be dominated by their theological oppponents. Paul uses sacramental teaching to stress community in Christ and to draw out the ethical implications for the individual as a member of the body. On the other hand, evangelicals tend to be very much people of corporate prayer meetings and group activities apart from set liturgical occasions, and this is where they must be recognized as having a high view of the visible people of God.

Evangelical Anglican doctrines of the sacraments are criticized from right and left as either failing to deliver grace in the actual elements or sufficiently to test the reality of faith: both see receptionism, with Quick, as divorcing spiritual reality and outward sign.[134]

E. ALL THE KING'S MEN

A group of reformed Canadian writers criticize all the churches, evangelicals in particular, for failing to be the church in the world, for being too cultically complacent.[135] The churchman is the church at his or her place of work in the world. The body of Christ exists not only as the Christians worship on Sundays, like bees converged, humming and well structured, in the hives. Evangelicalism can become in effect pietism, failing to be the body of Christ beyond the institutional church, failing to be concerned to witness to the world and to get into the structures of every area of human life, from politics to the arts. Here is a particularly deep critique of evangelical ecclesiology.

'The Identity of Christianity' is not simply a question of a dialectic between personal prayer and public liturgical worship, as Sykes concludes:[136] it is the saving reality of the royal priesthood transforming the world to approximate more closely to the kingdom of God. This line of critique compels evangelicals take up the creation aspect of the biblical message and to integrate salvation and church with it. The church is not so much a cultic sacrament to the world as the prophetic transformer of the world, living out the word in the sinful world to reclaim it for the creator. Again the criticism raised is whether the evangelical is biblical enough, or too much controlled by the ecclesiastical agendas of the past. Evangelical Anglicans, the laity especially, need to believe their doctrine that they are the covenant people of God, in the world and for the world.

Conclusion

Evangelical Anglican ecclesiology hinges on the categories of word and covenant; authority, structure, ministry and sacraments flow from them. Interpretation of the family of God goes back into ancient Israel and understands the living church as in this flow of promise, consummated in Christ. The centre-circumference model predominates, but with a clear complementary view of apostolic foundational gospel and canon at the base of the church for her teaching. The notion of growth and evolution works not in terms of developing binding *structures* so much as of a history of the covenant faithful down the generations.

The church now listens, rather than sees, as the way of knowing and following her Lord; she listens and then speaks her word of worship and witness. The greatest danger is that the evangelical, confident in being declared right with God, will only listen, and fail to act; will neglect the gospel in social and political life. This has led to a distinct ecclesiological reaction, to which we now turn.

END NOTES TO CHAPTER 4

1. Ephesians 5:31–3; 1 Cor. 7.
2. Article 18.
3. 1 Corinthians 10.
4. *The Household of God* SCM, London, 1953 p. 45.
5. Romans 9:4.
6. Newbigin op. cit. p. 47.
7. See Articles 19 to 21.
8. *The Principles of Theology* Longmans, London, 1930 p. 271.
9. *The Great Acquittal* ed. Gavin Reid, Fount, London, 1980 p. 31.
10. op. cit. pp. 27–8.
11. *Knowing God* Hodder and Stoughton, London, 1973 p. 224.
12. Galatians 4:4.
13. *The Forgotten Father* Hodder and Stoughton, London, 1987.
14. Romans 8:15.
15. Romans 8.
16. Galatians 4.
17. *Knowing God* p. 226.
18. *Outlines of Christian Doctrine* Hodder and Stoughton, London, 1902 p. 102.
19. ibid. p. 103.
20. ibid. p. 103.
21. G. Aulen's *Christus Victor*, SPCK, London, 1931 (1970), gives a vivid account of this theology.
22. Romans 8:3.
23. John 16:7.
24. *Evangelical Anglican Identity*, Latimer House, Oxford, 1980 p. 15.
25. ibid. pp. 15–16.
26. ibid. p. 16.
27. ibid. p. 16.
28. L. Newbigin *The Household of God*, SCM, London, 1953.
29. A. M. Ramsey *The Gospel and the Catholic Church* p 197.
30. A. Dulles *The Catholicity of the Church* Clarendon Press, Oxford, 1985 p. 40.
31. ibid. p. 40.
32. *Ephesian Studies* Hodder and Stoughton, London, 1900 p. 54.
33. Jeremiah 31:33–4.
34. *Introduction to Dogmatic Theology* 3rd edition, ed. H. G. Grey, Robert Scott, London, 1912 p. 363.
35. 1 Corinthians 15:45.
36. 2 Corinthians 4:17.
37. Hebrews 12:1.
38. *Ecclesiastical Polity* Book III chapter 1.9 Hooker's *Works* Clarendon
    Press, Oxford, 1890.
39. *The Church in the Theology of the Reformers* Marshall, Morgan and Scott, Basingstoke, 1981 ch. 5.
40. Avis op. cit. p. 116.

41. ibid.
42. S. Sykes *The Identity of Christianity* SPCK, London, 1984 p. 106.
43. Article 19.
44. John 17:21.
45. 17:20.
46. *Ephesian Studies* op. cit. pp. 184–5.
47. *On The Thirty Nine Articles* Paternoster Press, Exeter, 1988 p. 93.
48. *Fundamentalism* SCM, London, revised edition 1981 p. 288.
49. Fairbairn *Christ in Modern Theology* 2nd edition, London, Hodder and Stoughton, 1893 p. 505.
50. Hebrews ch. 1:1.
51. Romans 9:4.
52. *Introduction to Dogmatic Theology* 3rd edition, ed. H. G. Grey, Robert Scott, London, 1912 pp. 13–14.
53. Revelation 3:20.
54. *The Work of the Holy Spirit* (1900) Eerdmans, Grand Rapids 1956.
55. ibid. p. 141.
56. ibid.
57. ibid. p. 142.
58. ibid. p. 142.
59. The Doctrine Commission of the Church of England *Believing in the Church* London, SPCK, 1981 p. 74.
60. *The Riddle of the New Testament* Hoskyns and Davey, Faber and Faber, London, 1931,
61. *Introduction to Dogmatic Theology* p. 25.
62. *Interpreting the Bible in theology and the church* The Edwin Mellen Press, Lewiston, New York, 1984 p. 3.
63. Article 20, The Thirty Nine Articles of Religion.
64. *Institutes of the Christian Religion* ed. Battles, Westminster Press, Philadelphia 4, 3.
65. *The Tiller Report* Church of England Information Office, London, 1983.
66. P. T. Forsyth *Church and Sacraments* Independent Press, London 1917.
67. *Book of Common Prayer* Ordering of Priests.
68. M. Green *Freed to Serve* Hodder and Stoughton, London, 1983 p. 37.
69. B. Milne *Know the Truth* IVP, Leicester, 1982 p. 226.
70. N. T. Wright *Evangelical Identity; the connection between Bible, Gospel and Church* Latimer House, Oxford, 1980 pp. 32–3.
71. *St John* James Clark, London, 1880 (1958) p. 295.
72. ibid.
73. ibid.
74. Moule *Outlines* p. 225.
75. Moule *Outlines* p. 225–6.
76. 'The Christian Ministry', in *Dissertations on the Apostolic Age* Macmillan, London, 1892 p. 236.
77. op. cit. p. 144.
78. op. cit. p. 236.
79. ibid.
80. op. cit. p. 145.
81. ibid.

82. op. cit. p. 145.
83. ibid.
84. *Church Order in the New Testament* SCM, London, 1969 p. 219.
85. *Outlines* pp. 119–220.
86. Partners in Mission Report *To a Rebellious House* Church House, London, 1981.
87. *The Form and Structure of the Visible Unity of the Church* unpublished paper p. 12.
88. *Freed to Serve* p. 48.
89. ibid. pp. 93–4.
90. ibid.
91. Thirty Nine Articles of Religion.
92. E. Schweizer *Church Order in the New Testament* SCM, London, 1969.
93. op. cit. p. 147.
94. See *The Memory of The Christian People*, E. Hoornaert, Burns and Oates, Tunbridge, 1989 pp. 187–8.
95. op. cit. 154.
96. ibid.
97. ibid. p. 155.
98. ibid. 193.
99. ibid.
100. *The Reunion of the Church* SCM London 1949.
101. *The Church in the Theology of the Reformers* p. 121.
102. Moule op. cit. p. 231.
103. op. cit. p. 39.
104. ibid. 398–9.
105. *Church Order in the New Testament* p. 211.
106. op. cit. p. 239.
107. *The Doctrine of the Sacraments* N. Dimock, 1908, Longmans Green, London p. 19.
108. *Baptism in the Book of Common Prayer* Fellowship of Evangelical Churchmen 1974.
109. Moule op. cit. 242.
110. Calvin *Institutes* 4, 14, 17.
111. op. cit. p. 20.
112. op. cit. pp. 20–1.
113. ibid.
114. *The Great Aquittal* ed. Gavin Reid, Fount, London, 1980 p. 33.
115. Galatians 3:26, 27.
116. Motyer op. cit. p. 25.
117. Romans 6:3, 4.
118. Romans 6:11.
119. *The Great Acquittal* p. 35.
120. Motyer op. cit. p. 19.
121. P. Marcel *The Biblical Doctrine of Infant Baptism* James Clark, Cambridge, 1953 (1981).
122. Dimock op. cit. 48.
123. Moule *Outlines* op. cit. p. 246.
124. Tiller in *The Great Aquittal* ed. G. Reid op. cit. pp. 56–7.
125. Dimock op. cit. 237–8.
126. op. cit. p. 474.

127. *The Great Aquittal* p. 57.
128. ibid.
129. M. Green op. cit. p. 78.
130. Lightfoot op. cit. p. 229.
131. *The Identity of Christianity* p. 106.
132. op. cit. p. 165.
133. O. Weber *Foundations of Dogmatics* trans. D. Guder, Eerdmans, Grand Rapids, 1983 vol. 2 p. 642.
134. O. C. Quick *The Christian Sacraments* Nisbet, London, 1932 p. 213.
135. *Will All The King's Men* A. De Graaff et al Wedge publishing, Toronto, 1972.
136. op. cit. pp. 282–3. Rawlinson chillingly cites Wakeman's criticism of evangelical Anglicanism: 'no sooner had Evangelicalism become popular than it ceased to produce great men. . . . Their best men devoted themselves to mission work, like John Venn, or set up proprietory chapels in fashionable watering places. . . . They failed to lead the Church just when it most needed leadership.' *The Church of England and the Church of Christ* Longmans Green, London, 1930 p. 57.

5

FAITH IN THE CITY: RADICAL ECCLESIOLOGY

1. Anglicanism, church and society

A. CHURCH AND STATE

The Church of England established herself under the monarchy and parliament as the national church. The Godly magistrate, a reformation concept necessitated by the break from Papal political and spiritual power, was acknowledged as important for the church and not only for society. Secular society did not exist, and the lay leadership had to have a part in the church's deliberations. The sanctions of the law to maintain order and restrain chaos were part of the scheme of things under God.

This religious settlement readjusted the interweaving of state and church. Formally the 'supreme governor' of the Church of England is the monarch. She is anointed and crowned by the Archbishop of Canterbury, so consecrating her to Godly government. The highest office in the land, therefore, is committed to God and is invested with a spiritual and moral authority, rightly above party politics.

Theologically, God relates to the state as well as the church: 'Let every person be subject to the governing authorities,' wrote Paul to the Romans, 'for there is no authority except from God, and those that exist have been instituted by God. Therefore he who resists the authorities resists what God has appointed, and will incur judgement. For rulers are not terror to good conduct but to bad . . . he who is in authority . . . is God's servant' (Romans 13:1ff.). The Church of England takes up this positive Pauline strand of teaching by recognizing the supreme and constitutionally Christian authority in society as having an office in the church as well as the society. Society is sacramentally or symbolically being treated as if it were church, church as if it were society. This arrangement differs from that of the Church of Scotland, the established church North of the border, which is Presbyterian and of which the monarch is an esteemed member, rather than formal governor. Other members of the Anglican Communion, of course, have episcopal headship and no link with the British Crown.

Some relationship must be worked out between church and state. Paul's injunctions had to be qualified when the authorities of Rome turned on the church in savage persecution under several emperors, who earned themselves the label of anti-Christ, agents of the devil rather than of God, enemies of the people of the Holy God, in the book of Revelation. The rise of Nazism badly found out all churches of all polities, but the Lutherans were in the position of having bishops imposed who were definite Nazis, as a result of the system whereby the state controlled the appointment of bishops. Barth's criticism was unrelenting. The church is the church and must not be controlled by the state. This is the Reformed approach of a more independent attitude, as opposed to Lutheran and Anglican polity, although the Church of England procedures are designed now to give only formal involvement to the Crown in choice of bishops.

The Church of England, while having the closest possible relationship with the authority of the land, has had a record of failing to match this formal link with her ministry to the poor. Reformed with the aim of providing common prayer, of encouraging regular communion, of setting forth the true and lively word in ordinary language, by the eighteenth century the church had grown largely to neglect the common man and woman. When a ministry to them arose through Methodism, Anglicanism failed to embrace it. At grass-roots level the working classes were never systematically catered for in a sufficient way.

B. EVANGELICAL AND TRACTARIAN PATTERNS OF SOCIAL ACTION

The history of the rise of the industrial revolution does report some significant church action for the poor. The evangelical Anglican tradition can point to instances of their spirituality working out into practical measures. The small, late eighteenth century lay group, the Clapham Sect, proved to be an important

Christian impetus to social legislation. A particular piece of economic structural change of the time was fought for by Wilberforce in the Commons, eventually abolishing slavery. Lord Shaftesbury, in the Victorian era, from similar evangelical motivation, promoted vital Factory Acts to prevent appalling abuse of humanity. The evangelical theology of bringing the kingdom into these areas is, and was, that of encouraging the faithful to be 'salt and light' in the world, after Matthew 5 in particular. But the Clapham Sect and evangelical theology generally often attracted the criticism of being 'other worldly' in attitude to the social problems of the poor, of not grappling with the problem of what the gospel has to say about society and industry. 'The Evangelicals dismissed the social problem by denying the reality of it, as so many Christians have done, with less excuse, since their day,' judges Maurice Reckitt.[1] The National Evangelical Anglican Assembly at Nottingham, 1977, stated a commitment to 'putting flesh' on the gospel in urban areas and identifying with the underprivileged, with a dose of repentance for complacent attitudes,[2] although at the start of the conference this topic was originally scheduled as a fringe interest.

The interdenominational assembly of evangelicals, the Lausanne Congress of 1974, resolved to commit evangelicals to social justice as the outworking of the gospel in the world, and it expressed repentance over evangelical failure in this area in this century. 'Here too we express our penitence both for our neglect and for sometimes having regarded evangelism and social concern as mutually exlusive. Although reconciliation with man is not reconciliation with God, nor is social action evangelism, nor is political liberation salvation, nevertheless we affirm that evangelism and socio-political involvement are both parts of our Christian duty.'[3] Anglican evangelicalism theologically echoes this approach, its traditional stance, to the problems of deprivation.

The Anglo-Catholic tradition developed a strong 'incarnational' theology of the priesthood living and working in parishes of very poor people, a tradition at its height with the work of Headlam and Scott Holland, who sought to appropriate socialism for Anglo-Catholicism. London's East End remains a testimony to the willingness of such celibate priests to serve in areas where often others would not go. Theologically this strand of Tractarianism developed the idea of incarnation, the sacrificial dwelling among the needy, identifying with their needs and being a sacrament of the incarnate God caring for the lost and the hungry. This tradition, never as shy of left-wing politics as the evangelical, welcomed the Jarrow marchers in the 1920s into church halls for food and shelter, for example.

Evangelical theological instincts stress the atonement and the cross of Christ as a way of discipleship, and this has fuelled important social action by the church, rather than a social theology. But the theology of the incarnation also seems to be essential, especially in seeking to frame a social theology, as opposed to motivating individuals into working for change. It was just this enterprise that engaged the passionate concern of the next subject for brief consideration, who, although not a Tractarian himself, has influenced the Anglo-Catholic tradition heavily.

C. MAURICE AND CHRISTIAN SOCIALISM

The most distinctive name in Anglican theology for developing a social ecclesiology is that of F.D. Maurice of the mid-nineteenth century. Maurice developed a wide perspective, yet one he sought to keep focused in the central tenets of the faith. He taught that Christ, the second Adam, was the head of all humanity and that the distinction between the church and the world amounted to that between humanity not worshipping God and humanity which did. The 'world' was a principle on which men were naturally apt to centre their lives, from which they needed to be turned to the true heart of all things, the Word made flesh. This principle of the world exists also in the church, which witnesses against it for the light. People need to be told what they truly are, sons and daughters of God. The church's task is to tell them and incorporate them by the sign of baptism, which tells of God's grace already within.

The church knows that all humanity is a great brotherhood, all related to the new head, all constituted at the deepest level by this real bond of kinship. Humanity consists in a great catholic body, the church knows this and is the first fruits, the sign to all who do not yet count themselves inside this fact. The natural social groupings are not to be ignored from this scheme of humanity. Nature must not be split from grace. Family and nation, therefore, are proper ways of living and learning this brotherhood. This, after all, was the pattern of divine self-revelation, working through individuals, families, clans and tribes, finally widening out into the universal kinship shown and brought about through Christ. National life does not mean secular life, it is God-given and to be lived out in the spirit of cooperation, it guards against exclusive Protestant sectarianism on the one hand, and against the tyranny of Pontifical world dominion on the other. In terms of church polity, the national church is inclusive, not sectarian, and it is free from domination by imperial spiritual and temporal power, as wielded from Rome.[4]

The national government arranges the externals of society, the church supplies the inner resources reflected in the national institutional decisions. Catholicism stands for the whole church, protestantism for the national distinctiveness of each. The signs and witnesses of catholicism were those of the creeds, sacraments, historic ministry of the episcopate, and the scriptures. The church must be acknowledged, before parties within the church, for the good of the whole national community.

Maurice held a relational ideal of society as bonded together in the manner of the medieval community rather than the modern individualistic 'contracting in' social pattern, '*Gemeinschaft*' rather than '*Gesellschaft*' in modern sociological terms. But he grounded his social theory in classical theology of God first and foremost, and sought his justification from scripture. Ramsey, in his book on Maurice,[5] stresses that the Trinity was particularly important in this respect for Maurice's social thought. He worked this out in terms of the life of the triune God. The Trinity includes an aspect of self-subordination, revealed in Christ historically, and this must be lived out in cooperative social brotherhood. The life of God, reflected in the created order, is a reality of charity, trinity in unity, and this grounds cooperation as the basis of all human life at its truest. On this theological basis Maurice worked with Ludlow and Kingsley at pioneering efforts with 'Christian Socialism'. He wrote to Ludlow that his mission was theological, 'to show that economy and politics . . . must have a ground beneath themselves, that society is not to be made anew by arrangements of ours, but is to be regenerated by finding the law and ground of its order and harmony, the only secret of its existence, in God.'[6]

Archbishop William Temple stands in this tradition of social theology. He was not content simply to denounce what was evil in industrial society and to regard the church as called out from an ungodly world. 'Temple, possessing as he did a doctrine of the State as well as the Church, was more ready as a social thinker to trace the lines of a divine order of society, and as the ground for this he turned increasingly to the concept of Natural Law. He saw Natural Law as giving the key to the proper functions of State, family, property and trade. . . . Believing in a divine order he had a high conception of the Church's role to permeate society with the right conviction of its possibility,'[7] and this led him to see potential in the establishment of the Church of England.

This distinctive strand of Anglican social thought has primarily developed in the Anglo-Catholic soil, the seeds having been sown by Maurice. Incarnation and Trinity lie close to its heart. How should the church regard itself in view of the continuing social and economic pressures experienced by very large numbers of poor people in cities up and down the land? The issue of what the church is, let alone what her mission is in this context, remains alive and has been addressed by a major and controversial Anglican report, *Faith in the City*.[8]

2. Faith in the city

This report, 'ACUPA', analyses the conditions prevailing in England's inner city areas. These have become centres of population which are poor, with much unemployment, crime and youth alienation. Socially and economically there is 'multiple deprivation'. The church, of any persuasion, fails to reach more than one per cent of the population on average. The massive problem and scale of human misery revealed itself to a largely middle class Church of England, together with proposals for a fresh way of looking at the church and her presence. The particular chapter of the document relevant to the discussion of ecclesiology is chapter 3 'Theological Priorities', prefaced by a quotation: 'The Church seems to offer very little to people in the inner city, but surely Christianity has a lot to say?'[9]

The obvious point that the church is called to help the poor and those in need is made; charity must be enjoined on all Christians. But this is just one way of helping individuals. Faced with the scale of deprivation, the church also has to face issues of the structuring of society, issues of economic policy and decisions over such worldly matters as taxation. The individual must remain a focus for the church, each person is precious. But also the structural questions involving political choices cannot be ducked by the church. This is a more difficult and threatening proposition since it will involve sacrificial choices which may reduce advantages presently enjoyed by the more prosperous, in order to transfer more resources to the less well-off.

ACUPA, then, rejects private Christianity which imagines that the faith is a matter of the soul with God, not bound up with the reality of society around. No such dualism can be allowed for the church, which is flesh and blood and lives in genuine communities with genuine conditions. Although ACUPA does not use it, the Marxist thought that religion is the opium of the people, might well have been brought in at this point of the argument! 'We have seen areas where unemployment, poor housing, and the threat of criminal violence have reached such proportions that they are like a disease: they so dominate people's thinking and feeling that no presentation of the gospel is possible which does not relate to these material deprivations.'[10]

The economic and social structures must therefore be addressed, since evil lies in these as well as in the hearts of men and women. All societies legislate to ensure that the successful and wealthy do not over accumulate property so as to reduce all others to penury. The Old Testament notably provides for the stranger, the fatherless and the widow. Although no fixed blueprint can be reached, central principles must obtain. The notion of wealth creation cannot be absolutized if it means reductions for many to a low level of life. Efficiency, likewise, cannot become a rigid criterion for what is right in industry, since it can infringe human worth and dignity. The cost of efficiency also needs fair consideration, and simply to reject people as redundant and make them bear this burden of streamlining flies in the face of the Christian ethic of human worth. The consumer economy, presenting a fantastic array of desirable commodities before people by powerful media, cannot be the mainspring of a healthy society. Pure competition, as unfettered as possible, seems to offend the Christian way of looking at humanity and cannot serve as the engine of life together. ACUPA sounds the warning that society in the inner city is becoming too poor and degraded as a result of social and political choices. The church is called upon to question many political assumptions in the interests of the poor nationally.

Locally the church is already in the communities of the deprived areas, and is called to foster community among all sorts and conditions of men and women. 'A Christian community is one that is open to and responsible for the whole of the society in which it is set, and proclaims its care for the weak, its solidarity with all, and its values which lie beyond the mere satisfaction of material needs.'[11] The church herself must show that she is really a community accepting all, so as to enable people to overcome their sense of alienation from society in which they exist.

The inner city context contains large religious minorities, and the question arises as to the proper attitude of the church to other faiths. ACUPA advocates respectful co-existence and sharing of resources, while ascribing ultimate authority to the claims of Christ. Traditional evangelistic attitudes need revising in terms of dialogue and discovering what we share in the common quest for God.[12]

Theology and training for the ordained ministry need revision in this environment. Traditional theology, it is stated, centring on the study of Bible and traditional doctrine, is too intellectual, ill fitted to inner city people. Theology must begin from experience, from the needs of the poor in particular, and relate this experience to the Bible. The 'liberation theology' of Latin America works out this pattern of a problem-centred approach. Using small groups of people, they can learn how God transforms life in practice and brings about improvement socially. Telling of personal stories and matching these with biblical material, forms an important way of doing theology, 'narrative theology'.

The church, urges ACUPA, must fan into flame the embers of folk religion already present in the majority of the population, however alienated they are from the official church. This must be nurtured informally, not addressed academically, since that would be a culturally alienating process. The ministry in this environment must correspond culturally with the context.

Not claiming to present a blueprint theology of the city, nor of the shape of the church in the inner city, ACUPA has laid out some clear patterns for the church in society and some telling critiques of the *status quo*. It is in the heritage of Maurice in that it stresses the common humanity under God of the whole community, the church serving as a focal point of fellowship and catalyst for hope. Unlike Maurice, however, its *theological* reflection on the situation, as opposed to its *sociological* analysis, is hard to find.

3. 'A servant model'

A. THE FORM OF A SERVANT

The lines traced by ACUPA correspond with those of what Dulles has called 'the servant model' of the church, deriving this title from Harvey Cox's words, 'The church's task in the secular city is to be the *diakonos* of the city, the servant who bends himself to struggle for its wholeness and health.'[13] ACUPA argues that society has a relationship to God the creator, as does the church, and that the two must therefore relate to each other positively and not simply critically. The church comes alongside the world, society, as the Good Samaritan, to help the bruised reed and the dimly burning wick, to bring healing and wholeness and not just on an individual basis. The church in particular must be prepared to be the suffering servant in society, being broken in order to permeate and influence structures for the good of all.

'Church as servant' means that the authoritative aspect of the church diminishes, both in terms of organizational authority and teaching authority. The church must serve, listening and learning humbly from the world. The laity should be released to minister locally in the local idiom of life, the clergy being as little directive as possible. The church should be more responsive to social need, to the local voice.

Here the work of the radical ecclesiologists can convey genuine insight which the more traditionalist view might welcome in terms of the depth of the gospel. Gibson Winter, in his analysis,[14] made the point that the local suburban middle class church, being distant from usual places of work of the members of the congregation, ministered only in the context of their family lives and leisure time. The inner city local church has to ensure that this pattern is broken in its context and rejects this privatization of church life. 'It is not that pastoral concern with people's private and family lives is wrong; but exclusive identification with the private sphere encourages the widespread idea that Christianity is irrelevant to all other areas of man's life and activity.'[15] The fact that the inner city demands gospel involvement through the whole of life reminds the rest of the church of its narrow impact and contentment with marginalization.

Lesslie Newbigin makes this point on the global canvas in charging western Christianity with complacency at being allotted a place by secular society, a place on the margins of things where it can do no harm and affect life as little as possible. This allows the basically individualistic enlightenment anthropocentrism to continue its course of acquisition and suffering, quite unchallenged and unreformed by the gospel. The world is left to the devil. This terrible dualism is far from authentic biblical faith.[16] Church life has to have an impact in and on society, locally and nationally and, Newbigin reminds us, globally. The servant model of the church is getting this message through, with some difficulty, to the churches.

The church must not only allow her practical agenda to be affected, if not controlled, by social needs and tendencies, but she must listen to what God is doing in his creation in her interpretation of the faith. The church must discern what the Spirit says locally and, unavoidably, nationally, according to ACUPA and to this whole family of ecclesiology. Teaching cannot be handed down from the pulpit to be kept and applied; rather God reveals his will equally the other way round, the people, church and secular, will set the theological agenda from their practical concerns.

The theology of Vatican 2 moved official Roman Catholic attitudes along this line in its 'Pastoral Constitution on the Church'. That promotes an optimistic view of human culture outside the institutional church, and encourages a vision of the church as part of the one human family, sharing the general concerns of humanity. Conversation, not rejection, patterns the church's activity with the world, even to the point of dialogue with enemies of the church. 'We include those who oppress the Church and harass her in manifold ways. Since God the Father is the origin and purpose of all men, we are called to be brothers. Therefore if we have been summoned to the same destiny, which is both human and divine, we can and we should work together without violence and deceit in order to build up the world in genuine peace.'[17] Dulles describes the new approach as 'secular-dialogic': 'secular, because the Church takes the world as a properly theological locus, and seeks to operate on the frontier between the contemporary world and the Christian tradition (including the Bible),rather than simply apply the latter as a measure of the former.'[18]

The servant church serves in action and reflection, joining all humanity in the common quest for peace and harmony of life, for a common brotherhood embracing many diversities. Although not as radical as Harvey Cox's ecclesiology, the Vatican 2 servant model agrees with him, and with ACUPA, that 'The Church is first of all a responding community, a people whose task it is to discern the action of God in the world, and to join in his work.'[19] The marks of the true church today cannot be those, for Cox, simply of preaching and sacraments. Proclamation, servanthood, and community replace these, '*kerygma, diaconia* and *koinonia*'; the church appears where these signs appear, 'where tribal and town chauvinism are left behind along with their characteristic mythologies, and a new inclusive human community emerges.'[20] The servant church serves as a kind of catalyst for the brotherhood of humanity, disclosing evils and helping to eradicate and absorb them, or to 'exorcize' them, as Cox puts it. Perhaps the Johannine term for the Holy Spirit, 'paraclete', having a variety of meanings including 'strengthener', 'guide', 'advocate', and 'helper', sums up the type of service urged by this family of ecclesiology.

B. RADICAL SERVANTHOOD

Various degrees of radicalism flow from the servant model in ecclesiology. The Vatican 2 framework remains that of the papal and episcopal structure, whatever contradictions that may involve. ACUPA does not spell out a blueprint for the structure of the church or of society, but readers may assume that the structure of authority in the church remains as the framework for the Anglican community of faith. The lines set out by ACUPA have been taken forward and logically worked out in more thoroughgoing and radical directions by other theologians, notably, but not exclusively, on the protestant side.

As regards ecclesial structures, J. A. T. Robinson, former bishop of Woolwich, argued for the self-destructuring of the church so that she might more truly enter the life of the secular world, a true servant does not live in his own house but in another's. The church therefore must abandon the security of her own structured institutions and exist in the structures of the world. The total self-giving of the visible church's structures for the sake of total servanthood is the logic of this suggestion, a kind of self-emptying or 'kenosis', after Philippians chapter 2, 'taking the form of a servant'.

This reflects the influence of Bonhoeffer and the post-war theology constructed from his writings in his Nazi prison, which has come to be called 'religionless Christianity'. Bonhoeffer, who was finally executed by the Nazis, expressed the view that modern humanity was patently able to function 'as if' God did not exist, and he scorned apologetic that sought to find 'gaps' which necessitated the existence of God. The world has come to the point at which all the gaps have been closed by man, who 'has come of age.' Bonhoeffer regarded religion as a hindrance to God, who was present in society but in powerlessness and weakness, as revealed in Christ. He wrestled with the issue of how to express this religionless Christianity, and felt that 'The religionless man of today must not be asked to become religious first, in order to believe in and follow Christ. Similarly the man who is an inheritor of the religious culture of Christianity can be set free from it by Christ, and liberated for fuller participation in the world.'[21]

The world ought not to be regarded as incomplete without God, and God must not be defined as the completing aspect of the world. The world is the world in completeness, it is autonomous and the religious hypothesis has been ousted. What we are taught to do now is exactly to live as if God did not exist,

> 'And the only way to be honest is to recognize that we have to live in the world *etsi deus non daretur* (as if God were not given or did not exist). And this is what we do see—before God! So our coming of age forces us to a true recognition of our situation vis-a-vis God. God is teaching us that we must live as men who can get along very well without him. The God who is with us is the God who forsakes us (Mark 15:34) . . . God allows himself to be edged out of the world and on to the cross. God is weak and powerless in the world, and that is exactly the way, the only way, in which he can be with us and help us.'[22]

This differentiates the true God from the religious God of power. Discipleship is to enter the life of the world and so participate in the sufferings of God, not religiously, although Bonhoeffer ambiguously seems to reserve a place for the secret disciplines of prayer.

This proposes the radical suggestion that the world, as world, is where God is in powerlessness, while man is present in his technological and industrial strength. To participate in the godless world on its own terms somehow participates in God, who is nevertheless there right in the centre of things and not just in a religious marginal slot as was thought before. God is where mankind is strong as much as where he is weak, and one of the emphases coming through these writings is just that religion tried to reduce humanity to a guilt-ridden, problematic state, whereas Bonhoeffer sees God in the strength and joy of secular life. The church must exist non-religiously, therefore, as did Jesus, who was closer to the godless than the religious. The church is the church only when she exists for others. It should give away all its property to those in need. The clergy should live solely on the free-will offerings of their congregations, or possibly take secular jobs. The church must share in the secular problems of ordinary human life, not dominating but helping and serving. Bonhoeffer seems almost to make the world into the church, creation and history the cathedral of God. Certainly he abolishes the distinction of religion from the secular, church from the world, as strongly as possible. The deep influence of being steeped in Hegel in his early education may perhaps be emerging here, in an unusual form. World spirit or mind permeates in the world, hiddenly united with the spirit of humanity; men serve it unwittingly even, by their everyday participation in the world's developments and advances. Anglican diocesan industrial missions and chaplaincies commonly advocate this type of theology pioneered by suggestions from Bonhoeffer.

C. SIN AS SINNED-AGAINSTNESS

Raymond Fung, a World Council of Churches theologian, in a paper presented to the Anglican Evangelical Assembly, gave his theology of mission along with his personal story. Having worked with an evangelical student organization in Hong Kong he changed his understanding of the gospel message when he began working among very poor slum dwellers on industrial estates. There he found that the misery and lostness of the people did not permit of his former appeal to turn from sin and to Christ. The focus of his ministry was shifted into the view that 'Human lostness is primarily human sinned-againstness'; like Jesus, he saw the people as sheep without a shepherd, lost and helpless.

'Sinned-againstness' in such urban poverty is common ground with all kinds of ethnic groups and ideals, or lack of them. Fung's role became one of fostering community so that by corporate strength some of the exploitative structures might be alleviated and resisted. 'On this common ground, Christians stand with our neighbours, Hindus, Muslims, with people of no faith, to resist the forces of sin against us, to build a human community in a secularized and pluralistic world. The common reality of sinned-againstness makes nonsense of a mission of the privileged to the underprivileged. Christians reach out to others because of shared hurt.'[23] Here is a vision of ministry and mission quite close to ACUPA. Fung regards the non-Christian neighbour as part of the community which forms in order to help one another in the situation of poverty and powerlessness, against the weight of the industrial system.

Fung's understanding of mission aims to cut through the racial and social barriers separating people in their plight, and to offer them the good news that in community each has a responsible place towards making a better social environment in which to live and work. In this venture some will come to faith in Jesus and some will not: 'The task is the building of a human community together with all people of goodwill . . . inviting them into the community of faith. Not all will accept the invitation. They remain our friends and partners in the neighbourhood.'[24] But that does not invalidate the mission which seeks to bring about the kingdom of God on earth, a call with particular impact in the third world and inner cities of the world. The church serves to build an inclusive community with improved conditions to make decent human life possible, she is a sign and an instrument for this activity of fostering God's kingdom on earth. The church's gospel is freedom from sinned-againstness, liberation in the broadest sense. Fung faithfully represents the trend of World Council of Churches theology, reflecting its statements at Uppsala in 1968, and Bangkok in 1973 in particular.

D. LIBERATION THEOLOGY

Fung's paper gives the heart of what is called liberation theology, a general term covering a wide movement with different shades of radicality and orthodoxy. Latin American churchmen especially have developed a far more practically oriented view of church and theology than has been traditionally held. Gutierrez, the Peruvian theologian, insists that proclaiming the kingdom of God must reveal the roots of social injustice and oppression, and that the church must foster awareness ('conscientize') in the people of their state of being oppressed, of being sinned against. In her context of severe injustice the Latin American church must side with the forces of change and revolution which attempt to do away with the old order, even to the extent of supporting armed revolution. Also the church must learn to do away with oppressive ways of governing herself. Gutierrez identifies these emphases with the principles of Vatican 2 that the church is a sacrament of liberation and unity of humanity. The church in Latin America was generally felt to be bolstering the dictatorial regimes which liberationists find to be responsible for the plight of the masses, therefore the new analysis and action proves a major reversal in many ways.

Theology must arise from the practical situation of the people, hence the term 'praxis', in conjunction with the church traditions and biblical text, which will come alive as read with this practical need in mind. The well known interpretation of the Exodus, as a political and social liberation from an unjust oppressor, exemplifies this line of biblical interpretation, which takes the current political situation as the lens through which the interpreter must look. The revelation of God is not something to be known and pondered intellectually, it is to be done, enacted, lived out. It is to be done corporately in order that humanity may move from the current state of division and oppression on to a phase of unity and harmony. The strong influence of Marxist thought emerges plainly, but the shades of opinion vary as to how critically it is accepted and baptized into the church. Most Latin American liberationists would agree that the goal of economic and social harmony needs to be pursued in an ongoing way, as in the Marxist analysis of class struggle against oppressive and divisive powers of resistance.

European theologians well known as committed to the political dimension in theology and church are several. Johannes Metz, a Roman Catholic, probably introduced the concept of 'political theology'. Political theology for Metz displaces the purely private personal religion taken as Christian faith which only encourages the individual to stand apart from the world. Political theology also aims to overcome the purely passive interpretation of current Christianity, which tends to be content in standing by and watching events take their course without actively seeking to influence them. Passivity is as much a choice as positive involvement in the social and political structures.

Political theology for Metz measures all reality in the light of the promised kingdom of God, which has not yet come but toward which the church and the world moves, and this is the great hope of which the church is the sign to the world. Metz is anxious to avoid political theology being defined as a rigid political ideology of some kind, it is rather part of how the church functions: 'Political theology claims to be a basic element in the whole structure of critical theological thinking, motivated by a new notion of theory and practice, according to which all theology must of itself be "practical", oriented to action . . . It is in fact one of the aims of political theology and its society directed thinking to prevent the Church and theology being saddled as it were unwittingly with this or that political ideology.'[25] All theology now must have the formative factor of Christian political impact, the church must conduct herself in the light of society directed thinking compelled by attention to the kingdom of God. Political theology sees everything in the light of the eschatological message of Jesus, which is a critical criterion for church life at all times. The church serves the kingdom, her goal is the kingdom, and she lives as 'the liberating and critical force' of society to this end.

Political theology 'insists that the trial is on, on a capital charge, between the eschatological message of the kingdom of God and any given form of social and political life, in its various historical changes.'[26] The individual relationship to God remains important but 'the central promises of the reign of God in the NT—freedom, peace, justice, reconciliation—cannot be made radically private affairs. They cannot be entirely interiorized and spiritualized . . . they make the invidual free with regard to the political society around him, in the sense of committing him to it in a free critique of it.'[27] Political theology, for Metz, has a very critical function, not wishing to replace or 'undermine a secularized and religiously emancipated society and infiltrate it with "restorative" tendencies.' Instead it 'tries to take this "secularized" world seriously, as the starting point of theology and preaching.'[28] This critical role may flare up into revolutionary proportions, but the kingdom of God must evaluate revolution in terms of faith, hope and love.[29] The church acts as the prophetic, liberating, critical force prompting constant change for righteousness.

E. ESCHATOLOGICAL ORIENTATION

Moltmann and Pannenberg voice much the same kind of concern in their notions of the church and society, with even more stress on the dynamic eschatological dimension of divine presence in history as God, the 'God of hope' for Moltmann, the 'God of the open future' for Pannenberg, continually sustains the flow of history and involves himself in it in his very being. Both these theologians, in their different styles, reject the classical idea of the transcendent deity 'above' the changing world and instead develop God's relation to the world in terms of history, whose final end will bring in the kingdom, anticipations of which are always presenting themselves in advance.

Jesus' death and resurrection decisively brought in the initial impact of the kingdom of God. His trust in the God of hope was vindicated, he walked towards the future in trust and obedience, through suffering and godforsakeness, to constitute new potentialities for humanity and also to affect the very being of God.

These two theologians are not identical, but the similarity in the structure of their whole approach is striking. Both owe much to conversation with Marxism, which Pannenberg criticizes on the grounds that its determinist system, everything being decided from the past, cannot account for the genuinely new and cannot really account for hope. God, the God of future who brings new events about as humanity advances forward to the future, is the ground for speaking of what is novel and politically hopeful, the free God alone can be the source of human freedom.

Jesus ushers in the new freedom in a radical way, anticipating the final liberation of the universe. Moltmann stresses the identification of Jesus with the lost, forsaken, and the suffering. Jesus guarantees and reveals God's solidarity with them. As a result of Jesus' life, death and resurrection, not only is there forgiveness and hope for the sinner but also 'Then the new future comes in the mission of the community of Christ, which as "the new people of God" drawn from all nations and tongues, is the vanguard of the new humanity and the representative embodiment of freedom from the coercive powers of this world. Then it arrives in the new obedience of the believers, who in ordinary life refuse to conform to the scheme of this world, but anticipate the coming freedom.'[30] In waves or concentric circles, the advent of freedom through the messiah and his community comes to the church and the world. The church receives what it marches towards, the anticipation of the kingdom.

In her life, the church, living out this kingdom presence, must act politically and socially, must be as the Marxists are and seek to penetrate all aspects of the world and transform it. The church exists to mediate this kingdom, which she recognizes but the world does not, into the world. The kingdom which will finally come and complete the process of history with its anticipation of the kingdom, 'already but not yet' finalized, will bring about the unity of mankind, as mankind goes to meet this future. 'The church,' says Pannenberg, 'is an eschatological community pioneering the future of all mankind.'[31] She is true to her vocation only as she 'anticipates and represents the destiny of all mankind, the goal of history.' When she narrows her vision so as to become a kind of private chaplain to selected souls she fails to be what she really is and loses her social significance and 'humanizing vocation'.[32]

Moltmann, who has paid more attention to the significance of the cross, strongly makes the point that a mark of the church is her identification with the poor and forsaken, a feature of Jesus' life and death. The church exists for the kingdom, a far wider category than the church herself, who represents, pioneers, interprets, and serves the whole of humanity. It is important to note that the kingdom embraces other great world faiths, dialogue with which for Christianity 'is part of the wider framework of the liberation of the whole creation for the coming kingdom.'[33] The kingdom also embraces the world's secular institutions 'which can neither be ecclesiasticized nor Christianized, but to which the Church adapts itself and in which Christians adopt particular viewpoints.'[34]

The church like her master is kenotic, she lives to give herself away, unsung and untriumphant, serving the interests of the kingdom wholly. She is not for herself but for others and the future of God. She does not seek to draw all into her ambit necessarily, but to serve the diversity of humanity as it will ultimately come into a unity which is not an authoritarian uniformity. Ultimately the church will merge into the greater kingdom of which she is an imperfect anticipation.

Pannenberg radically claims that there would be no need of the church if the structures of society were adequate, 'For then the kingdom of God would be present in its completeness.'[35] This is also the logic of Moltmann, who believes in the presence of the kingdom hiddenly wherever harmony and liberation exist. As Marx's state will 'wither away', so it seems to be for the church, which will dissolve into the kingdom. Pannenberg also makes more conservative remarks about the structures of the church, even allowing the possibility of acknowledging that a non-authoritarian papacy might stand as representing unity, unity of the church and of humanity.[36] Further, he makes the important criticism of the classical Reformation definition of the visible church, included as we have heard in the Anglican

Articles, of 'the congregation of the faithful where the pure word is preached and sacraments ministered', on the grounds of its total lack of reference to the kingdom of God and all implied in that. This is a telling point and part of the Reformation's general weakness on eschatology.[37]

The church is open-textured, the servant of all mankind, whose mission is self-giving, to spend and be spent at the behest of the kingdom, which is wider than herself, in solidarity with Jesus, delighting in other faiths, secular culture and the harmony of mankind. The messianic impact of Jesus pointed forward to the kingdom with the impulses of the anticipation of the kingdom; the church has tended to look back and reverse the true dynamic of God's continuing advent. 'And above all,' says Pannenberg, 'the mission of the apostles which has been passed over to the church (since it cannot come to end until the consummation of history) is directed to the future of God's kingdom. This future brings about change for every present situation.'[38] Moltmann sees the future of God as the agent of transformation of the past into what is new and hopeful, but also that God is identified in the misery of humanity, since he is always the crucified God.

The engine which purrs away beneath this theological enterprise is trinitarian and dialectical. The hope of the future, which is freedom and liberation, comes from God who invests himself into the historical process. This is the Fatherhood aspect. The Spirit knits up the past and the future into the present, to create new configurations of history. The Son is the human Jesus, now constituted one in being with the Father, utterly open and trusting, representing all humanity in its quest forward towards the kingdom, and bearing the pain of negativity, suffering and disappointment, the cross. The dialectic, the transformation of the past by the arrival of the future of God, shuttles onwards in the Spirit towards the climax of total unity in diversity, perfectly reflecting the life of God. In fact the history of Jesus is the life of God: divine history chooses to work itself out in and through human history.

This eschatological servant model points unashamedly to its deep relation with Marxist thought with its dialectic advancing onwards to the perfect society. This strand of theology stands in what Macquarrie calls the 'Hegel—Marx—Bloch' line of thought. Both the theologians and Marx share a considerable debt to Hegel, whose theology of the trinitarian life of God was picture language for the diversities and negativities of the world process being knit together and reconciled by the cosmic spirit, or mind. Whereas Marx abolishes the spiritual dynamic and puts it into the purely material process of history, the theologians here utilize the eschatological categories and insist on a free God who is himself participating in the whole process. To use the philosophy of Hegel or the thought of Marx is not necessarily any bad thing: the early church fathers used Plato, and Aquinas Aristotle. But is this type of system too controlled by this dialectical historicist dynamic? The great merit of such theologians for the social issues facing the church is that they are theological, they seek to address the question from the perspective of the God who comes from the future to bring hope and transformation. They offer more than secular social analysis in this enterprise.

4. Appraisal of ACUPA in the light of the servant models

A. ACUPA AMONG THE SERVANT MODELS

While being far from anything like a detailed ecclesiology, ACUPA has the clear theological lines of the servant model of ecclesiology, not so much in the eschatological version of that model, although some common points emerge there also.

The proposals of Bonhoeffer's religionless Christianity go beyond anything attributable to ACUPA except a presumption about the capacity of secular society, given the right adjustments, to take care of itself sufficiently, the church somehow acting to heighten the social conscience. Certainly ACUPA does not in any way commend dissolving church structures into the general political and social structures. Man has not definitely come of age for ACUPA, although it is not certain that man needs to know Christ. The resources needed to pull humanity from its predicament can be purely secular, it seems, for ACUPA, the church perhaps being one agency among others to enable improvement.

The approach of Latin American liberation theology seems to involve a definite blueprint for alternative structuring of society to which the church ought to be committed, a thoroughgoing Marxist pattern. Plainly ACUPA distances itself from proposing a definite social plan which would improve on the present one. Perhaps here ACUPA resembles rather the European teaching of Metz with his notion of the permanent socially directed critical function of political theology as an inherent formative factor of Christian theology, trying to avoid saddling the church with a particular ideology; although in general ACUPA's social recommendations all tend in one political direction. The ACUPA methodology for theological interpretation of society and for involvement in the city avowedly makes links with liberation theology: the call for less academic theological training, for the agenda of theology, not just local parish strategy, to be set from life experience or praxis, and for the traditional sources of theology to be read in the light of that experience, all this equates very squarely with the liberationist method.

ACUPA shares with the eschatological servant models of Moltmann and Pannenberg the acceptance of the pluralism of the modern world as a good thing. The church forms part of the kingdom, but by no means the whole of it and needs to affirm the great world faiths and secular institutions as somehow secretly ordained to serve, Cyrus-like, the purposes of God, rather than needing to be Christianized. The traditional dictum, 'no salvation outside the church', does not hold for ACUPA any more than for these modern theologians. The church can help the other factors of the kingdom and vice-versa, but the church is not, it seems, necessary to people in the sense that they must join her and accept her gospel as a matter of eternal consequence.

B. CRITIQUE OF ACUPA

The essential criticism of ACUPA's line of vision is that it seeks proper Christian ends with means that could cut the nerve of the gospel which constitutes the church. It is hard to conceive of any Christian ecclesiology or theology which would deny that the concern for the poor must take a high profile in Christian ethics. How ACUPA relates that vital ethic to Christian doctrines of salvation and inextricably to the definition of the church forms the subject for discussion.

In what I take to be a typical overstatement of his point R. A. Knox, then a witty young Anglo-Catholic don, made his conservative response to what he took to be a similar line of thought to that of ACUPA:

> 'It may seem captious to observe that in ordinary old fashioned Christian theology our religion is said to save us not from a situation but from sin. "Being then made free

> from the Situation." . . . "You being dead in your Situation" . . . "Where remission of these is, there is no more offering for the Situation" . . . it hardly rings familiar,' says Knox. 'But there is ground for emphasizing the point. If by situation we mean the general atmosphere in art, politics, and science; the problems that call for solution, the questionings that most occupy men's minds: then I think it is true to say that the Christian revelation came into the world at a time when there was a situation, and did not save people from it; or rather, it saved them only by carrying them out of it and beyond it. It came at a time when the armies of the world were continually on the verge of mutiny, and all it had to say was, "Be content with your wages." It came at a time when slaves suffered revolting ill-treatment, and said "Servants obey your masters." It came when the problems of Imperial Government were very much in the air, nowhere more so than in Palestine, and gave oracular advice, "Render to Caesar the things that are Caeasar's." The salvation it brought was altogether on a different level: it insisted, with obstinate irrelevancy, on the good fight of faith with its crown of life, on the glorious liberty of the sons of God, on a citizenship in Heaven.'[39]

Knox is not arguing for the retention of slavery and bad conditions in the interests of sanctity, 'that grace may abound'! But he is pointing out the central orientation of the Christian gospel of salvation and the complexity of linking this with politico-social concerns and theories;

> 'And if it is true to say that the present aspect of politics constitutes a very grave feature in the modern situation, now that the comfortable optimism of the Manchester School has died out, and a strong passion for social justice has set in, though the effect of this may be to make us feel nervous, and give us the impression that we live in stirring and changeful times, it is by no means clear that such considerations are relevant to the position of modern theology, or the need for its restatement.'[40]

Presumably Knox would have pointed out that the institution of slavery, like the Roman empire, was 'washed away by the waters of baptism', and argued that the church's calling is to produce converts to Christ whose life and witness indirectly whittle away the evils of society. In other words, Knox conservatively insists on the orientation of the praxis as being 'inside out', on grace working itself out in terms of Christian decisions in society which eventually produce transformation of society. The conservative theologian must be troubled by any suggestion that the gospel of salvation in Christ, with its scandal of particularity, is now to be redefined in terms of social action. If it is to be Christian social transformation, then the praxis needs to emerge from the gospel as the fruit of the Spirit.

In a formal expression of this concern over liberation theology from deep inside the Roman hierarchy, Cardinal Ratzinger formulated it in these terms:

> 'The acute need for radical reforms of the structures which conceal poverty and which are themselves forms of violence, should not let us lose sight of the fact that the source of the injustice is in the hearts of men. Therefore it is only by making an appeal to the *moral potential* of the person and to the constant need for interior conversion, that social change will be brought about which will truly be in the service of man. . . . The inversion of morality and structures is steeped in a materialist anthropology which is incompatible with the dignity of mankind.'[41]

Ratzinger calls for the teaching of the whole doctrine of salvation which must include the transcendent Jesus and liberation in him. He warns against the sacralizing of politics.[42] He clearly states the conservative worry.

Similar cautions are entered from the evangelical wing. Bruce Milne shows a real appreciation for the concerns of the political theologian and finds biblical warrant for them: 'God has a particular concern for the poor and oppressed as scripture constantly repeats . . . We must therefore be very sensitive, as God clearly is, to the cry of the wretched and downtrodden.'[43] But Milne, like Ratzinger, rejects the method of theologizing which claims to start with human experience as the grid for interpreting revelation, a method, he thinks, which leads to a humanistic appraisal of human problems. This method leads to the central weakness of much political theology.

> 'In its view of mankind's need, political theology is particularly inadequate. The human predicament cannot be reduced to social and political alienation, even assuming we can be certain of their root cause and of the correct social and political means of dealing with them—which is not infrequently a deceptively subjective issue.'[44]

It is sin which constitutes the central disease of humanity. 'Political theology does not touch this dimension. Insofar as it makes reference to man's deliverance from sin at all, it commonly assumes the truth of universalism: all men are already saved from sin, so that the question of our eternal standing with God can be put to one side, leaving us free to concentrate on salvation in this-worldly, socio-political terms.'[45]

Milne makes an interesting point about the analysis of the roots of poverty and the opinion as to its cure in a society. Here is a very difficult question for ACUPA. There is a legitimate debate over ways of working to improve the lot of the underprivileged. Here too pluralism exists but this pluralism fails to gain recognition. Political parties of the left and the right claim to be working for the good of society and can point to their achievements. Increased material benefits form the aim of the major political options in the West, but the proposed methods differ. ACUPA seems to assume that the real answers lie left of centre while not attempting to prove or discuss this assumption. Is the Christian to vote for an emphasis on individual freedom, opportunity and achievement as a way forward, or for increasing state control and involvement? This debate, each side of which can adduce biblical support, seems to be passed over. This is a practical criticism rather than a theological one, but since the very point of ACUPA's rejection of conservative theological method rests on praxis it is a major weakness since praxis becomes something of a 'nose of wax', movable in several directions. The related paradoxical question arising is whether ACUPA would endorse a right wing policy of individualist enterprise if it proved successful in creating more material prosperity in the inner city, while failing to create increased community.

The question of a presumed universalism lies near the centre of the deepest conservative unease with the servant models, and ACUPA, while acknowledging the primacy of Christ, seems to share this optimistic view of humanity under God. God's activity in creation, in other faiths and in worthy secular activity, appears to suffice, and hence the church serves this presence of God wherever it may be. Archbishop George Carey criticizes this tendency of liberation theology which he says confuses creation and salvation.[46] From the conservative, particularly the evangelical, God's presence in creation, his immanence, is not to be denied, but not necessarily as his redemptive, saving presence. The patristic dictum, no salvation outside the church, proves to be the corollary of the 'scandal of the cross' here. Can the church act as the church if she contents herself with the idea that helping socially brings the salvation of God to bear on the lives of people? Traditional theology distinguishes divine activity in sustaining creation from the more personal divine activity of salvation in creation.

This point applies in all aspects of soteriology. The view of sin as primarily sinned-againstness, as socially structural, draws the fire of the conservative who makes the distinction between sin and the effects of sin. Attacking social evils is a Christian calling, but it is not the same as, and must not be confused with, salvation from the state of sin. If the church thinks she can withhold the word of the cross and offer as a valid *alternative* the word of friendship, then she is failing to be the church. Affirming other faiths and secular solutions looks like an alternative gospel from a legitimate menu. For the conservative, to stop short of presenting the message of pardon and salvation in Jesus Christ is patronizing and dehumanizing: it is allowing a kind of spiritual apartheid to develop, those who need material amelioration in one camp and those who need a personal relationship with Jesus in another. To treat sin as a sociological entity may well fail to attribute sufficient dignity to humanity, the burden of Ratzinger's complaint. The Holy Spirit, to take another aspect of traditional soteriology, becomes available universally outside as well as inside the church. In other words nature and grace merge.

This conservative critque of the servant model, institutionalized in Anglicanism by the ACUPA theological suggestions, finds some support in Dulles's remarks on the servant ecclesiology. Of this model he says it 'could easily give the impression that man's final salvation is to be found in history, and could lure the church into an uncritical acceptance of secular values, thus muting its distinctive witness to Christ and to its own heritage.'[47] Praxis has to be Christian praxis, informed by the gospel. There are many ideologies which seek to create unity, community and social solidarity which are based on ideas at odds with Christian faith: Nazism being a fairly obvious one, but, more insidiously, secular utilitarianism.

Dulles points out that the servant role of the church to transform the world and serve it is hard to ground directly in the New Testament, where salvation is individualized and spiritualized;[48] it is very hard to interpret the kingdom as having agencies or stimuli other than the church from the New Testament data:

> 'Interpreted in the light of the gospel, the kingdom of God cannot be properly identified with abstract values such as peace, justice, reconciliation, and affluence. The New Testament personalizes the Kingdom. It identifies the Kingdom of God with the gospel, and both of them with Jesus. As Paul says in 1 Cor. 1:30, God has made Jesus himself our wisdom, our justice, our sanctification, and our redemption. Not to know Jesus and not to put one's faith in him is therefore a serious failure. It is not to know the kingdom as it really should be known.'[49]

Here a modern Roman Catholic ecclesiological authority makes a very evangelical critique of servant models. This voice wants to keep the concerns of the servant church, but in the context of the gospel of Christ as well as that of social analysis.

Vatican 2 authorizes the servant model with its affirmation of sectors of the life of the world as reflecting the divine at work in creation, orienting the church towards humble service and partnership with the world in many respects. It is no accident that Jan Luis Segundo SJ has met Ratzinger's Vatican critique by appealing to Vatican 2 and even warning the church that Ratzinger and the Sacred Congregation for the Doctrine of the Faith may be seeking to renege on the teachings of the Council: 'It is not hard to see that he feels, at least implicitly, that the Council went too far and that today the Church is suffering the consequences.'[50] Segundo, whose argument might be pitted against Dulles's criticism of the servant model, cites text after text from *Gaudium et Spes,* the Pastoral Constititution on the Church, of Vatican 2, to rebut Cardinal Ratzinger.[51] '*Everything,* secular and religious, that good will has sown in it will be reaped in the new heaven and the new earth, purified and transfigured (*Gaudium et Spes,* 39). The historical work of all people will lead, by the grace of God, to a new metahistory.'[52] Segundo makes a point which seems flawless in the context of current Roman Catholicism after Vatican 2, and he cites the authority of Pope Paul Vl in denying that the Council deviated toward anthropocentric positions of modern culture.[53]

As Dulles said in his critique of the servant model, it must have the kerygmatic, herald model at its side at the very least, preferably in its centre. It is the evangelical tradition of proclamation of salvation in Christ alone which logically baulks most at such models and at the universalist tendencies of Vatican 2. Barth queries the optimism of the teaching of the Council on the church in the modern world, *Gaudium et Spes*, as not reflecting apostolic teaching and insists that proclamation to the world taks priority over dialogue with it.[54] Likewise Barth rejects theological method which seeks to coordinate revelation and experience, the former must take priority as the self-attestation of the word to humanity.

The optimistic approach of Vatican 2 implicit in the servant models and ACUPA fits more readily with Roman Catholic ethos than evangelical. Thomas Aquinas's famous dictum, 'grace does not destroy nature but perfects it', retains its validity in modern Roman Catholic thought. One of the deepest differences between Roman and Reformed theological orientation has been over the definition and relationship of nature and grace; the former having a more, the latter a less, optimistic understanding of the fallenness of nature and its capacity to be a partner of grace. This was precisely Barth's great critique of the Roman medieval synthesis, that it took too rosy a view of the innate capacities of nature. He finds precisely the same issue at stake in his reservations about *Gaudium et Spes*.

It can be argued that Vatican 2 in this respect changed nothing, however much certain conservative Papal encyclicals may have misrepresented the essential orientation of the medieval theology. In Karl Adam's Roman Catholic apologetic work, *The Spirit of Catholicism*, we can find an ethos quite similar to some of Vatican 2, when he speaks of

> 'that fundamental Catholic conviction that every genuine value, everything that comes from pure and uncorrupted nature, belongs to God and has citizen rights in His Kingdom. Therefore the Church sets up no barrier against non-Christian culture, and no barrier against antiquity. She sets up her barrier only against sin. . . . Such is Catholicism: an affirmation of values along the whole line, a most comprehensive and noblest accessibililty to all good, a union of nature with grace, of art with religion, of knowledge with faith, "so that God may be all in all."'[55]

This all-welcoming spirit of Roman Catholicism needed merely to be developed into the realms of politics, sociology and economics by the fathers of Vatican 2, to be developed by the theology of liberation. Segundo therefore appeals to a massive weight of Roman medieval tradition, claiming that liberation merely unites the prayer with work towards a better society and the elimination of terrible political and social evils.[56]

The universalist strand of thought in Vatican 2 claims for God whatsoever things are noble and of good report, blesses God for all human activity, genuinely seeking after truth and community. The whole world can be said, according to the optimistic stream of medieval thought, to be a sacrament pointing to its creator and ready to be lit up by the touch of grace, to be completed. The very centre of this sacramental universe is Christ, the human who is also divine. From him radiates out the sacramental grace informing all creation, through the church and into the world of human activity and natural beauty. This system of sacramentality, of concentric circles narrowing down to the incarnate Lord, lends itself well to a servant model, to blurring the boundaries between church and world. It makes it easy to regard the world of secular affairs as secretly in the whole pattern of God, and needing only to be told of the fact.

For evangelical theology it is more difficult. The central categories of nature and grace have been amended, in the light of Romans 1, and Augustine, to those of sin and grace. It is not so easy to baptize the world and its better values, to regard them in the more optimistic light of the traditional and modern Roman and Anglo-Catholic sacramental view. Sinful nature cannot be topped-up with grace unless and until nature has been renewed by saving grace. This is still the basic difference in orientation between the Roman and the evangelical world view, and it means that for the latter there is a real distinction between the church and the world. Men and women who exist in the purely secular mode, dying without Christ, face eternal consequences and the church fails if she does not bring the saving word to all, calling them by all possible means to faith and repentance. The line between church and world therefore cannot be blurred: the church has no mandate to encourage speculation that salvation may be available elsewhere, or that there are degrees of grace.

Evangelical ecclesiology cannot avoid the scandal of the one way street from grace to sinful nature; from there grace, proclaimed by word and deed, moves out into the world telling out the good news and living out righteousness. Grace leads to ethics, and the movement from God to man leads to the responsive movement of mission and righteousness. This parallels the evangelical view of sacraments: they are means of receiving from God, not offerings of the church, in Christ to God. The message is that humanity needs the saving grace of Christ and has nothing to offer; this applies all the more strongly to the world which cannot be recognized as somehow hiddenly baptized.

This point holds good also for evangelical theologizing. ACUPA's attack on traditional theology is hard to swallow because the gospel does have a content which needs to be communicated, taught and lived out. It is not transformable and it is found in the Bible. Experience is important to relate to the gospel, but the gospel cannot arise from neat experience, whether corporately or individually. Rather experience needs to be tested against the gospel and canon. The ACUPA rejection of cognitive theology, of teaching which can be taught and learned, of a fundamentally clear Bible, finds opposition with traditional evangelicals. Any appeal to praxis as against theory is regarded as bogus, as an appeal to the way and the life without the truth. This falsifies the situation since there is never a possibility of praxis uninformed by truth or theory, indeed to pretend that there is, merely misinforms in a highly authoritarian way, since it forecloses the possibility of debate and criticism of that chosen particular praxis. Any programme of practicality contains within itself a theory, an idea, and needs to be scrutinized unless freedom is to be denied and the praxis is dogmatically imposed. To bury cognitive, normative revelation inside praxis cannot commend itself to conservative methodology. Therefore the proposals for alternative theological method in ACUPA, although often unspecific, run counter to evangelical conviction that theologizing only from experience, and looking to an unreal 'raw praxis', will leave open the possibility of compounding failure in the cities with losing the gospel to the cities, by cutting loose from cognitive truth.

The evangelical Anglican ecclesiology, with the stress on the proclamation of the word and on grace coming to save humanity, with its insistence that ethics is the application of the gospel, must be said to face the criticism of ACUPA most sharply, and to be challenged to see that this application is in fact carried out. To hold that social action is not sufficient as a definition of the gospel is valid, but to decline to put what is necessary into practice is not. Indeed it is hypocrisy falling under the kind of condemnation found in Amos and James. With their formal declaration of the priesthood of all believers both evangelical Anglican clergy and laity perhaps need to listen to the voice of ACUPA as a summons to move into the structures with the living word, not sacramentally to represent the church but practically to do what has been heard.

The Old Testament, read in church services far less proportionally than the New, is the best source of stimulus to care for the oppressed. What horrifies the prophets, according to Stephen Neill,

> 'is men's disregard of the elementary principles which alone make life in community possible—accumulation of great landed estates, the denial of brotherhood shown in refusal of justice to the poor, luxury and wantonness on the part of some while others starve. The nature of this ethical protest is summed up in the sorrowfully weighty words of Amos, "They are not grieved for the affliction of Joseph."'[57]

Neill points out that the distinction between personal and social ethics in the Old Testament was almost unthinkable, that breaches of the social order undermined what God had established in creation. Those who cannot follow the means of ACUPA must share its aims, those who stress the hearing of the word must become doers of it. The Word, at the culmination of revelation, became flesh. Packer closes his remarks on the incarnation by reminding his readers that the Christmas spirit

> 'ought to mean the reproducing in human lives of the temper of Him who for our sakes became poor at the first Christmas. . . . It is our shame and disgrace today that . . . so many of the soundest and most orthodox Christians go through this world in the spirit of the Priest and Levite in our Lord's parable, seeing human need all around them, but (after a pious wish, and perhaps a prayer, that God might meet them) averting their eyes, and passing by on the other side.'[58]

Biblical faith cannot be purely inward any more than purely cultic.

Evangelical theology also faces the challenge of developing a theology of God's activity in the world as well as in the church. Public affairs have been excluded from consideration and need somehow to be brought into the evangelical view more clearly. Conservatives continue a policy of attacking social evils as they present themselves, and indeed often perceive the powers of darkness at work in them. The spiritual battle underlies the political and social. But this approach does not usually address socio-economic structures, in the context of a European Parliamentary democracy. It might well be different in an oppressive regime, in another context, where evil operating through the structures, as John the Divine perceived evil operating through the Roman Imperial structures, simply needs to be addressed on a corporate, political level.

Perhaps the outstanding piece of *evangelical* wrestling with the issue of God and politics this century, written in a time of acute crisis, is Forsyth's *The Justification of God* written in 1916, in the terrible First World War. Forsyth rejects the easy immanentism of God at work in history in one way only. He insists on coming at the issue from the cross of Christ, the great regenerating judgement of history by God. This act of God is the way God judges and deals with the process of history as well as individual souls. Conservative Christians have over-individualized the cross, he argues, and severed it from the broader process of public issues. Indeed, this consistent failure to press the principles of the atonement into public policy was bound to lead to victory for militarism and tribal aggression as a good. Evangelical theology today could well profit from taking up Forsyth's summons to go deeper into the great crisis of the cross, and find its wider power and its eschatological judgement. 'The Cross of Christ, eternal and universal, immutable and invincible, is the moral goal and principle of nations and affairs.'[59] God is the personal king of history whose saving judgement and battle with evil now, will find its climax in the final judgement. This has the *seeds* of an authentic evangelical approach to a theological reflection on public policy issues, an approach going much beyond moralism and into redemption by the living Christ.

Troeltsch closes his *The Social Teaching of the Christian Churches* on this note: 'One of the most serious and important truths which emerge as a result of this enquiry is this: every idea is still faced by brutal facts, and all upward movement is checked and hindered by interior and external difficulties . . . For every threatening abyss which is closed, another yawning gulf appears.'[60] This truth of history and society needs to be remembered by all concerned for the church's servant role socially. Utopianism has no place here, and yet this is often too quickly invoked to hinder action. Perhaps the role of the churches in Eastern Europe in those nations currently undergoing massive social reform after years of strict state socialism can help us. Although some churches simply seem to have baptized the existing order, many persisted with their critique of social structures, providing a 'new forum'. Their insistent, while powerless, voice sought to obey the Christ of the regenerative cross and resurrection, the second Adam, true humanity. At the moment we do not know whether they will be called to play that role again as new structures and systems crystallize.

'The common purpose of man is relational, '"Rightness" for man—or "wholeness" or "holiness" . . . is not a matter of some private and inner consecration; it is primarily a matter of relationships—first to the one who made him, but this involves also a right relationship to all other men about him; the one cannot be maintained without the other.'[61] How ecclesial humanity can best affect socio-political structures to this end remains an issue of debate for every historical and geographical context, a vital point made by ACUPA. That the church cannot avoid choices in the matter is a theological fact, particularly for a church closely linked to national structures. That these choices need to be conditioned to faith in the crucified and risen Lord makes them Christian. The cross of Christ 'is the active principle which slowly brings to book the devices of men, the enterprises of heroes, and the adventures of nations. It is a creative revolution, which inverts the values that fired their passion and converts to God's kingdom their egoist schemes'[62]; adapting to this personal, and absolutely holy, king must form the central impulse of the church's servanthood.

In terms of our models adopted for describing the shape of the church, servanthood wishes to claim that it is a return to the earliest foundation church. The first church had its base communities, was composed of those on the margins of society, was small and without power. This sort of ecclesiology claims a radical return to the roots of the church in the lifestyle of Jesus himself.[63] Subsequent developments in church history soon distorted this simple vision into hierarchy and institutional power. The servant vision has to have a high place in any ecclesiology, the question is whether this form of it maintains a sufficiently full Christological centre-circumference content.

END NOTES TO CHAPTER 5

1. M. Reckitt *Maurice to Temple*, London, Faber and Faber, 1946 p. 41.
2. *The Nottingham Statement* Falcon, CPAS, London, 1977 pp. 69–70.
3. Lausanne Covenant, section 5.
4. *The Kingdom of Christ* Everyman's Library, Dent and Dutton, London 1838.
5. *F. D. Maurice and the Conflict of Modern Theology*, London 1951.
6. Reckitt op. cit. p. 85.
7. Ramsey *From Gore to Temple* op. cit. p. 154.
8. *The Report of the Archbishop of Canterbury's Committee on Urban Priority Areas* Church House Publishing, London 1985.
9. ibid. p. 47.
10. ibid. p. 51.
11. ibid. p. 59.
12. ibid. p. 61.
13. Dulles *Models of the Church* op. cit. p. 89.
14. *The Suburban Captivity of the Churches* New York, Macmillan, 1962.
15. Eric Jay *The Church* vol. 2, London, SPCK, 1978 p. 128.
16. For example see *The Other Side of 1984* WCC Geneva, 1984.
17. Article 93 *Documents of Vatican 2* ed. Abbott and Gallagher G. Chapman, London, Dublin, 1966 p. 307.
18. op. cit. p.86.
19. *The Secular City* London, SCM, 1965 p. 105.
20. Cox op. cit. p. 145.
21. W. Nicholls *Systematic and Philosophical Theology* op. cit. p. 218.
22. *Letters and Papers from Prison* 16 July 1944, Fontana, London, 1953 p. 122.
23. *The One Lord Jesus in Contemporary Pluralism* address given to the Anglican Evangelical Assembly, 1985. See also Fung's article 'Sinners and the sinned against in Hong Kong', *Third Way* October 1981.
24. ibid.
25. Article 'Political Theology' in *Sacramentum Mundi* ed. K. Rahner Burns and Oats London, 1970 vol. 5, p. 35.
26. ibid. p. 36.
27. ibid.
28. ibid.
29. ibid. p. 38.
30. *Religion, Revolution and the Future* New York, Scribners, 1969 p. 137–8.
31. *Theology and the Kingdom of God* op. cit. p. 75.
32. ibid.
33. Moltmann *The Church in the Power of the Spirit* SCM, London, 1977 p. 163.
34. ibid.
35. op. cit. p. 82.
36. ibid. p. 99.
37. op. cit. p. 74.
38. *Spirit, Faith and Church*, Panneberg, Dulles and Braaten, Westminster Press, Philadelphia, 1970 p. 113–4.

39. *Some Loose Stones* Longmans Green, London, 1914 pp. 1–2.
40. ibid.
41. *Instruction on Certain Aspects of the Theology of Liberation*, Sacred Congregation for the Doctrine of the Faith, Catholic Truth Society, London, 1984 pp. 31–2.
42. ibid. p. 34.
43. *Know the Truth* op. cit. p. 168.
44. ibid.
45. ibid.
46. *The Gate of Glory* Hodder and Stoughton, London, 1986 pp. 179–180.
47. op. cit. p. 184.
48. op. cit. p. 94.
49. op. cit. pp. 95–6.
50. *Theology and the Church: A response to Cardinal Ratzinger and a Warning to the Whole Church* G. Chapman London, 1970 p. 162.
51. op. cit. ch. 2.
52. op. cit. p. 69.
53. op. cit. p. 70.
54. *Ad Limina Apostolorum* John Knox Press, Richmond, 1967 p. 27.
55. *The Spirit of Catholicism* Sheed and Ward, London, 1929 pp. 188–9.
56. op. cit. p. 53.
57. *Christian Holiness* Lutterworth Press, London, 1960 p. 18.
58. *Knowing God* op. cit. p. 65.
59. *The Justification of God* Duckworth London, 1916 p. 202.
60. *The Social Teaching of the Christian Churches* vol. 2, trans. Olive Wyon George Allen and Unwin, 1931 p. 1013.
61. S. Neill op. cit. p. 17.
62. Forsyth op. cit. p. 208.
63. See Eduardo Hoornaert *The Memory of the Christian People* Burns and Oates, Tunbridge Wells, 1989 for a full statement of this claim.

6

ESSENTIAL ANGLICANISM: ORIENTATION FOR THE FUTURE

Aspects of the church

The three images of centre-circumference, foundation-superstructure, and biological growth, usefully describe aspects of the church and we have seen how various important interpretations of the Church of England make use of these ideas in their own ways. Theologically the model of the Christological centre has a certain priority, since it focuses the dependence of the people of God on Christ and his gospel. The foundation idea shows the commitment to the authority of the canon for evangelical Anglicanism, and for the Anglo-Catholic it also represents the base of apostolic warranty for the succession of bishops; the radical wishes to appeal to the earliest church, a simple, powerless community, the base community of base communities, as the foundation. The growth idea expresses the church's institutional and conceptual development through the centuries, the life of faith and the development of structures, forms, and customs of all kinds; ARCIC 1, in particular, depends upon this line of theologizing.

These various aspects cannot be finally separated, as the current debate over the ordination of women shows: is it a natural development, is it consistent with the canonical witness, is it an expression of the gospel of Christ? But the Anglican heritage implies these three models as useful descriptions of the dimensions of the church. Relationship to Christ, to the apostolic teaching and ministry, and to the process of the history of structures and movements, these questions will focus the discussion of the nature of the Church of England and her options for her future.

1. Christological koinonia

A. CATHOLIC KOINONIA

The primary truth and reality constituting the church is Christ. All the types of ecclesiological interpretation considered would agree on this basic statement. ARCIC begins its ecclesiology, like Barth and Ramsey, in terms of *koinonia* or fellowship with Christ and so with fellow Christians. This accords with the New Testament, which constantly appeals to this fact of the common union with Christ to regulate the church's life, mission and ethics. Union with Christ rules out religious syncretism: communion with Christ at the eucharist and partaking in pagan rites are incompatible; union with Christ and sexual immorality, union with prostitutes, is a contradiction. Church worship and ethics are brought to the test of Christ and our relationship with Christ.

Likewise the unity of the church is a question of Christology: is Christ divided? The idea of splitting into splinter groups of Christians seems absurd because of the constitutive Christological relationship among the faithful. The catholicity and unity of the church is not firstly organizational, but Christological. This catholic unity will of course endeavour to keep the unity of the Spirit in the bond of structural peace.

The Christological centre means that the circumference in principle opens out to all humanity. In this sense also catholicity rests on this particular *koinonia*. Gentiles enter into full fellowship on conversion to the Messiah. This implication flows from the fact of Jesus' life, death and resurrection. *Koinonia* with Christ proves to be decisive in ordering the progress of the church because Christ, living in the church by the Holy Spirit, defines the church. The holy God of Israel astonishes the conservative apostles by declaring the common or unholy, to be holy. As Quick reminds us,

> 'Just as in English the words "communion" and "common" are cognate, so in Greek the word koinonia is allied to koinos, which means "common" or "unclean", the very

> opposite of hagios, "holy". And the connection is not purely verbal, but has a basis in ideas. In the Old Testament the notion of the holiness which is the essential characteristic of God excludes the notion of a common sharing. The holiness of God means his awful, mysterious separateness. The holiness of God's chosen people meant that they were separated and set apart from all the nations. The holiness of the inner shrine in the Temple meant that it might not be entered by all and sundry even of the holy people.'[1]

Jesus Christ's royal and priestly judgement of humanity makes the unholy holy and brings in the end-time kingdom of God. The Holy Spirit dwells within the faithful who have direct access to the Father. This radical deepening of relations with God also extends the scope of holiness to all people, who can in principle now become living stones in the temple of the Holy Spirit. Now everyone, Jew and Greek, slave and free, male and female, 'are to stand on common ground and equal footing, first as alike sinners, and then as redeemed members of Christ's body to which the Spirit gives its common life.'[2] The unholy, the unseparated, can now become holy; the common has become consecrated: the church is the royal priesthood in her sanctified *koinonia*. The Johannine statement of this was made in the story of the woman at the well: no longer are the Jerusalem Temple or the Samaritan Temple of significance, for 'God is Spirit and those who worship him must worship in Spirit and in truth' (John 4:24). God's direct spiritual contact with mankind, through the sacrificial 'going away' of Jesus, simultaneously widens the scope of Israel to all humankind. This is the basis of the church's catholic mission into the common world.

Koinonia with God, the fellowship of the saints, and the mission of the church therefore must be regarded as inseparable. It is probably false to speak of the the mission of the church: the church *is* mission, necessarily, if she follows her calling of bringing the consecrating Holy Spirit out into all corners of creation, incorporating all peoples, tribes and tongues into the regenerating Messiah, so grafting them into the olive tree of faith. The common, the unclean, becomes consecrated and holy: the non-people become God's people in the messianically re-vitalized tree of the Hebrew tradition. The people of God, finally, must be defined in terms of the nature of God, holy love: merciful and gracious, abounding in steadfast love.

Here we seem to reach the essence of the church. The church can be defined as the communion of the sanctified in the

Spirit, consecrated by Christ for 'real', rather than formal, relations, with God and creation. However idealistic it may sound, the church is an end-time reality in advance of the end, as was Jesus himself. Jesus is the kingdom of God, and his church is the kingdom by status, the kingdom in the making by moral reality. The church is moving towards her final destiny, is becoming what she is. She will become perfected as covenant partner of her Lord, the bride of Christ. It may be that the 'church at present' compared with the 'church of the end-time' proves a more helpful distinction than that between the 'visible versus invisible', which tries to express the fact of the visible church known to God, and preserved by God as the elect through all the tribulations of the 'last days' (Mark 13:20). The church moves toward her reward which will consist of what she has become. The fruit on the branches of the vine, often known to God alone, shows the presence of the faithful. Grace, in the depth of its Christian meaning, not only centres the church but emanates from her circumference—and this makes the circumference an open border.

B. PERSONALLY SACRAMENTAL KOINONIA

The church seeks actually to live the life of Christ in history. This is prior to any sacramental notion of the church as symbolizing the presence of the Lord. To regard the church as a sign and symbol, first and foremost, is to miss the essence of the *koinonia*, the holy love in the blood and sweat of human history. Such *koinonia* is real, committed care and self-giving. It issues in flesh and blood moral actions, in 'the fruit of the Spirit'. Only if the church is this reality can she be said to provide a sacramental picture of God for the world. The world is not to be consecrated by erecting charming or moving religious buildings or statues. Neither will impressive structures of ministry, nor the most artistic liturgies, themselves bring Christ to society. Only if such images communicate the gospel, only if the erectors of the signs live out the gospel in concrete, costly, unromantic, historical fashion, will the world be reached with the holy love of God.

This seems to me a very serious point indeed for all churches, and vital for Anglicans to grasp at this time, when so many options are facing them. Avery Dulles argues that the central model of the church is that of sacrament, which subsumes his other models of *koinonia*, the herald, and the servant.[3]

However weighty, this view needs to be challenged in the interests of the true depths of what the church is. The *koinonia* of the gospel means the very real relationship of the church to God based on grace. Newbigin correctly stressed that the church is united on the common basis of free pardon in Christ, justification by faith.[4] Echoing Quick, he said that all stand on the same footing of being forgiven through the cross, bringing about a new common humanity, the church. The church is the community of riff-raff, astonishingly given priestly ordination and placed in the holy of holies, given direct relations with God. This is the ontology of the church. Her very being is sinful, pardoned, and *en route* to eschatological perfection through the way of the cross.

Because she has not yet reached the state of perfection, she often displays the signs of anything but a sacrament of God in the world. Because her status rests solely on what is given her, on the basis of the work of the risen crucified Lord, she points to her own incapacity. Like John the Baptist, she must decrease that Christ may increase. She is not sacramentally identical with the saving work of Christ as are the sacraments of baptism and eucharist, on which she feeds from the hand of the Lord. She herself is the recipient of grace, her only ground of boasting is in her own inadequacy and her Lord's gracious and costly love. Her testimony is that of the tax collector: 'Lord have mercy on me a sinner.'

The church may become sacramental of Jesus, as she actually pursues her calling to realize, in human life, the life of the Holy Spirit. As she shows the world real costly love; as she lives out the communion of the saints, the sanctified, the consecrated, she will serve to attract the peoples of the world to her Lord. The church is often very unattractive, unsacramental of Christ, to those within: she becomes helpful to her members when spirituality, Christ-like *koinonia,* takes place; tragically she so often fails to be this sacrament—but the sacraments of Christ, with the word, correct and revitalize her as they bring her, corporately afresh, to the risen Lord and his renewing grace.

Only as she lives and speaks and acts outwards to the world, the 'non-people' who need to be claimed as Christ's, is the church sacramental to anyone outside faith. Dulles fails to escape from an insufficiently biblical Roman catholicism when he relegates *koinonia* behind the sacramental model. He also, probably unconsciously, identifies the church with the ministerial structure of the church in making his central model: how is the whole church, the whole people of God, sinners justified by grace through faith as ARCIC 2 says, necessarily sacramental of God? The answer must be only as they actually become holy and loving, only as they herald the gospel, not only with their lips but in their lives, by giving up themselves to the Lord's service—and this is perhaps the distinctive point—attributing all to the grace of God in Christ and nothing to themselves, by precisely *not* attributing to themselves, nor to their structure of ministry, the honour of being a sacrament. Perhaps this was Barth's point when he talked sometimes of the church as a 'becoming' in the Holy Spirit. The church is the church, and yet she needs constantly to become herself.[5]

The purpose in disagreeing with Dulles is not polemical but theological and therefore practical. The church is divinely constituted, the royal priesthood ordained out of the gutter, and her essence is real communion with God. She is also the body of Christ in a purposive, dynamic way. The New Testament depicts the various aspects of the body in terms of the purposive life of Christ in the church. This is essentially Hebraic and historically purposeful. Salvation is worked out by Christ, but is to be worked out by the church with Christ in the practical events of social, historical life, in the face of evil. The church is the 'church militant' with a real commission of holy love to carry out, in identification with Christ.

The church is best described as sacramental in the personal sense advocated by Forsyth. He speaks of the minister as a personal sacrament.[6] God acting through the consecrated will and life of his ordained servant. This, he argues, goes beyond the traditional notion of sacrament, which concerns institutions and symbols rather than persons. Biblically, the Holy Spirit works not upon things but people. The church might be defined as the people of God whose personalities, lay or ordained, communicate the word of grace to others. Potentially the church is indeed a point of contact with the world, but only as she is in communion with Christ and her neighbour in a real way. Sacramental definition, unless renewed in terms of personal act and word, remains too static and passive as a first order ecclesiological category. The church is the divinely human missionary fellowship, worshipping in Spirit and in truth, she works towards the eschaton while seeking to live out the relationships which will be finally validated and perfected at the end-time, face to face with God.

C. TRINITARIAN KOINONIA

In the second Adam a new humanity rises, from the verdict of the resurrection on the judgement born by the true Israelite. Ecclesiology, therefore, must mean a new anthropology in Christ. Fulfilling the destiny of the historical Abrahamic people, Christ restores Adam, a restoration of life in the image of God, in relation to God. Of the ecclesiologies considered earlier, Ramsey set out this radical understanding most clearly. In Christ a new race is born. Israel gives birth to the source of human regeneration. The more catholic tradition sees the church as the new humanity more clearly than the evangelical.

Recently this ecclesial anthropology has been emphasized in a style similar to that of Ramsey by the Orthodox bishop John Zizioulas.[7] True being, for Zizioulas, is relational; it comes only from the free person 'who freely affirms his being, his identity, by means of an event of communion with other persons.'[8] Nothing exists alone, 'communion is an ontological category;'[9] paralleling the existentialist insights of Buber for whom 'In the beginning is relation,'[10] and of Heigegger who claimed that true being 'is being—with.'[11] But for Zizioulas Greek patristic thought developed the ground for this anthropology, and this ground was the existence of the personal God, whose triune being is communal. This necessarily underlies free individual being as communion. Tillich tells us that existentialism 'has no legs,'[12] and the classical trinitarian tradition provides these on which it can stand! Ecclesiology is founded on the being of the free God, united with his human creatures, and this leads to a renewed humanity. The church is both a corporate entity but utterly personal and freely individual. Zizioulas stresses the fact of the Spirit indwelling the whole church as the divine presence implementing this truly authentic existence as communion; 'Spirit is not in the "I",' said Martin Buber, 'but between the "I" and the "Thou".'[13] Zizioulas gives this a thoroughly Orthodox twist by insisting that the eucharistic assembly makes the future present, enables ecclesial humanity to occur, since at the eucharist biological definitions are transcended: there we are all related, 'every communicant is the whole Christ and the whole Church. The ecclesial identity, consequently, in its historical realization is eucharistic.'[14] Here is a heavily eucharistic definition of the ecclesial humanity.

Herribert Muhlen, a German Roman Catholic theologian, has also developed a trinitarian ecclesiology, interpreting the fundamental being of the church as communion, 'a countless community of persons, united with Christ yet distinct from him, having the Spirit as the principle of unity and somehow also forming a corporate entity, the "corporate I".'[15] He too focuses on the Holy Spirit, in less heavily sacramental terms than Zizioulas, rejecting the traditional Roman Catholic notion of the church as the extension of the incarnation; it is the Holy Spirit's work to unite persons in the triune life of God and in the church, therefore, the Spirit unites persons into a corporate person. The same Holy Spirit who inhabits the life of Christ exists in the church now: Jesus was baptized in the Spirit and we now receive what was given to Jesus. The church is not the continuation of the incarnation but the continuation of the anointing of Christ and the church shares in his anointing and mission. Grace presupposes person, rather than nature, according to Muhlen, a position which Zizioulas also adopts. The Holy Spirit, identical in Christ as in his church, constitutes the church as being in communion, as related uniquely through the self-consecration of Jesus. The church is mysteriously a corporate person, yet preserving free creative individuality and magnifying it within herself.

D. THE CROSS AND THE WORD: EVANGELICAL KOINONIA

This fundamental notion of the church's identity as spiritual *koinonia* constituting humanity as its true self has been taken up at times by the evangelical tradition. Bonhoeffer, in his earliest publication, makes precisely the same point, rejecting 'any mystical ideas of a final absorption in God', like Zizioulas he looks to the doctrine of creation as the background for the church's unity. 'The creator and the creature remain distinct as persons. But the creatures too are distinct from one another, and yet taken all together form the mighty unity of the congregation of God. They are now entirely justified and sanctified, one in Christ and yet all individuals. . . . They surrender themselves to each other and to God, and thereby form one community both with man and with God.'[16] Bonhoeffer, with Forsyth also, injects the evangelical note of the cross, which Ramsey also brings into focus, but eucharistically. This aspect must be prominent if the *koinonia* is that of the Holy Spirit of Christ. The relationality of the church must be defined Christologically in terms of the crucified and risen one, otherwise the idea falls into romantic idealism. The new race receives the Holy Spirit from the cross, and *koinonia* means sacrificial love, costly and reconciling and actual.

Christ remakes humankind as the church, against the background of the covenant and creation destiny. The doctrine of the creation of mankind in the image of God, as Barth points out, concerns, at least, relationships between humans, male and female as the classic paradigm (Genesis 1:27). Love in the biblical sense 'is simply the translation of holiness into terms of personal relationships,' in Bishop Stephen Neill's wise opinion.[17] Catholic and Orthodox theologies summon our evangelical attention to the seriousness of the church's being as new humanity, a corporate as well as an individual reality. Few evangelical thinkers, Forsyth, Barth and Bonhoeffer being notable exceptions, have articulated this important and biblical fact. Bonhoeffer's later classic *Life Together* conveys the sense of huge privilege of all Christian fellowship; even amid the trying sinfulness of the community of faith, the wrongs of a fellow Christian can 'be a constant occasion for me to give thanks that both of us may live in the forgiving love of God in Jesus Christ.'[18].

Evangelical ecclesiology must gain a new hold on the nature of the one church, through the cross as the central dynamic of the unity, linking gospel and church more powerfully. Forsyth comes nearest to spelling out this evangelical catholicity, bringing the grace and judgement of God in Christ to bear not only on the church but public affairs generally.

The great moral act of atonement shattered the power of sin, dealt with the judgement due to the race corporately, rent the veil between God and man, and regenerated humanity. God's making himself commonly holy involved the commonality of the race. Church life is the Christ life at work in the world, is the life of costly, reconciled relationships. Christ's body also faces decisions, taken under the judgement of the cross, about political and social affairs. Here is a potentially vast canvas of ecclesial life, linked to salvation but also to creation and its eschatological renewal. Christ crucified and risen takes us to the depth of ecclesiology, but also gives it a massive scope, beyond our current horizons and commitments.

Evangelical Anglicans can blow the dust off their Hooker and rediscover many statements of this rich ecclesiology:

> 'Thus we participate in Christ partly by imputation, as when those things which he did and suffered for us are imputed unto us for righteousness; partly by habitual and

> real infusion, as when grace is inwardly bestowed. . . . The first thing of his so infused into our hearts in this life is the Spirit of Christ. . . . From hence it is that they which belong to the mystical body of our Saviour Christ, and be in number as the stars of heaven, divided successively by reason of their mortal condition into many generations, are notwithstanding coupled every one to Christ their Head, in as much as the same Spirit, which anointed the blessed soul of our Saviour Christ, doth so formalize, unite and actuate his whole race, as if both he and they were so many limbs, compacted into one body,by being quickened all with one and the same soul.'[19]

Classical Anglican ecclesiology, evangelical and catholic, can reach this huge scale of view, centred not only on the Logos, as in the neo-Platonic vision of reality, but on him crucified and risen, and therefore reaching into our moral and spiritual darkness.

Baptized into the death and resurrection of Christ, the church faces the world and wants to gather all into Christ. Fellowship and mission, often alternative strategies in local church life, if they are truly Christian, are very much the same because they are both concerned with *koinonia* of Jesus. The church's life and work, her being and act, cannot really be split. The Johannine motif of the Father sending the Son and the Son sending the church in His name goes hand in hand with that of the unity of the Father and the Son as the ground of the unity of the church and, inseparably, her mission into the world. This life and mission is that of the Son, sent by the Father.

This unity is no mere mutual social commitment, but springs from the regenerative impact of Christ, from the decisive act of the absolutely holy in sinful humanity. This *koinonia,* as Bonhoeffer knew and lived, must not be confused with sociability and the warm cosy glow of mutual companionship. Dulles is correct to reject this humanistic *koinonia* as the essence of the church. The life in unity with the Son can mean much coldness and absence of companionship; any Christians who criticize and leave their God-given brothers and sisters in Christ for other groups must always ask themselves what precisely they are looking for, and whether they have faced up to the depths of mature fellowship with Christ.

Church being as communion is eschatological, not primarily sacramental although the sacraments express this fact, but primarily in the 'real relations' established in the Holy Spirit in actual regenerate human lives. Human decisions and deeds incarnate the ecclesial life of the new race: this is where the Spirit of Christ dwells in his temple of living stones; the coming of the Spirit is upon 'all flesh' rather than on sacramental elements. The branches stemming from the vine bring forth fruit, fruit which endures. Here is the correct basis for the undeniable claims of the radical liberation theologian: Christological *koinonia*, real relations which, because they open the individual out to his neighbour in every sense, cry out for expansion to the ends of the earth and the end of time. Just as fellowship within the church cannot be true if it does not turn outwards in mission, so mission can only be Christ centred if it includes the material well-being of all. Fellowship with Christ also means sharing with the victor over the powers of darkness, and knowing that behind much of the evil and conflict there lies a personal hostility to humankind which Christ alone has overcome.

A. E. Garvie, a Congregationalist Scottish theologian, marvellously grasps this truth that the church is on her eschatological journey, and his exposition helps us glimpse a way forward for defining the relationship between church as a unity and as a communion of the redeemed, and also between church and creation as each moves towards the eschaton, the 'inner basis of the covenant' expanding to transform the outer basis.[20]

> 'Because human personality and human society are both so imperfect, the two conceptions for us still lie apart; but even we in an ideal can observe their convergence, and they meet in the perfection of God. It is the Christian life in its distinctiveness as individual and collective in which both ideals should find their realization. As the individual Christian loves others, he gives his life to them and finds his life in them, and his personality becomes increasingly social. As in the Christian Church the community of the Spirit is realized in the virtues and graces, the society will become more personal, with a unity and a continuity of life which raise it above all atomic individualism, and give it a common aspiration, purpose and activity. The Christian is perfected in his unity in the Spirit with all other believers; and the Church is perfected into unity through the fullness of its personal life. To speak of the Church personally as the community of the Spirit is more than poetic personification. As the Christian perfects himself in love, and as the Church has a universal destiny and obligation, the ideal

> can be realized only as men become one in love, and the Church becomes the society which embraces all mankind.'[21]

For the church, 'dying to live' can never become simply a principle, separated from the person of the risen Christ, as if it were a cosmic secret of universal harmony, following Hegel. But given the fact of reconciliation, flowing from the act of Calvary, and communion with the Lord of the church, Garvie's vision of the destiny of the church has real value.

Garvie, fundamentally agreeing with Zizioulas, Muhlen, Ramsey and Bonhoeffer, touches the heart of ecclesiology and finally links the church's historical life, mission and worship with the transcendent God: 'The revelation of God as Father, Son and Holy Spirit can be completed only as humanity is redeemed to be the temple of God, filled with his Spirit; and until that consummation we shall not realize in experience so as to be luminous to our thought the ideal of social personality and personal society, the two converging conceptions which are leading our thought into the holy of holies — Father, Son and Holy Spirit as one God.'[22] Garvie moves us towards the concrete problems of the historical church living out this spiritual ecclesial *koinonia* and developing her institutions accordingly, as new situations and opportunities arise in the blood, toil, tears and sweat of the events of real life. The temple of the Holy Spirit proves to be no beautiful sacrament, but a rough-hewn people, full of the unattractive, marked with the sign of the cross.

The church, rather more aptly than Jesus, might be described in terms of 'the paradox of grace' because she is set apart, consecrated and redeemed from her sin, renewed by the Holy Spirit, and yet remains sinful, needing constantly to repent and stand only on the cross of Christ for her salvation rather than her own 'spirituality'. It is this paradox which makes practical or structural ecclesiology so difficult. The church in Eastern Europe knows deeply about her life hid with Christ in God, as a terrible and physical thing. One of the very few Czech theologians whose work is available in English, Jan Milic Lochman, tells us that the Czech Reformed tradition includes 'obedience to Christ's gospel and law, with special emphasis on love between Christians; and suffering (cross) and persecution for the truth and kingdom of God', among its marks of the church.[23]

Ecclesiology of spiritual *koinonia* commands a massive consensus which the Anglican can confidently share as utterly consistent with the scriptures and the centre of Anglican tradition.

New wine will need wineskins, and the wine of the new covenant demands that the process of embodying the ecclesial life institutionally will continue. This is precisely the point at which the Church of England finds herself, and she must look ahead, not only backwards, for her orientation. She is currently a church very visible, with many magnificent cathedrals and parish churches across the land and a physical pastoral presence everywhere. She is a church visible and pastoral, with an incarnational ethos and an overriding ministerial and sacramental commitment.

Perhaps, in addition to this catholic-orthodox mores, she now needs to appropriate her reformed tradition and become also the church audible and personal, geared to evangelize as well as to worship and pastor. The covenant tradition of bringing the word personally, rather than just sacramentally, needs restating; and this means a far greater stress on the *whole people of God* having their part to play in lay witness to the Lord of creation. It also means encouraging people to bring gospel values to play in society generally. God dwells invisibly and in his visible church by his Holy Spirit, not in objects but in the hearts of people, the living stones of his temple. The living Word, from the heart of the Father, spoken and sacrificed in personal dialogue, remains Christ's manner of presence to his church. Christ inhabits his faithful people redemptively, by the Holy Spirit in a personally saving manner, distinct from the way in which he sustains creation. Blurring this distinction, so clear in the New Testament gospel, has led to some Anglicanism ceasing to act ecclesially by melting into a general religious mixture and failing to proclaim the saving uniqueness of Christ's death and resurrection. It is precisely an over-concentration on the church as a static sacrament, reflecting religious consciousness, coupled with a purely pastoral goal, that can allow this radical failure of the church to proclaim the gospel of grace for sinful, and religious, mankind. The church must be visible but dynamically audible, to lead people from natural religion to Christ, from the circumference to the very centre of true faith.

2. Institutions for koinonia

A. INSTITUTIONAL STRUCTURES: DEVELOPMENT IN HISTORY

The church's life of 'reconciled and reconciling' *koinonia* has to be lived out in history. The model of growth and development applies particularly to this dimension of the church's being. The tradition of the Church of England, while being conservatively reverent to the wisdom of the past, does not absolutize it and acknowledges institutional development for the sake of the Christological centre. With Newman, Anglicanism knows that living in history entails change. But with Barth 'the community knows perfectly well that it cannot exemplify the law of God directly, but only in the broken form of its human law in which it can only point to the law of God.'[24] The gospel must be served by the institutional arrangements of the church. The growth of structures and institutions needs to be consistent with the Christocentric *koinonia*.

The church is the church of Jesus Christ, a Christocracy according to Barth, who surely is correct to stress that the question of institutional order in the church cannot be dismissed.

> 'Is it not wiser,' he asks, to argue . . . that juridification and bureaucratization, ie the reduction of Church life to a matter of forms and techniques, are symptoms of disorder which we can counter, not by a rejection of the problem of law or a dissolution of order, but only by a recognition and assertion of the true order of the community; that they constitute a lawlessness of the Church in face of which we have to maintain the form of law which corresponds to the substance of the matter, and therefore the true Church law . . . ?'[25]

Here Barth teaches something akin to the classical Anglican principle, seeking to avoid ecclesiastical absolutism on the one hand, and an anarchy of the pure spirit on the other; he talks of church law being based on 'confessing law', that is on the community's commitment to listening to the testimony of the prophets and apostles. Church order and structure are vital, necessary, while never sufficient in themselves, and the community must seek to form itself with reference to faith in Christ. This is precisely the message of Paul's olive tree image: historic pedigree has immense value, but faith in Christ must be the central defining criterion for the church.

Michael Ramsey's plea to evangelical Anglicans was to relate the visible, historical, institutional church to the gospel, and he strove to show how the Anglo-Catholic vision of the institutions of the threefold ministry, its succession, and the sacraments were the necessary embodiments in history of the death and resurrection of Jesus. His theology was correct in insisting on the link, the way he worked out that link remains in dispute. Newman also insisted on the priestly sacramental shape of the church as the providentially-wrought expression of the gospel community, essentially ARCIC's understanding of the case. Zizioulas has offered a Greek Orthodox statement of a very similar line. With Barth, he affirms the Christological centre of the Church, but with Ramsey he stresses that this is primarily a eucharistic reality: the eucharist, representing Christ and his sacrifice, constitutes the institutional church and is an institution logically prior to the ordained ministry. But the eucharist and the threefold ministry cannot be separated: the sacrament requires its proper priestly officiant as well as the whole congregation of the faithful. The church as the many has to be defined always along with the one, the local bishop: there cannot be one without the many, nor vice versa, for Zizioulas.

This applies for the consecration of bishops and the ordination of presbyters, people and local leader are always both equally necessary for perpetuating the historical church. The eucharist also is even more basic and actually constitutes the church. No important church act, including ordinations, can happen outside the eucharistic context. The eucharist, for this Orthodox theology, is not in the hands of the church so much as the very point of contact with God for the body of Christ. Here heaven and earth meet, here the things eschatological cohere with the temporal and historical, here the Word is incarnated at the centre of the church. In this sacramental act the Christological *koinonia* gains primary expression in the church, according to the Anglo-Catholic and Orthodox.

But this heavily sacramentalized focus can only be accepted by Anglicans if it does not dominate or relativize the reality of the church's life of faith and walk in the Spirit, daily and not necessarily sacramentally, taking up the cross into the world. If eschatology is so concentrated into the eucharist that the common life and mission of the people of God is downgraded into a status of awaiting the next eucharistic event, then ecclesiology has become distorted away from apostolic catholicity. Eucharistic Christological *koinonia* plays a vital part in the Anglican tradition, and evangelical Anglicans may still need to gain a fresh appreciation of its centrality as the institutional structure sacramentally uniting the church in the redemption of Christ. But the eucharistic community, the community created by the life laid down of the suffering servant, is the community of the Spirit. The Spirit dwells in the hearts of the faithful who therefore constitute the church, which celebrates the sacraments. The problem with the rationale for sacraments and ministry offered by Ramsey and Zizioulas for evangelical Anglicans is that it seems to render the priesthood of the whole church a symbolical formality. *Koinonia* in the Spirit, including mission, goes beyond the sacraments; the church is not 'episodic' or punctiliar, she remains the Spiritual *koinonia* inside or outside the eucharistic celebration. An over-emphasis on the sacramental elements turns the church inwards and clericalizes her priesthood. Eschatological eucharistic celebration is not a fresh incarnation of the Word, in an impersonal static sacramental mode.

Baptism into Christ commits the church to a life of conflict against sin, the world and the devil and to a life of faith which is confessed, to the mission of Christ in the world as well as to fellowship in the church. If evangelical Anglicans must appropriate the eucharist, focused on relationship with Christ and relationships governed by the sacrificial principle, catholic Anglicans have to take seriously the confessing, witnessing, praying character of the whole baptized community.

Quick, perhaps influenced by Forsyth, grasps the nature of the church's historical, eschatological character of conflict with the fallen world.

> 'There can be no gradual evolution or transformation of this world into the next, or of the temporal into the eternal. And yet the harvest of eternity is the harvest reaped and garnered from this world, in which and for which the Son of God was content to die. And those who by faith in him are willing to surrender all this world's life and goodness in the spirit of his love, are those in whom the life and fellowship of the world to come are already real.'[26]

Only the people of God themselves, living in the world with all its temptations and conflicts, can go this way. It may be eucharistically presented, but lived out only through the higher, because personal, 'sacraments' of Christian people. How are church structures to serve the whole people of God in their discipleship?

B. PARISH AND PASTORAL PRESBYTER

At present the parish structure revolves around the presbyteral sacramental ministry, with the implication that the whole country is Christian and simply needs pastoring. The reality is very different, with continuing decline in participation of the Church of England. Plainly a 'post-Christendom' missionary church is urgently needed, and a church which at her heart will provide community, *koinonia*, for those converted from the secular culture to Christ. The ministry of the presbyter, the pastor-teacher who presides at the sacraments, has been almost exclusively that of the *'didache'*, of the theologically trained teacher of the faith and to some extent builder of community, although in Anglicanism this has been often a symbolical rather than real role, the priest 'representing' various functions sacramentally in himself.

The needs of the day, our present horizon as well as the apostolic horizon, call for a massive emphasis on the *'kerygma'* as well as *'didache'*, for gospel evangelization outside the walls of the churches, for trained evangelists and even more for a 'confessing' church membership. In addition to the evangelistic priority, in terms of God's creation the church has to begin to foster the consciousness of lay people acting and thinking Christianly in their secular employment and the wider world. The church has to start to be the church in the world which God made, if that world is not to spiral steeply into totally secular materialism. The ministry of the word must be both *didache* and *kerygma*, teaching and proclamation to the unchurched, not simply proclamation to the insiders. The Church of England desperately needs to acknowledge this plain fact and to take evangelism and real community in Christ with utmost seriousness.

Anglican clergy arise from the church, their call by the Spirit tested by the whole church, lay and ordained, and their appointment made by the whole church, represented by the bishop. This goes beyond a congregational appointment. The ordained minister not only arises from out of the whole body, but also is sent to the congregation. This valuably rules out any hint of the minister being *hired* by a local congregation, and *fired* should his ministry prove disturbing of complacency! Anglican principles resist commercial, contractual ideas of ministry as being secular and anthropocentric. Ministry comes to the church, as well as from it; it also comes from the wider church as well as to the local outcrop. Anglican ministry in structure is not only connectional, but prophetic and apostolic in the sense of representing the word coming to the people.

The Church of England falls clearly into the 'church' type according to Troeltsch's classification, by which 'the Church is an institution which has been endowed with grace and salvation as a result of the work of Redemption.' His other type, 'the sect is a voluntary society composed of strict and definite Christian believers bound to each other by the fact that all have experienced "the new birth".'[27] The Church of England, the established Church by law, is open to all comers and could hardly place fewer demands or qualifications on her members. In a real sense the church of England is open to all citizens of the land. Her ministers have to assent to a basically orthodox faith, and her laity to the baptismal vows, without much teaching or 'discipling' in the faith. The establishment formally places all the country under the pastoral care of the church. However small the congregations may be in a place, a minister has responsibility not only for the congregation, but formally is available for the wider community. Troeltsch finds the 'church type' likely to endure as the basic form of Christianity since 'it is able to receive the masses and to adjust itself to the world, because to a certain extent it can afford to ignore the need for personal holiness for the sake of the objective treasures of grace and of redemption,' although this has its price, since 'it cannot be denied that this does mean a modification of Christian thought in order to bring it down to the average level, the level of practical possibility; and it is a principle of far reaching adjustment and compromise.'[28]

Such words, although written in the spirit of careful analysis, sound the terrible theological warning note of the Apocalypse, 'you are neither hot nor cold', for the Church of England, with her commitment to being 'user friendly' and undemanding. Her strand of Reformation tradition is that of Luther and Calvin, who do stress objective grace rather than the subjective sanctification constantly pressed home by the radicals of the Reformation, the Puritans and the Wesleyan tradition. If she is to avoid dissolving into a social religious phenomenon, she has to develop ways of teaching the faith and of forming disciples in her open type framework. She has to be constantly serving the Christological centre of herself. Theologically it is arguable that the Church of England accepts her flock on God's own terms of acceptance, the principle of justification by grace. Given this, the theme of sanctification has also to be taken seriously in structures for specifically Christological *koinonia*.

Given this open parish structure, there have to be ways of nurturing deeply Christocentric community within the parish and for the parish. Fellowship and mission in the triune life of

God cannot accept dilution and compromise if the church is to have anything to offer to the world, or indeed to her own people. Such adjustment and compromise seems precisely the religion expounded by the Grand Inquisitor to the anonymous Christ. It is because she is suspected of compromise that evangelical Anglicans see many zealous members joining house churches in search of real community life and heavy ministerial discipline for spiritual growth.

Such secession, perfectionist in character, received its theological rebuttal by Hooker, still the classical statement of Anglican institutional order, against the radicals and the Romans. But if the Church of England fails to take her members' fellowship with Christ seriously, she will remain vulnerable to the criticism of not being faithful to the gospel. Effective structures to promote mission and fellowship within the parish are a priority. Here is a difficult spiritual and ecclesial balance: spiritual pride by an inner ring of the parish is a danger, a 'true church within the church', in reaction to the spiritual sloth of identifying the church with casual, uncommitted, 'cultural Christianity'.

Newbigin teaches that the church exists as a justified sinner, standing as the the publican rather than the pharisee.[29] When the church is truly focused on Christ, walking in the Spirit, there is no place for dividing off a spiritual elite:

> 'the mark of the man in Christ will be that he is more eager to claim freedom for his brother than for himself, and more ready to submit himself to good order than to impose it on his brother . . . the fundamental principle will always be the love which seeks not its own good but the common good of the body. When the claim to possession by the Spirit, attested perhaps by abnormal signs of spiritual power, is made the ground for treating the unity and order of the church with contempt, and for despising the great mass of "nominal Christians" in whom only the virtues which we have come to regard as normal for a Christian are to be seen, we must say bluntly as St Paul did, that this is not the work of the spirit but the flesh.'[30]

The Church of England is structurally committed to this broad charitable approach towards her flock; but must therefore develop effective means for fostering real relations with Christ, for turning the formal into the actual. No doubt the sacraments play a part in this, but living faith in the heart is how we feed on Christ, as the words of administration of the BCP tell us. If Newbigin is right about justification being the key ecclesial model, then all the more strongly must sanctification and real faith be fostered as the spiritual counterpart to the forensic aspect. Because the Church of England declines to judge the sheep from the goats, preferring to leave that to Him who knows the heart, she has all the more responsibility for developing all possible means of spiritual renewal, for giving every opportunity for the outward and visible to become inward and spiritual in individuals.

Such structures arise naturally in each locality to meet increasingly particular situations: small sub-units of many kinds and at several levels of mutual commitment. An important unit is the family, a unit in need of particular attention at present by Anglicans who are not strong at handing on the faith to the children; again the more this is a church unit, the less exclusive will it become. Fostering faith at a family level, perhaps drawing on Jewish traditions of weekly meal and prayer for example, would enrich the life of the church, and the evangelical tradition of daily prayer with the scriptures seems increasingly important for all strands of the church to learn. It is important for the clergy not to block the development of new forms of fellowship and mission, which may be the Spirit at work in the growth of the church. In this the charismatic movement has often been of real benefit, when prompting initiatives within the church family, but in a spirit of humility rather than of bombast. One utterly key point arising from such suggestions is that church structures do not only mean *ministerial* structures, but structures for and from the *whole* people of God. In *principle*, the Church of England, with her lay representation in the synodical system, realizes this. But structures must develop to foster all the ministries of the whole body.

C. FLEXIBLE AND CORPORATE MINISTRIES

The official Anglican-Reformed agreement *God's Reign and Our Unity*, stresses this need for flexibility, for institutional development:

> 'Except in very simple static societies, modern communities consist of various overlapping groups whose members are related through language, work, culture and common interest. In order to be effective in missionary outreach the

> church may have to encourage the formation of distinct forms of ministry and eucharistic fellowship for different groups in the same area.'[31]

The rigid application of the system of the parish and incumbent, already breaking down in favour of a more corporate clerical form of team ministries, may need to be yet more flexibly interpreted. The fixed form of ministry centring round the one and the many, ordained and lay, needs to be complemented with more corporate models of leadership. In addition the ministry of the word, both inside the church congregation and outwards as proclamation to the world, needs re-emphasizing by the Church of England. The heart of the ordained ministry is not, for Anglicans, sacramental but primarily the apostolic calling of 'fishing and shepherding', of communicating the faith, of building up the faithful in the faith and summoning the world to faith in Jesus.

Eduard Schweitzer's work on church order in the New Testament found that pastoral ministry, local to one place, was but one line of ministry. Many others existed, notably the travelling charismatic prophets, and the apostolic church planting missionaries. The church needs to accept that the local presbyteral-episcopal ministry is not the only, nor necessarily the controlling, line of ministry. Travelling ministries, such as missionaries sponsored by missionary societies, are equally apostolic and to be recognized as such. What are often dubbed 'para church' organizations may often better be recognized as wider forms of mission and ecclesial care, which are fully apostolic 'church' ministries although different from that of local presbyters in the parish. One disastrous move the church can seek to make is to bureaucratize such ministries, reorganize them, put them under the control of the episcopal line, rather than simply acknowledge and encourage them as apostolic in themselves, as 'charismatic' promptings of the Spirit.

D. THE MINISTRY OF WOMEN IN THE CHURCH

Adopting a more corporate approach to church leadership brings the issue of ministry and ordination into a new perspective. Rural situations in England seem to be stretching the current pattern to breaking point, so that duly commissioned lay presidency of the eucharist seems a pressing question, if truly local leadership is not to be disconnected from presidency.

In urban situations, where the percentage of the population attending church is tiny, matching levels in the communist bloc, there is a desperate need for the church to invest in evangelists to work in tandem with the pastorate. These are two examples which might be multiplied. The point is that a more flexible approach needs to be taken to ministry: the body of Christ has more functions than the presbyteral and episcopal, the two currently operating formally in the Church of England, and operating with a very sacramental focus.

The ordained pastor-teacher and normal president at the eucharist, remains indispensable but not without some form of eldership, some corporate complement beyond the curate who is training to move on to another pastorate. Green points out that the New Testament refers to elders or presbyters in the plural, suggesting a more corporate original understanding of this ministry.[32] This also surely is the current way ahead for the issue of women's ministry. If the Church of England is serious about this ministry, then she must set about financing posts for women in many more parishes as the norm, alongside incumbents as part of the leadership team. Only in this way will the church as a whole grow to appreciate the distinctively feminine contribution, and grow to evaluate precisely the right steps forward in terms of complementarity and headship. Whether it is right simply to graft women into the currently individualist, western clerical leadership model is highly debateable: the opportunity for widening the whole notion of ministry and so bringing the distinctively feminine into a complementary pattern for the mission of God seems a truer Christian development, in that it would more precisely reflect the relational quality of communion which should colour all aspects of church life. Such a move would be meeting the needs of the whole church, in establishing complementarity, rather than simply addressing the issue in terms of the single line of ordained ministry.

Here is an opportunity to appraise the very character of Christian leadership. 'Team ministries' developing in the church currently mean a series of clergy, each pastoring one congregation, linked only for administrative convenience. Genuine relationship as leadership is a much more real affair, and the presence of women could enable this to become a reality and to break down the masculine individualist approach. To take this chance to discuss 'ministry' and to bring more women into ministry, would ensure that the Church of England does not simply 'masculinize' women's contribution in parishes.

E. EPISCOPACY AND SYNODS

The personal and relational character of the church in Christ points towards the increasing use of teams of leadership. Again *God's Reign and Our Unity* looks forward with this in mind when it advises the Anglicans to take seriously the corporate aspect of leadership, while the Reformed agree to take up the personal aspect, eldership and episcopate respectively.[33] This looks like a more grass roots, lay, expression of the conciliar–primatial distinction made by ARCIC. It does not, however, involve the unique spiritual charism claimed for a topmost personal expression of leadership, and does not assume that such a role is needed at a global level.

In practice the Church of England is gradually tending to increased use of teams. Bishops have suffragan bishops for example, a development of the classical threefold order pattern and a necessary development born of the need to minister in very large dioceses. Anglicanism probably needs to increase real relations of actual contact between bishops, who are formally pastors, and clergy whom they pastor, as well as between bishops and people. There is a real need to emphasize the bishops' function, beyond the strange notion of *episcope* as some sacramental abstraction, vested in the bishop, who focuses the church in himself and *creates the church* by virtue of his power to ordain and confirm. It may well be true that larger numbers of bishops should be appointed, who will have purposive ministries of diocesan, and national mission and building of fellowship rather than exclusively symbolical functions. Here again the notion of church as primarily 'sacrament' is unhelpful, leading to the corollary of bishop as sacrament.

Anglicanism has a form of episcopal government closely akin to English constitutional monarchy. Bishops have authority in their dioceses, and Archbishops have a national moral authority, although not one which overrides diocesan episcopacy. The Archbishop of Canterbury has a sapiential authority, but cannot create new doctrine, as can the Roman Pontiff. The bench of bishops meets separately from houses of clergy and laity. But the system of electing representatives to synods means that the whole church has a voice in the decision making. Bishops have a great authority, but they have to accept decisions of General Synod. Personally vested authority is balanced by the electoral system of synods. The balance is hard to state because bishops have a moral authority and respect, just as at parish level the vicar has a pastoral authority in the relationship with the elected Parish council. In theory the Anglican system combines what Dillistone called the 'organic' and the 'covenantal' means of church order: the episcopate representing the ongoing ministerial order tracing back down the centuries; the synodical representing the voice of the whole people of God. In principle this development of the old episcopal power by means of synodical government seems not only fair but theologically well oriented. It provides the personal and the corporate aspects and ensures that the leadership cannot dominate the people.

The problems with this system lie in its adminstration rather than its principle. Dr. Gareth Bennett's *Crockford's Preface* expressed deep disquiet over 'fixing' of committee memberships, over unchristian party domination of key committees nominating bishops, over the timing of synods which in practice exclude ordinary working lay people. Like the operation of the British constitution, a degree of secrecy at high level committees was detected, with a liberal oligarchy pulling the levers of power.

The paradox of the church remains her imperfect nature in covenant with her Lord, who is perfect and gives his Spirit, yet who is failed time and again by his people, and the church at every level needs a continuing repentance. But that is not to say that the attempt at complementary structures of leadership and decision making is wrong, in fact the episcopal-synodical structure has much to commend it. It has the potential to provide not only negative balance against powerful leadership, but positively to provide several avenues through which the word of God may be given to the church.

Episcopacy at home and global Anglican episcopalianism appear to be rather separate phenomena in Anglicanism. In England bishops form an interlocking instrument of regional ministry and ratification of ministry through the years. With the synodical system, not in a wholly neat way, bishops under the archbishops provide a coherent form of leadership and decision making. As for the worldwide Anglican Communion, 'The truth is that the Anglican Churches are not held together by any outwardly constraining bond. They cohere, as a loose knit family of Churches, because they desire to cohere; and they remain in communion with one another for the same reason. Yet there are tensions within Anglicanism; and it is conceivable that in the ten years' interval between the Lambeth Conference just ended and the next . . . the sense of internal tension and strain may be even intensified.'[34] This was written forty-one years ago by the then bishop of Derby, who added that the current Archbishop of Canterbury felt that inter-communion should be pursued rather than a single organically united Church of the nation, since the Church of England was insufficiently unified internally to pursue schemes of constitutional unity with other denominations. Anglican ecclesiological problems remain the same; the Lambeth Conference of 1988 broke up with precisely such issues troubling it. What kind of episcopal system is the Anglican Communion?

The basic choice lies between the Tractarian view and the Elizabethan view expressed in the work of Field and Hooker. The Tractarian view, which seems currently to determine ecumenical attitudes, has received the most damaging criticism of being an oddity among ecclesiologies, permitting the episcopal schism it claims to overcome. It is time for the Church of England to return decisively to the ecclesiological principles developed by her second generation reformers in the interests of integrity and mission. That is to say, the episcopal form of government continues to serve the gospel by providing a wide framework and instrument of order and mission in complementarity with local congregations and their ministry. The organic wholeness of the church of God finds protection and expression in this episcopal form. Newbigin argued powerfully for this position from his Presbyterian tradition at the formation of the Church of South India.

The episcopate subserves the whole church rather than creating her, therefore Hooker and the great weight of representative Anglican theology did not unchurch continental non-episcopal churches. Anglican ecclesiology does not, classically, hold the view that the church and sacramental grace depend upon the episcopal succession from the apostles. Bishop Bell, in the opening chapter of his book on Anglican ecumenism, cites text after text from the history of Anglican ecclesiology demonstrating this position, that while episcopacy has divine sanction there is no sweeping conclusion as to the absolute and invariable necessity of it.[35] Rawlinson echoes Bell's expression of the classical Anglican view when speaking of

> 'the principles of the classic Anglicanism of the past, to bear witness . . . to the principle that a bishop is the proper minister of ordination, without pressing the logic of neo-Anglicanism to the extent of requiring other Churches, as

> a condition of inter communion with Anglicanism, either to unchurch their own past or to break such present communion with Churches not yet brought into the episcopal family as they . . . may desire to retain.'[36]

Hooker recognized both Rome and the Puritans as churches, seas as part of the one ocean, some seas being muddier than others.

This heritage of Hooker and the Anglican tradition needs to be underlined both for the high and low constituencies of the Church of England. The New Testament, against Rome and the Puritans then, and today against the Restorationist movement, lays down no strict *blueprint* of church goverment. Anglican ecclesiology preserves this instrument of the wide organic principle of the wholeness of church and of the wisdom of her history by her episcopal loyalty. As Dillistone argued in his work focusing on Anglican and Presbyterian ecclesiology, the organic or holistic aspect of ecclesiology, that which features the visible church's overall being, finds most powerful expression in the episcopal systems. The Roman system of ecclesiology, with its hierarchical structures descending from the bishop of Rome downwards, true even for the post Vatican 2 era, exemplifies this organic principle to the highest degree.[37] Complementary to the organic is the covenantal principle, most highly developed in Presbyterian church order: the covenant between God and his people in Christ is lived out in congregations who enter into relationship with each other, characteristically bearing allegiance to a common confession of faith.

Dillistone regards the Church of England as built primarily on the organic principle but strongly embracing the covenantal, particularly since she is committed to the scriptures as containing all things needed for salvation, and to faith as the means of receiving salvation. On the face of it the Church of England enjoys the double aspect of the organic and the covenantal. One unique factor also involved is the established character of the Church of England, woven into the constitutional fabric of the country, which gives distinctively organic definition.

The recent Lambeth Conference of all the Anglican bishops worldwide demonstrated the strengths and weaknesses of the organic framework of the global episcopalian system. Episcopal Anglican churches across the globe gathered together represented by their bishops, presided over by the Archbishop of Canterbury, each church recognizing the others and accepting the ministry of the others. But is this truly an organic unity as Dillistone supposed, rather than a covenantal one, a 'loose knit family of churches' as Rawlinson put it? The reason why this question arose very forcibly had been accurately predicted in the tragic *Crockford's Preface*: some episcopal churches already ordain women as priests and proposed to consecrate women bishops, while the majority still do not and some bishops fail to agree that women bishops can possibly stand in catholic and apostolic succession. Within this loose knit family of churches, which have different ways of selecting bishops and different liturgies, for example, a serious point of dissension has to be dealt with. Some bishops might not recognize others within the 'organic' episcopal structure and this causes one to ask whether the Anglican Communion is in fact more of a federation, a covenanting community of episcopal churches, rather than an organically integrated body. Some bishops are considering not recognizing consecrations of women, as if such consecrations breached the terms of the covenant or communion. The conference visually brought home Newman's point that 'the branch theory', or the episcopal pedigree theory, does not achieve unity; episcopal schism is possible and is solid historical fact.

In the same year that the Lambeth bishops gathered, Archbishop Lefèvre was excommunicated from the Roman church for consecrating bishops in defiance of the Pope's instructions, causing another kind of episcopal split. In that case, the organism of the Roman episcopal system showed its own particular character: the episcopacy stands under a prior controlling system, the papacy. The Pope adjudicates when disputes arise between bishops and decides who are genuinely part of the organism. The Anglican Communion has no such personal judicial primary norm to define the episcopal fellowship. The Roman papal system would solve the problem of whether or not to recognize a woman bishop; the ARCIC version of the primacy would also decide the issue, since the ARCIC primate is chairman of brother bishops but also has an *independent* charism for decisive action. Any primatial power less than this would not provide a neat solution to the Lambeth problem, since it would leave the bench of bishops in disagreement. Anglicanism recoils from judicial primacy in the sense of a divinely gifted official whose decision, like that of the football referee, is always right. The awkward fact is that the interpretative authority of church leaders must, for Anglicans, appeal to the apostolic gospel for justification.

This makes things far less neat and tidy than for the Roman church, whose primate has jursidiction everywhere, and power of the most penetrating kind. Anglicanism seems to be left agonizing over hard issues, seeking gospel illumination for the way ahead, and also having to listen to the voice of the laity, not only the clergy, although this principle needs stressing more plainly at occasions such as Lambeth conferences. Anglicans recognize tensions and disagreements in interpretations of the gospel, but can appeal finally only to the gospel and the canonical scriptures for the way ahead, just as in the Acts of the Apostles church leaders agonized over issues thrown up by the gospel encountering new situations, such as the need to keep the Jewish food laws and the acceptance of Gentile converts.

Anglicans have no neat interpretative norm to cut through such problems; they trust that over a period of time, given genuine commitment to listen to the scriptures at the same time as concentrating on the contemporary issue in question, the right apostolic way ahead will emerge. As the Church of England, General Synod with the episcopate and the archbishops combine to produce a coherent system, as the Anglican Communion worldwide, things are not so easy: an authoritative central body or person does not exist.

As in the post apostolic centuries when dioceses debated issues and sought support from brother bishops of large prestigious sees, so the Anglican bishops are in a state of episcopal debate among themselves without a final mechanism to decide the issue. Anglican episcopacy regards itself as patristic rather than medieval, a natural instrument for continuity and fellowship in time and space which the church needs. It is a flexible instrument for communion rather than a hard-edged judicial tool. The bishop has to stand for apostolic way, truth and life, very much in the way that Irenaeus regarded the office. In a sense the Church of England behaves as if she were a second-century church: trinitarian doctrine and the threefold structure of ministry are presupposed, the former apparently under more threat than the latter, but not at the deepest level of her being.

The Lambeth bishops committed themselves to communion, albeit 'impaired communion' caused by the consecration of women bishops. The *'Eames Commission'*[38] was set up as a body of bishops across the disagreement, committed to mutual relationship despite the debate. This may lead to a more organic worldwide Anglican Communion, since it has led to the system of 'episcopal visitors' sharing in ordinations of priests. A woman bishop, therefore, would always have a male bishop sharing in the ordination. This effort at preventing disagreement freezing into a complete break-off of relationships between dioceses could be argued as a gospel principle. Should disagreement result in turning away institutionally?

It is arguable that the theological coherence of this Anglican episcopal family rests on pastoral charity and acceptance: it certainly does not rest on a judicial legal base. This rationale suits the Anglican ethos of tolerance and acceptance but is far more profound and challenging in every sense. The worldwide Anglican Communion clusters around a common confession of faith only in a very general sense of being a 'reformed catholicism'. The criterion of truth is largely presupposed: the scriptures and creeds as mediated in the BCP's theology must form this presumed core, and the Thirty Nine Articles remain formal doctrinal standards for most churches in the Anglican Communion.[39]

The appeal to the unwritten Anglican ethos, claimed to enshrine a particular style of worship and spirituality, begins to sound increasingly hollow in the light of the ever increasing diversity of liturgical rites found among the Anglican churches internationally. It may be true, however, that bishops in the Church England, share a common liturgical practice, whereas they no longer share a common theological role as pillars of the common faith. An early significance of bishops was their role as teachers of the catholic faith in a context of much syncretism and gnosticism. Today on the other hand, many bishops would not wish to draw hard and fast doctrinal lines between Christianity and other faiths.[40]

F. ECUMENISM

The key concepts developed by the *Eames Commission* of 'impaired communion' and 'episcopal visitors' seem to apply more widely than just to the intra-Anglican family disagreements. Just as the socio-political dimension cannot be ignored in any theological method now, so the ecumenical reality increasingly has to be seen as a central 'formative factor' of all ecclesiology. The ecumenical awareness has made theologians sensitive to their own denominational inadequacies and challenges them to find new initiatives to go beyond the previously established lines of disagreement. Now the Anglican Communion has developed the notion of 'impaired communion' between disagreeing churches, the question arises why this cannot be used towards churches outside the Anglican family, and why episcopal visitors could not begin to visit and invite the ordaining ministers of other denominations to ordinations? The Eames principle of commitment to mutual commitment could be applied in conjunction with the call from the movement coming from 'Not Strangers but Pilgrims', *Churches Together in England* being the English branch.

Given the fact that the global Anglican episcopal communion exists on the basis of unwritten conservative fundamentals, mutual recognition and love, rather than on a form of law, the challenge must be to extend this attitude in Christlike fashion to other church bodies, to pursue recognition along the lines of the characteristic inter-Anglican recognition. This would involve a more eschatological and less historicist view of episcopacy. The fourth leg of the 1888 Lambeth Quadrilateral, 'the historic episcopate' as a mark of the church, does not claim an absolute status in the true Anglican heritage, which allows for the impact of historical change. If the Anglican Communion can produce a formula to save communion with the American episcopal church, while upholding the doctrinal difference over women bishops, then surely the door to recognizing other denominations willing to accept episcopacy is wide open?

The 'historic episcopate', shorn of uncatholic Tractarian exclusivism, can become an instrument of unification. In his prophetic book, *The Reunion of the Church*, Lesslie Newbigin, standing in the Presbyterian tradition, argued for a return to the historic episcopate as the means of reunifying the churches. 'So long as episcopacy is accepted and cherished as the organ of the Church's continuing unity from the Apostles in Palestine to the Christian Churches in every land today, it will offer a centre round which the Church may be visibly reunited;'[41] but the exclusivist notion of Anglican episcopacy, designed to attract the approval of Rome and Constantinople, and succeeding with neither, merely cuts off all other Christian denominations.

At this time when it seems that several Free Churches are open to taking up the episcopal system, without their former ministry being denied in any way, Anglicans face the opportunity for a truly catholic and apostolic advance into the future of God. It is time to look into the future of the church, at home and abroad, and to adopt a far more open and welcoming approach to millions of church people who wish to integrate into a Reformed episcopal-synodical system. Unity seems there for the asking with the major Free Church denominations, with what enormous impact for the church's mission and worship in these days of dwindling faith. Were Hooker and Field ministering today, not in a context of Calvinists constantly attacking episcopal order but of Free Churches seeking it, there is no doubt that they would be advocating intercommunion, as an initial step at least. Given fundamental doctrinal agreement, and this would need carefully securing, there is every reason for regaining the broad charitable approach that used to characterize Anglican ecclesiological attitudes, attitudes which accorded far more with Christological *koinonia* than the current 'neo-Anglicanism'.

God's Reign and Our Unity looks to the future of the church and her mission, seeking to define and adapt structures accordingly while maintaining loyalty with the past. The church is a foretaste of the kingdom of God, therefore formalized disunity must be transcended: the message of the gospel proclaims that barriers are broken down in Christ crucified and risen. Here is the challenge to the church for the future. Anglican episcopal theory, desperately needing a theological rationale for the future and relying on the Elizabethan, rather than the Tractarian theory, must become Christianly charitable and accepting and go the way suggested by *God's Reign and Our Unity*, forgetting former exclusive rigidities and moving forward in the Spirit, rather than being obsessed with the 'fleshly' desire for historical pedigrees. To alter the Anglican character by indulging in a juridifying of the episcopacy would be a retrograde step and not one for wholeness but for exclusivity.

Dillistone identified the weakness of a purely covenantal system:

> 'The remoteness of the representatives from their accrediting groups, the tendency of conferences to deal in abstractions which have no vital relationship to existential situations and the powerlessness to implement in practice what may have been agreed upon in the central assembly . . .'[42]

On the other hand 'in Catholic circles overmuch reliance has been placed upon the organic (and often mechanistic) principle in isolation,'[43] which leads to rigidity and clericalist hierarchical institutionalism. Anglicanism must resist the impulse after Lambeth 1988 to seek the ARCIC solution of accepting a version of Roman Primacy, as a divinely inspired focus or point of the pyramid, as an easy way of rationalizing her apparently illogical episcopal system. This would be to move towards the over-organic and mechanistic, at the expense of the covenantal. ARCIC 1 starts with the category of *koinonia* or fellowship, but develops it into a clericalist form of ascending, or descending councils. Such a move would indeed be the rescue of the Tractarian programme, but would not be true to the Anglican heritage of Hooker, nor to her responsibility to the future to pursue wholeness under the influence of the prophets and apostles, for Christians in England.

Anglicanism has to recover her ecclesiological charity, and covenant with all churches who wish to join in this organic episcopal structure, while upholding the trinitarian, incarnational and redemptive faith, the apostolic faith which constitutes a church. From being structurally closed and tempted into ever more doctrinal openness, she needs to become structurally more open and keep a firm hold on her apostolic faith.

This will really only continue the Anglican practice of governing the church by both bishops and synods, not simply synods of clergy, but of all sections of the church. Already there is a complementarity of the organic and personal, along with the corporate and covenantal, forms of oversight. It is now time to become porous to other great, and small, denominations. To go along this path will also match local English ecumenical life and forward the impact of the *'Churches Together in England'* movement, impatient now of what are felt to be clericalizing impediments at the top being put in the way of grass roots Christian fellowship in mission.

The issue of a primacy for such an open welcoming episcopal family will not raise the question of a judicial, so much as a presidential, office acting in concert with fellow bishops as a matter of human church order, since the church 'hath power to decree rites and ceremonies'; but such a presidential office cannot, for Anglican tradition, be invested with a special divine charism, it would be of human arrangement, *de iure humano*, and not divine, *de iure divino*.

Paul's picture of the olive tree in Romans 9–11 speaks of the grafting onto the ancient stock of Israel the Gentile believers by faith in the Messiah. Paul says that all live in this tree of the covenant people because of grace, not because of some inherent historical right: those who rely on status of historical pedigree are deluded. This principle of church life needs reappropriating at the very heart of Anglican ecclesiology. Not only are all church people grafted onto the Abrahamic stock by faith, receiving the free gift of God in Christ, so all are one in having no grounds for boasting; but the olive tree principle compels us to a free acceptance of one another. There are no degrees of better or worse churches as churches. Each will have things and experiences to share. Anglican Lambeth Conferences in future must open themselves to a process of mutual recognition of acknowledgement that we all have been grafted in; once we were 'no people', now we are 'God's people'. The organic episcopal structure must commit itself to its true root in the ecclesiology of classical Anglicanism, rather that the rigid, exclusive Tractarianism which continues to rend the body of Christ.

The gains from following the policy of a less historicizing episcopal theory and uniting with the Free Churches would be immediate and would go to the very core of visible unity. To follow the path of ARCIC 1 would distance the Anglicans from the Free Churches at a subtle but huge doctrinal cost to the Anglican inheritance, and the gains are wholly unknown. The most that is suggested is that Rome would recognize Canterbury as she does Constantinople, far from a true integration and sustaining visible disunity in a major way. It is very hard to disagree with Newbigin that 'the first steps toward that goal must be rather in the direction of that South India has taken than in the direction of those who find in the Church polity of Cyprian the last and unalterable word about the nature of the Church.'[44] An episcopal-synodical church, open to all who wish to integrate, standing on the principle of acceptance by virtue of commonality, *koinonia* in Christ and him crucified, this prospect could be attained and soon, given a return to classical Anglican principles, which point to the relative nature of outer structures in comparison with the central Christological *koinonia* of the church of the people.

Anglicanism was not born out of an attempt to create a new church. It always saw itself as the ongoing church in England, the catholic church reformed, continuing from the past in the gospel of Christ. To open her episcopal instrument to all freely and without condition simply stands in that tradition of building the church in England. Now we must look to the future as much as to the past, to the eschatological dimension of unity. The gospel points to eschatological unity, a unity of Christians which will transcend the divisions of church order and pedigree claims. Then Christological *koinonia* will be all in all, the sole criterion. Modern theology has reminded the churches of the significance of eschatology, of the coming of the Lord of the church. It is time to refashion encrusted structures to serve the mission and unity of the people of God, to open Anglican episcopacy up to all wishing to use it as a time-honoured means of ministerial order, a means to an end, the end which is Christ. At the same time Anglican episcopacy must learn to be more Irenaean in character, to stand as a teacher of the apostolic word, entrusted with fostering this message of salvation, at least as much kerygmatic as sacramental.

The ecumenical life of the Church of England at grass roots level rather contradicts her official preferences for liaison with Rome. Much common church life already takes place and is formally recognized by Local Ecumenical Parishes where Anglicans work, witness and worship alongside other denominations. The demand for increased mutual church life also came to focus in the *Not Strangers but Pilgrims* report, which set in motion proposals for institutionally backed common life at local level. Such movements will increase and raise the issue of the recognition of ministries of Free Churches, who have both men and women ministers. According to the principles of the *Eames Commission*, communion could be initiated however impaired, on precisely the grounds applying in the case of the American episcopalian church.

Given the fact that the church is constituted by Christ's presence in the Spirit to the covenant people, that this is the very essence of the church, it seems to verge on disobedience to remain separated institutionally. The reason for the continued separation hinges on the theology of divine immanence in church history and structural development. There may be no disagreement over Christ as the head of the church: in each denomination people truly know the Lord, in word and sacrament and sacrificial life. But has God been immanent in the structural changes of all the denominations over the years? Have some developments been providential and some not? Was the Reformation compelled by the word being rejected by the medieval church? Has an ongoing institutional unity with the bishop of Rome, or with the family of the Eastern Orthodox, been the only proper institutional embodiment of the knowledge of God in Christ?

Plainly Anglicans think not. For their ecclesial tradition, the divine immanence in historical developments is of a different order to that of Christ's spiritual communion with his people. God works in different ways in creation: his redemptive presence by the Holy Spirit in the hearts of the people is of a higher order to his ordering of events, which is often a total mystery to us. The face of the historical record is as inscrutable as the sphinx, how churches have got to their current positions is also of that nature. The past career and pedigree of churches anxious to reverse schism has to be a secondary issue. The Old Testament shows us the principle of the driest of structures still being capable of renewal by the Spirit of the Lord. This insight into the faithfulness of God towards even the most apparently dead wood, that he can cause the sap to flow, means that no church can be written off by other churches, neither the mainline denominations by the radical housechurch restorationists, nor the latter by the former. Promoting structural division, splitting from the trunk of churches whose formularies are apostolic, offends the faithfulness of God. One structural principle we can derive from the gospel must be that inclusion, grafting in, at different levels of agreement or impairment, is a commitment for the Church of England, starting perhaps with intercommunion as a realistic goal.

G. CHURCH AND STATE

The global Anglican communion, opened up to all sharing in the trinitarian faith and life, would accept varying kinds of links being formed in different countries, and this would in no way harm the family acceptance of Anglican churches any more than do current differences of emphasis within that family. The effect of a coming together of denominations at regional level, in ways appropriate to each, could be dramatic both for mission and pastoral development. The church visible, it must be remembered, is visible and audible regionally, in time and place. It exists within a given culture. It will worship and witness in a given language, understood by the people. This was a central principle of the Reformation, and now, of post Vatican 2. The church must be structured in a way suited to the language and temper of the people of the place, the region, the country. Church life in each place will best serve its Lord when most united and most attuned to reaching its population. The notion of the church in a nation remains very important structurally, indeed inevitable.

In England the impact of restoration of visible *koinonia*, by way of intercommunion and even union, would possibly be heightened in view of the establishment of the Church of

England. Given the fact that the church and state are deeply woven together historically, the monarch being vested with power by the church which in turn cedes formal headship to the crown, it is only appropriate for the church to be as wide and comprehensive of Christians as possible. The Church of England, originally envisaged as the church continuing in England, has no moral right to exclude denominations who desire real relations as fellow members of the body of Christ. As a national church she has to lengthen her tent cords and be as unsectarian as possible.

The establishment of the Church of England cannot be considered now apart from the 'formative factor' of ecumenism. Which way the Church of England decides to go ecumenically, to ARCIC and a papal allegiance or to a deep-seated organic unity with non-episcopalian churches, will deeply affect the relationship of state and church. The ARCIC way of being incorporated into the Roman system of hierachy resulting in being recognized, as Rome recognizes the Eastern Orthodox, would almost certainly cut the nerve of the state link. It is hard to imagine the Parliament of the United Kingdom, which is for the English, Welsh, Northern Irish and the Scots, countenancing a monarchy deriving authority from an archbishop bound to obey the Pontiff.

Donald McLeod, Professor of Theology at the Free Church College in Edinburgh, regards the carrying through of the ARCIC proposals as entailing a massive legal and constitutional dismantling.

> 'At the moment the Queen is the Head of the Church of England, and that to me is just about acceptable. If the Pope were to become the Head of the Church of England and the Queen were to remain within that Church and become therefore a subject of the papacy, it would cause ominous rumblings in many sections of the Protestant community . . . As for myself I would probably abandon the monarchy if these proposals were to be carried through.'[45]

McLeod thinks that the Church of England is behaving as if she were a 'Free Church' which she is not, she is this established church; therefore any adoption of primacy outside Canterbury affects the nation as a whole, and cuts the knot tying together the British Constitution. There is little doubt that McLeod is correct in saying that far too little attention has been given to this national, constitutional aspect of ARCIC. To put the matter crudely, it seems doubtful whether the gains promised to the Church of England, that is the status of something less than a uniate church in the eyes of the Vatican, can possibly be worth such national upheaval, let alone the distancing effect from the Free Churches.

The question must be raised whether the current system whereby the monarch is the formal head of the Church of England may be too unrelated to the actual state of national life to be sustainable. The prospect of a future monarch with strange religious ideas may not be out of the question at all, and this could render the situation untenable. Although the state involvement is formal and instrumental to the decisions of church boards, nevertheless it may seem a symbolical control over the church of Christ, a control which Barth at Barmen in 1934 exposed as potentially disastrous and which the Oxford Movement criticized heavily.

Given the increasing formality of the link with the state, it is possible, for the present, to fend off such criticism, on the grounds that God is the God of society as well as of the church. The link with the state does not mean any real degree of state control or 'erastianism'. The monarch, a lay person, is only formally the supreme governor, and this has a distinct benefit for the structure of the church. This benefit parallels the constitutional benefit of the monarchy in relation to the politically elected prime minister of the day, the holder of actual executive power in the nation. Formally all power, and all judicial authority, in British constitutional law, is vested in the Crown. This is a vital negative function, denying that place to the holder of political power, as compared for example with the President of the United States. Likewise for the Church of England. Formally the monarch, a member of the church, is governor, meaning that this ultimate position is denied to the line of clergy. A *powerless monarch* occupies the place from which institutional authority comes, an arrangement acting against any tendency to prelacy in the church. In the appointment of bishops the monarch, through her agent the prime minister, can only agree to names submitted by church committees, ruling out state control.

From the angle of society, the state values the moral and spiritual involvement of the church. Why, then, should the church refuse her involvement, provided her freedom is safeguarded? Some relationship between state and church has to be worked out: certainly in this the New Testament once more offers no fixed blueprint. Paul tells the church that the governing authorities with their law-keeping function serve God's purposes (Romans 13.1 ff). Disestablishment of Irish and Welsh Anglican churches has not led to strengthening of churches and has lessened the cultural identification of people towards the church. It would be a highly negative gesture towards society as a whole, amounting to a pulling out of social responsibilities in order to adopt a more strident and judgemental attitude towards it. It would declare the state wholly secular, and the state could only respond by removing bishops from the House of Lords, for example, apart from a few who happened to be made peers. Any changes should take the nature of reform and not root and branch disestablishment. It is a considerable paradox that in an age when voices are raised for involvement of the church in society, some of these call simultaneously for her to pull out of key structures and points of legislative influence. One thing is plain, that establishment does not prevent the church from insistent criticism of government policy. Establishment must evolve and reform itself in a way that can bring Christians together as the people of God in this country. Perhaps the model of the Church of Scotland might prove helpful, in which the monarch is an esteemed member, rather than supreme governor, of the established church.

3. Authority in the church

A. FOUNDATION AND SUPERSTRUCTURE: A LEARNING AND TEACHING CHURCH

In England Anglicanism has always regarded herself as reformed catholicism, simply the ongoing stream of faith reformed under the testimony and teaching of the prophets and apostles. For the Church of England the canonical scriptures are the authoritative point of reference, the primary norm which the creeds and first four ecumenical councils of the church in turn reflect. The scriptures form the foundation on which the doctrines and practices must stand, against which subsequent developments, the growth of church order, ethics, liturgy and theology, must be measured—hence the term canon or rule. In this sense the church stands on the unrepeatable foundation of the apostles and prophets.

This principle finds thoroughgoing expression in the Thirty Nine Articles, and its orientation of the Church of England, accounts for Barth's judgement:

> 'As Reformed thinkers, it is impossible for us to say of the Anglican and Lutheran Church, as we do of the Roman Catholic Church, that in them also there is a Church; we must say of them what in view of their doctrine may seem strange and difficult to approve, that in another form they are the one Church of Jesus Christ just as much as is the Reformed Church.'[46]

This apparently polemical statement rests wholly on the fact that the Reformed, Lutheran and Anglican Churches are 'Evangelical' in that they claim to stand under the unique authority of the canon, they seek to scrutinize their way, truth and life according to the voice of the prophets and apostles. Anglicanism affirms this foundation, claims fundamental trinitarian doctrines which arise from the truth of the life, death and resurrection of Jesus.

Barth's apparently harsh comment, although no harsher than the formal attitude struck today by the Anglicans to the Free Churches, refers to the Roman Catholic coordination of living tradition with the canonical norm as a dual form of ultimate authority. His comment demonstrates the immense shift involved in the ARCIC 1 proposals for the future of Anglicanism; it means a move from regarding the canonical scriptures as occupying a higher level of authority in principle than the teaching tradition of the church down the centuries.

The debate about authority and interpretation in ARCIC 1 opens up the discussion of Anglican attitudes. Both Anglican and Roman theologies share a commitment to norms for teaching the faith. They share the presupposition of an inspired Bible as the '*norma normans*', the final source of authoritative teaching. They differ over the uniqueness of the way this functions as the normative norm. For evangelicals, and officially for all Anglicans, the canon of scripture operates uniquely as the supreme authority for teaching, the yardstick available for testing and checking. The traditional evangelical position stands with Barth in giving church tradition a place of honour as a tried and tested secondary source. But it denies the equal coordination of the scriptures with the interpretative tradition of the church, that is a coordination which fails to accord primacy to the written word and tends to equate living tradition with another form of divine word.

The problem with the ARCIC 1 method, and its concluding crystallization in the spiritually evolved primacy, lies in this area: the normative written word and the living traditional word become two strands or forms of inspiration, coordinated and mutually essential. There seems too little real chance of the tradition standing under the correction of the canon and being found mistaken, and there is the clear possibility of new developments, having the status equivalent to that of revealed truth, emerging from the dialectic, or interplay, of the clerical discernment focusing the *sensus fidelium*, the feeling of the faithful. For the evangelical, holding to the official formularies of Church of England, this is equivalent to fashioning another form of the word of God; it identifies the church, and the ministry, with the word. The ARCIC 2 agreement on salvation and the church, however, suceeds in basing itself securely on New Testament theology to which evangelicals would assent gladly.

But the notion of authoritative teaching, despite different views of how it is gained, unites catholic and evangelical. The church, for both, is a teaching church. The church does not create her message but is responsible to the apostolic witness, the primary source, the scriptures. The church learns from listening, listening to the consistent speech of the voices of the apostolic writers commissioned, as inheritors of the ancient Hebrew covenant tradition, to interpret and enact the way, the truth and the life. By listening, the whole church has her message, has something to impart and teach. The whole people of God, not only the ordained ministry, has this privilege.

The pastoral ministry is also a teaching ministry and has a special, not exclusive, responsibility for maintaining the truth in the church. Pastoral concerns cannot be divorced from doctrinal convictions. Theory will condition praxis, however deeply the theory may be buried and disavowed. The role of pastor is theological, if the pastoral praxis is Christian. To deny the presence of a theological, theoretical, aspect merely cloaks its presence and prevents free choice and the possibility of scrutinizing the praxis. The appeal to raw praxis can be, unknowingly often, a hidden form of dictatorial absolutism.

The Anglican faithful have recourse to the central norm, the scriptures, as the final yardstick. The *sensus fidelium*, however that may be discovered, perhaps in terms of synodical elections, may provide a useful guide. But it is not a primary source so much as a guide and factor to take into account. Likewise the teaching ministry stands under a norm. The Lambeth Conference 1988 raised the notion of 'reception' as significant: the idea that if a new development were gradually accepted, 'received', by the whole church, then that would be a sign of its validity. Such a notion falls outside evangelical Anglican ecclesiology, since it fails to stress that reception, as for the acceptance of a sermon, must result first of all from the apostolicity of the development as discovered from gospel and canon. The Spirit must not be separated from the Word, as if the experience of the spiritual body were a sufficient measure.

The ideas of Barth and Newman clash here, and Anglicanism has to remain committed to the unique normativity of the canonical foundation. But it is important to note that the connotation of a lifeless foundation stone is not appropriate. Rather than just this purely visual image, we must weave in the notion of the audible, the voices of the apostolic and prophetic witnesses speaking to us from the past. This witness is not a dead foundation, a dead text. To treat it as such is a reductivist move and forgets the ministry of the Holy Spirit bringing the company of voices to life. Newman was right in his vision of a living chain of church life, but wrong in his abandonment of the uniqueness of the decisive voices in this family of faith.

To say that Anglicans have a notion of 'dispersed' authority expresses just this principle. Rightly understood, this concept means that the whole church has access to the primary source of authority in the church, to God in Christ by the Holy Spirit, and to the apostolic scriptures setting forth this saving faith. The fundamental authority is directly in the hands of all. Here the centre-circumference idea and the foundation-superstructure idea coincide. Every phase of the superstructure has access to the foundation, can hear the voices of the original testimony to the God of Abraham, Isaac and Jesus.

Unlike our legal system, in which the individual has to rely on a professional lawyer for access to justice and the necessary legal knowledge, Anglicanism is committed to opening up the knowledge of God to all and to encourage all to refine their faith by contact with the scriptures. Authority of the highest level and personal human freedom coincide, for the Anglican way, at this point. On the one hand, there is an authoritative framework of faith, fundamentally the trinitarian scheme of creation, salvation and future hope, which draws on the whole scriptural kaleidoscope of content. On the other hand, this authority liberates the whole church and fosters rational, moral life, worship and thought. It also fosters enquiry into the authoritative revelation, enquiry of faith seeking understanding, which will never exhaust the riches of the depth of this mine.

This point is exceptionally important for Anglicans for whom the Reformation was a break with a normative tradition which suppressed individual free thought and chained the Bible. The claims made on people by the gospel are total: 'come follow me' involves self abandonment to Christ. Such a total moral claim for obedience goes to the free personal decision of an individual and requires the fullest information possible. The claim of the revelation is comprehensible and reasonable, it has a content for the mind to consider, a content which will enrich and nourish the commitment of the will. I need to know to what I am committing myself, I need authoritative help to interpret my way along the path, and such help in part is the comprehensible content of revelation. The gospel summons us to no blind faith, but into increasing clarity and truth. As for the idea of an unformulated, instinctive *sensus fidelium*, it will have to be focused time and again by the word, as will any attempt to thematize such a consensus by a clerical official. Like tradition, the *sensus fidelium* has authority only if it reflects the teaching and principles of the gospel and of the prophets and apostles, the foundational authority of the church's teaching.

B. THE HUMAN AUTHORITY OF THE CHURCH: HISTORICAL DEVELOPMENT

No one exists as a Christian purely individually; the individual is in the church, not submerged by the church but part of the communion of all the saints in the *koinonia* of Christ. The scriptures belong to the whole body and speak to the whole as the prophets spoke to Israel, as Jesus to the disciples, as the apostles to the congregations of the ecclesia of Jesus. The apostles, the twelve, with Paul who claimed a commission directly from the risen Lord, formed a unique body of opinion whose voice lives through the written scriptures by the Holy Spirit as the divine authority, in human form so as to be accessible to the human race. But the church is also the continuation of the apostles as fellow believers, as well as hearers of their word, and the authority of the church as an ongoing institution subserves the apostolic authority. It has the status of an historic, churchly authority.

The church has a definite authority of a qualitatively different nature to that of the scriptures. In the present she has the authority to order and adjust her forms of worship and her patterns of ministry. Her past has formed a vast treasury of thought, practice, liturgy, hymnody and biography which the present church draws upon in gratitude. We stand on the shoulders of faithful interpreters and worshippers. A *prima facie* authority attaches to theological formulations and creeds which have withstood the tests of time as faithful to the gospel and the canon. The Anglican knows this debt to the past and all the wrestling for the faith enshrined there. Particularly the Nicene and Chalcedonian formulations of trinity and incarnation stand as tested pillars of faithful interpretation. Also the Reformers' recovery of the truth of how we relate to God in Christ by the Spirit, on the basis of the reconciling death and resurrection, remains definite in the church's authoritative tradition of witness to God.

This human authority of the church, resting on the foundational apostolic authority, means that Anglicans commit themselves against schism. The apostolic gospel heralds Christ's reconciliation; presbyter and bishop have pastoral charge and authority in Christ's church, and to flout that authority is to offend against good order and therefore against the whole body of Christ. Paul directs much effort in his epistles to this end, appealing to all the faithful for unity, for mutual respect, for good order. This appeal rests on the fact of Christ and his reconciling death: bickering and squabbling contradict this fact which constitutes the church.

Christian maturity involves respect for duly constituted authority as part of self-denying discipleship, a point Ramsey makes so well. Such respect includes willingness to accept the authority of church custom and practice, handed down to us from the wisdom of the past. But it also includes the need to debate issues, under the common teaching authority heard from scripture. There are occasions for the asking of questions by the individual, in the interests of the gospel. In questions of church government and institutions, the Anglican view is that the New Testament provides gospel principles, rather than strict structural blueprints. Here the model of growth and development plays its part, and as a second order idea subserving the other two concepts, since it concerns the churchly authority to order the church in the present context using principles derived from the foundational witness.

Evangelical Anglicans do need to stress that this does not mean licence to ignore the authority of the church and her order. Such a view is not apostolic at all. The primary Christological centre forbids such an attitude as proud and 'fleshly'. Paul presumes unity and cannot countenance splits within the *koinonia* of Christ. As Barth said above, any church formally basing herself on the word of God must be considered apostolic and any disagreement within that overarching umbrella must be simply a relative disagreement. Evangelical Anglicans need to recall this fundamental stance that differences over styles of worship, over interpretations of what the Spirit is now saying, over introductions of new forms, cannot possibly ground any thought of leaving a church committed to Christ, according to the prophets and apostles.

The classical Anglican two-tier view of authority, the apostolic and the churchly, immensely revered the latter while relying fundamentally on the former. The issue of authority was the central agonizing issue in the *Crockford's Preface* tragedy. There a traditional Anglican high churchman, with a massive respect for the centuries old tradition of ministry and for the scriptures, rebutted the idea that change could take place in the order of ministry. He argued primarily on the grounds of tradition: the wisdom of the past cannot be treated with disdain but has a weight of authority not to be ignored. The liberal tradition was, for that author, overturning the church's wisdom because of contemporary social phenomena, notably American. The church stands under her own wisdom and her law, she is not free to break with it on the demand of a pressure group. Dr Bennett was clearly desperately anxious about the control of the Church of England exercized by theologians of the liberal modernist school whose influence, he warned, was eating away at the foundations.[47]

C. THE MODERNIST REJECTION OF DOCTRINE

Liberalism is engrained in Anglicanism; it presupposes the traditional faith so as to criticize and adjust it in tune with the needs of a modern mindset. It opposes fundamentals and foundations as dogmatic and corrosive of genuinely free thought. Faith bubbles up from within the human spirit, and classical dogmas provide useful pictures of the inner religious, or moral, sense but do not express metaphysical truths about God and mankind. In particular the Bible is a resource of such material, ancient parabolic religious texts, often claiming historical record but with doubtful truth.

Oliver Quick penetratingly sets out the new position, showing that historical criticism of the Bible cast doubt on the historicity of key gospel events which orthodoxy had taken as the basis of the fundamental doctrines of the faith.

> 'Now assuming that the original facts no longer justified the subsequent beliefs, and that a new kind of synthesis was necessary, there were two possible lines along which it might be attempted. (1) On the one hand it was possible to exalt the value and importance of the original facts as now modified by criticism, to maintain that in them is the essence of Christianity, and to disparage and discount subsequent doctrines, which they do not seem to justify, as errors . . . which . . . must now be discarded. (2) On the other hand it was possible to attach primary value and importance to the ideas underlying the developments of doctrine, to point out the error of confusing origin with validity, to seek a basis for the validity of these ideas independent of the alleged facts on which they had been thought to rest, and to find the essential truth of Christianity in their continuous growth and expansion in the minds of men.'[48]

These two modern approaches lead respectively to liberal protestantism and catholic modernism; the former focusing on the man Jesus and his value, the latter on the ideals, symbolically expressed in traditional doctrines, in the developing mind of the church.

The Bible, for traditional theology, contains a vast range of materials from centuries of time. Some is obscure and difficult to grasp; some is fairly plain. But whatever the type of literature in question, the mind can address it and seek to understand it, always taking account of context. The texts do say something which we can *understand*, therefore they are 'propositional' in the sense that they make statements or 'propositions' which the mind can understand. These statements mean something. They take a multitude of forms; they can be, for example, historical, moral, doctrinal. There will be debate over which category to use in interpretation. Whether or not the reader wishes to accept these statements is another matter, but the fact that he has something with which to disagree shows that the material has a cognitive element.

The traditional Anglican, standing on the Anglican formularies and the great bulk of Christian history, claims that the church can and must frame teaching or doctrine which is based on the scriptures, that this teaching has been accurately expressed by the church in the past to create a tradition of teaching usually reliable and very helpful. Scripture therefore has a clarity and a content: the real issue is whether one agrees with it or not, rather than whether it is comprehensible. As to its nature it is fully human, God reveals himself and his ways through the human medium to humanity. There are areas of teaching hotly debated, infant baptism for example, but that underlines the fact that the texts have something to say, something understandable about which we can disagree. Such disagreement does not go to the heart, but the edges, of the faith in Christ. It is also important that the vast scale of the biblical material be recognized, spanning centuries, and assuming that God acts and speaks in human history. *Prima facie* the historical character of scripture must be taken to match this religious frame.

This traditional position formally unites catholic and protestant orthodoxy. Vatican 2 calls the scriptures inspired and normative, as does ARCIC. Liberal theology breaks with this historic view of the supreme authority and intelligibility of the scriptures, regarding them as very fallible, flawed human texts, even where we have their original form. Texts register religious feeling at times in the past. The great systematizer of this position was Schleiermacher (1768–1834), who described Christian doctrines as 'religious affections set forth in speech'.[49] By this he meant that statements of truth for the Christian church were really reflections of religious experiences, very secondary and provisional expressions of the primary experiential reality. Christian doctrines, or teachings, turn out to be pale reflections of the immediate warm religious feeling of the heart. The individual personal feeling becomes the source of Christian statement about man, man and God, and about God. The distinctively Christian experience, is 'the feeling of absolute dependence', the Jesus feeling of total and unreserved surrender to the divine. From this central insight, Schleiermacher weaves his system of Christian faith. This experience of the absolute dependence of mankind on the ground of all being becomes the yardstick by which the church can select what is right and wrong in the scriptures. Immediate consciousness of the beyond, of what we call God, now is the norm for the faith. Religious sense of being at one with the divine, of personal participation in that great suffusing power behind all reality, this is the centre of the faith and its sole content.

ARCIC 1, despite flaws to evangelical eyes, formally acknowledges the principle of an external teaching authority. However hiddenly supplemented, the scriptures are affirmed to be inspired and intelligible. It is on this ground that ARCIC 1 has come in for criticism from the liberal wing for holding to definite doctrine, which is intelligible and authoritative. Avis regards the cardinal sin of ARCIC 1 as affirming a notion of propositional revelation, a notion he sees as hostile to Anglicanism and profoundly Roman: 'The root of the problem seems to be that the Anglican members of ARCIC have been willing to go along with a concept of truth (and error) that is deeply entrenched in the Roman Catholic tradition, but is profoundly inimical to the ethos of Anglicanism. It is the difference between propositional (or analytical) and a personal (or fiduciary) understanding of the nature of truth.'[50] This is quite a considerable misreading of ARCIC 1 which has adopted a far more sophisticated methodology than the old-fashioned, and probably caricatured, idea of revealed truth as divinely formed blocks of truth. ARCIC 1 employs a dynamic, evolutionary view of truth, truth which is not severable from the living experience of the church community. The Holy Spirit at work in the history of the concrete events of the community of faith brings fresh interpretations to light through the appointed channels.

The method used embracing the *sensus fidelium,* cannot be said to exclude the personal or fiduciary dimension of knowing at all: it merely uses a corporate rather than an individualistic mode of reflection on personal experience. Using Quick's analysis, it is a variety of catholic modernism. Indeed the more profound and accurate analysis is found in Barth's critique of Möhler: this method incorporates and coordinates too much, not too little, contemporary religious sense, the *sensus fidelium* in fact, into the ongoing interpretative formation of doctrine. ARCIC 1 methodology uses a subtle historical-analogical method, fusing the contextual community of faith with the apostolic witness. It is fundamentally in line with catholic modernism in its discussion of authority, since the ideal of Primacy, developing providentially over the years, is the basis of the argument, cutting away from the arguments from historical fact and received dogma.

This attack on cognitively comprehensible truth, or 'propositional' revelation, and consequently on intelligible doctrine, from the liberal wing of Anglicanism, while failing to touch the sophistication of ARCIC, represents the standard liberal protestant rejection of comprehensible doctrine, and the centuries-old view, held by Eastern and Western churches, that God has revealed himself to the human race in an intelligible form, which therefore includes a definite cognitive or informational dimension. This brings us to the very centre of the debate over doctrinal authority in the Church of England. Avis, exactly mirroring the approach developed by Schleiermacher, tells us, 'Theological statements, wherein doctrine is articulated, are inescapably existential. We have no wish to know, and cannot take cognizance of, what has no bearing upon our lives.'[51] Why the Almighty should forgo the ability to convey information to us concerning what may not be immediately relevant, not immediately transposable into existential testimony, has never been explained by this liberal protestant approach. No one living has ever existentially experienced, for example, the creation of the world nor the resurrection of the body, but that does not at all diminish either the factuality, clarity, nor truthfulness of these utterly fundamental doctrines of the Christian faith.

For Schleiermacher, doctrines which are not expressible as immediate products of the distinctively Christian religious feeling are only very secondary and dispensable. Schleiermacher aimed to interest the cultured despisers of religion in the faith by appealing to an innate, individual religious feeling, a feeling distinct from, and not reducible to, reason and morality. This personal feeling was for Schleiermacher utterly primary and the benchmark of Christian statements about God, man and Jesus. He was precisely appealing to purely personal feeling, personal piety, individual religious experience. In this he was a true son of modern romanticism in full reaction from dry orthodoxy, which had lost something of the vitality of living faith in a real God. Few now doubt that he over reacted by claiming to derive all statements about God, all doctrine, from our immediate personal experience. We can sum up the criticism of Schleiermacher by saying that he came to confuse statements about our religious feelings with statements about God. But 'statements' are, according to this school, analytical and dogmatic, dispensable for Christian faith, which concerns the heart rather than the head, feeling rather than reason.

Avis remorselessly treads the same path: 'Clarity, precision, distinctness, objectivity, are spurious when applied to statements of doctrine, since these are distillations of Christian experience—of the personal apprehension of God's truth and reality revealed supremely in Jesus Christ—and the personal dimension is not amenable to impersonal description without radical distortion taking place.'[52] The classical Christian position is built on the contrary view, that there are central fundamental doctrines of the faith which are intelligible, by no means all capable of being experienced personally now, and which are revealed by God, or can be reasonably inferred from revelation. Revelation has the primary quality of unveiling rather than mystifying and obscuring. Mainstream Anglican theology holds on *both* to the propositional, informative and cognitive nature of revelation *and* to its personal character, rejecting the sleight of hand which seeks to spin informative statements from undifferentiated religious sense.

This is a central difference between orthodoxy and modernism. Traditional Christian belief, Eastern or Western, has affirmed revelation to be both 'I–it' knowing, factual and not yet experienced, nor necessarily heart-warming, and, on the other hand, 'I–Thou' knowing, the personal kind of knowing, as we know, friends for instance.

In a very thorough examination of this issue, John Baillie rightly concludes that we do not know God first and foremost by working him out logically: we do not want inferred friends.[53] But to say this is not to commit the equal and opposite error of abolishing clear factual statements from revelation. 'I–thou' knowledge *presupposes* 'I–it' knowledge: knowing a friend entails knowing about her, factual information such as the colour of her hair, her height, moral character and all the other data without which she would not be herself. In technical terms, revelation is both a question of *fiducia* and *assensus*, both personal trust and information. Anglican theology has always held on to both, indeed has never seen them as separate. There can be no true personalism, a term with a host of different meanings in modern philosophy, without information. The Evangelical Anglican, the ARCIC Report, the Anglican-Orthodox Agreed Statement, concur that the church has a deposit of faith to pass on, has a gospel to proclaim which is quite clear—so clear that it attracts the disagreement of the modernist. The church is a dogmatic church in being charged with the preservation, proclamation and interpretation of the word of life: a word which is sufficiently understandable as to be preserved, proclaimed and interpreted and controverted.

Statements of doctrine, and of history, for the liberal, are false gods, baggage surplus to the Christian pilgrimage, a dead weight to be dropped as soon as possible for a mature experiential theology. Instead of this needless preoccupation with doctrines, the church should cleave to Christ as she ascends the path of the Christian journey. The obvious question occurs: how do I cleave to Christ without facts and doctrines about him? Can we begin to imagine a picture, or impression, of Christ without any informational content about this figure? Can the church begin to understand how to cleave to Christ, why she needs to do so, apart from some informative doctrine?

This liberal approach, superbly systematized by Schleiermacher, was transposed into modern existentialist mode by Bultmann in this century, the biblical statements being interpreted as myth to be re-expressed in terms of Heidegger's version of personalist philosophy. The Jesus event of the New Testament becomes the parallel to that moment of 'authentic' existence, the sense of coping against all the odds, of not selling out to mass pressures and simply becoming one of the herd, 'herd man'. Rather than the *sensus fidelium*, the innate instinct of the whole, we have here the *sensus individualis*, the inner religious instinct of an individual, what Montefiore once called 'protestantism cubed'! Only when the text of scripture, or a Christian dogma, 'rings bells' with my personal, modern religious experience is the tradition of any value: otherwise it is consigned to the rubbish heap of the out-moded past.

The purpose of revelation is relational. God speaks to man to elicit responsive trust: this is the covenantal framework found in the biblical witness itself and it forms the framework for Anglican ecclesiological interpretation. God reveals himself as the personal God, approaching mankind with the offer of fellowship. Personal faith is utterly central. But such faith requires truth about the speaker of the word, the giver of the covenant, the forgiveness of sins and gift of grace. Gospel and canon co-exist. All statements of belief necessitate doctrinal background, because to affirm our faith entails affirming it in someone who did something to some effect. To say we believe 'that' and to deny any content to 'that' is not sophisticated but banal. Anglicanism presupposes normative scriptural content, with orthodox trinitarian interpretation. Indeed, the objective content of the texts, taken as a whole, must be normative in measuring experience.

Commonly understood, shared beliefs are presupposed in the very idea of the church as opposed to a religious club of members sharing incommunicable, mystically personalistic experiences. Jerome Hamer has pointed out that God is able to accommodate his revelation to our human faculties. We could amplify this in terms of the incarnation. Written words are written words, and they tell us something, they have a content with which we may or may not agree. The devastatingly simple fact is that the whole Bible tells a story which is basically intelligible, and that the church presupposes this whole content. Traditional theology affirms the centrality of Christ as the absolute fulfilment of God's saving and revealing activity; but insists that scripture, the same scripture that Jesus knew, does inform us about God. Jesus seems to have patterned his life on scripture, to have lived it out consciously, certainly drawing upon it frequently. He used it radically. If it informed his mind, why not ours also? He interpreted himself to the disciples after his resurrection, according to Luke's account of the journey to Emmaus, with reference to 'a corpus of revealed propositional truths', which he claimed concerned himself.

Traditional objective content is inevitably smuggled secretly back into supposedly exclusively experiential, or 'personalist', views of revelation, as when Avis, for instance, produces as the 'determinative principle of Christian theology, the incarnation.'[54] It is doubtful whether the author has experienced incarnation, or has seen or touched the incarnate Lord. In fact he must depend wholly on information, on the dogmatic tradition, in turn appealing to data from the New Testament, which he has been able to understand and has chosen to trust, in order to use the complex theological construct of the incarnation as his central matrix. There really is no escaping an essential informational character of revelation and therefore of doctrinal statement. Cognitively true statements are necessary and indispensable for anything like an orthodox Christian faith.

Such information alone does not constitute Christian faith: the 'devil believes' purely factually in Christ, but 'trembles', says the Epistle of James. But the enterprise of denying the factual and informational dimension of revelation and doctrine, while trying to hold on to central Christian doctrines such as the incarnation, is wishful thinking, almost literally so. It amounts to sawing off the branch on which the experiential 'personalist' wishes to sit.

John McIntyre gives us a pointed illustration of the difficulty in retaining the traditional Christology with a purely 'personalist' method. 'In a recent discussion with David Frost,' he writes, 'Dr. Billy Graham came very close to admitting that if modern criticism should disprove the truth of the Bible, his faith, now so deeply personal a relationship with a really present Christ, would be unaltered. One cannot but admire the depth of such personal conviction, but one may be forgiven for wondering how long this kind of personal relationship with Christ could be sustained without the reinforcing structure of the biblical literature and its narratives about Christ. My own guess is that without the structure this sort of personal experience would very soon become a rather formless, if not also joyless, mysticism.'[55] Reformed and catholic faith knows that objective Christianity requires objective teaching rooted in the scriptures which themselves are both authoritative and intelligible.

The cause of informational revelation and doctrinal truth has had few champions in recent Anglican theology. But a compelling example of its necessity can be found in an essay of C. C. J. Webb and with reference to the gospel of John, a text often dogmatically labelled poetic and mystical, therefore not factual and 'propositional'. Webb talks of the intuitions of a prophet, but argues that we must be very careful over this issue and warns against exaggerating the incommunicability of the prophet's intuitions. It is prophetic religious men who found religious communities;

> 'But this is surely because they can and do communicate what they see. The writer of the fourth gospel makes Christ say, "All things which I heard from my Father I have made known unto you." And the same writer throughout this gospel evidently regards it as characteristic of the supreme inspiration of him whom he sets before his readers as the only-begotten Son or Word of God that it is no dim or obscure feeling, for which words cannot be found, but a clear knowledge which, where fit recipients can be found, can be without reserve or hesitation imparted.'[56]

Webb is no evangelical theologian, but his reading of the situation is that prophetic figures have something to communicate beyond ineffable feelings and intuitions of a vague and imprecise nature. The ordinary reader of that gospel will add that it speaks of 'what we have touched and heard', it purports not only to offer mystical poetic reflection but very importantly to convey information and teaching about the man who was full of grace and truth. Any theological system claiming to make the incarnation central cannot help depending on cognitive revelation to a great extent; if not, then it falls into a version of idealism and treats the life of Jesus as illustrative of a supreme religious idea rather than an historical, metaphysical and moral act that really happened.

So far I have argued that revelation includes an informational or, to use the old-fashioned and perhaps off-putting term, 'propositional' character. Even the poetic, aesthetic parts of scripture have something of this. Just because a text expresses itself in poetic form does not at all mean that objective data or affirmations of some kind are not conveyed. The idea that poetry is only the self-expression of the author's inner feelings is a very modern and narrow understanding of the genre, probably gaining dominance in the last century with the romantic movement. But we have only to think of pre-romantic poetry, making, for example, precise social and political comment, to shatter the myth that imagery and stanzas speak mainly of the inner self, in necessarily imprecise ways. Poetry can speak, and for the majority of history has spoken, of objective events and ideas, of battles in the past, of morality and of nature. 'Yea, though I walk through the valley of the shadow of death I will fear no evil, for Thou art with me, Thy rod and staff they comfort me', is not primarily an expression of the psalmist's psyche, although much can be said of that, but it is primarily a statement of the real presence of God with him in distress. When Shakespeare in his sonnet says, 'Love is not love which alters when it alteration finds', he makes a statement about an objective reality, even in the middle of a poem apparently written to foster a relationship.

Rikhof points out, in a discussion of the use of metaphors in defining the church, that poetic metaphors cannot be regarded as alternatives to conceptual, cognitive statements. 'It is because the thesis that only images can be used occurs in the context of the appeal to a mystery that surpasses all knowledge, that another aspect of these arguments is the contrast between cognitive (concepts) and non-cognitive (metaphors). But in metaphors,' he continues, 'as in most other sentences, one can discern a cognitive element.' This content aspect is precisely the aspect which is responsible for the peculiar feature of the metaphor, and it is precisely this aspect which makes a conceptual development possible, if required. 'So,' he concludes, 'instead of a sharp contrast between metaphor and concept on this point, there is more of a link, continuation, or transposition.'[57]

To reject conceptual doctrine in favour of poetry and metaphor is a confusion of major proportions; there is no escaping the cognitive, conceptual element of the Christian faith and revelation. And the bulk of biblical texts are not poetic and romantically aesthetic at all, but very robust, insistent testimony to events, often unsuitable for children, and to metaphysical doctrine, with an embarrassing amount of eschatological statement, for example, which can only await experience. Much of the text is plainly understandable, some of it will continue to puzzle interpreters, but the central points are clear. The problem is not so much their clarity but whether readers will accept what lies before them.

Biblical text informs the mind and speaks to the heart. Calvin, the systematizing mind of the Reformation, defined faith as a 'a firm and certain knowledge of God's benevolence towards us, founded upon the truth of the freely given promise in Christ, both revealed to our minds (in the Bible) and sealed upon our hearts through the Holy Spirit.'[58] Apostles and prophets are not Byronic figures darkly brooding on their tragic lot and giving forth from the heart of their frustration and aspiration. Prophets say what God tells them to say and enact what is commanded. All too often in the Bible these men would far rather remain silent and would not choose to give forth their oracles. God communicates to his people by word and event. The people are to 'hearken diligently and obey'. That which is spoken is understandable, but often not heeded.

But to state this very obvious, if very unfashionable tenet, is not to hold a 'Koranic' view of teleprinter dictation. Biblical information comes through human mediation. It has the character of the river rather than the canal blasted through the granite artificially. It magnifies the miracle of revelation that God communicates by the roundabout route of thousands of years of history of an otherwise small and petty race in a scrubby, arid patch of the Middle East. Within this historical continuum, of which we know a considerable amount, event and interpretation were the medium of divine action and leading. The word comes to the people through the person and personality of the prophet in particular historical circumstances demanding some response. The prophet does not distil messages out of his own religious genius. Nor can it be said convincingly that the interpretation of key events was the work of the people, while only the events themselves were the divine contribution. The word comes to the prophet for the whole people, often to interpret events with a fully 'natural' causation. Very often, indeed, the community experience at the time comes up with the wrong interpretation, a wrong reading of events; the distillation of their corporate experience produces false doctrine. The word is terrifyingly particular, an alien word to a disobedient religious people. Even the disciples, prior to Pentecost but after the resurrection, according to the book of Acts, could not distil a correct reading of the state of the church: they needed to be given the truth.

The fact that biblical revelation, and arising from it Christian doctrine, have a cognitive character and are primarily given to the church rather than being distilled from her experience, includes, rather than excludes, the historical personalities of the particular communicators of the word and the particular situations in which all were caught. Evangelical theology asserts that the existentially charged, informational word originates in God and in the messenger, without abolishing the human quality of the communication, the quality necessary for its being intelligible to the people of that culture at that time. The personalities of Paul, Jeremiah, and John, far from being obliterated as if they were merely the hardware for some computer print-out, play a decisive part in expressing what God intended should be communicated. They are personalities moulded and conditioned in the knowledge of God, therefore ideally and naturally congruent with God's message. Informational 'propositions' from the history of Israel under God do not infringe, but respect, the human historical and sociological status.

On the other hand, the prophetic and apostolic personalities chosen to bring the messages and interpretations to the people of God do bring these, rather than simply their own spiritual insights. It would be a version of the genetic fallacy to reduce the cumulative revelation of the canon to the personal and social histories of these personalities. God's revelation comes through human means of communication and interpetation, but cannot be reduced to these, nor to the springs of purely human religious insight. This parallels the obvious point that revelation is given in scripture, but is not reducible to ink marks on paper.

A certain irony lies in the denial of informational revelation by those who wish to state that the incarnation is the centre of the faith. However debateable may be the developments in the way it is done, in the catholic tradition Mary is rightly revered as the obedient servant, agreeing to bear the word into the world. This is quite a fashionable doctrine among the high and even liberal Anglican constituency. How odd it is, therefore, that the predecessors of the humble, frightened girl, the canonical prophets, should not be regarded with similar respect and for a similar reason: they bear the word of the Lord to the people, the word that has the same sifting, saving effect as the incarnate word. The word revealed through the messengers of the Lord is both theirs and His. They are committed to the words given to them and accepted by them. They sacrifice themselves to and for the message committed to them. Von Rad shows how prophets such as Jeremiah and Ezekiel live out the word in their actions and suffer for it, anticipating the ministry of Jesus the suffering servant.[59]

They were not acting out some unintelligible drama primarily to fulfil their private religious feelings, to distil their religious experience. They were trying to force home a highly intelligible, if unacceptable, message. Prophets were reckoned to be false prophets if their words proved untrue, clearly presupposing that they were conveying understandable statements, statements with a concrete reference, statements far from vague and imprecise. The word made flesh was given to the world while being utterly accommodated to it. Incarnation consummates the coming of the word, the word which was given less fully through the mouths of the prophets and seers for centuries beforehand. The shape of the coming of the given word into the community is common to both.

When Mary 'pondered these things in her heart', she had something definite to ponder; she was not undergoing a dawning mystical experience, despite the contrary vision of church art down the centuries of the wan, dreamy figure, alone and palely loitering. She was given a very defined message, a task, a child and hers was to deliver that child, the Word, into the world. The prophets likewise were to convey, to communicate, messages in their historical contexts, given form by their personalities. Revelation is then mediated to us, mediated by the whole vast range of literary types known to the ancient world and in types apparently unique to it. The library of the biblical books taken together, interpreted against our knowledge of their contexts, provides the church with the compass and map of her journey. Revelation comes mediated, in the sense of being in the form of human language given to the cultural historical continuum of the people of God tracing back to Abraham. The word of the Lord interprets itself in the life of Israel; a cumulative background building up, against which the focal and saving revelation is interpreted.

The church, like Mary and before her the prophets of Israel, understands and obeys, thereby keeping herself within the covenant relationship with God. This is very mundane, very unromantic, workaday and practical. Throughout the Bible, revelation very often fails aesthetically or intellectually to dazzle in form, although its very content often radiates through the historical, 'accidental', communicative medium of the human personalities in concrete situations. Revelation corresponds to an accurate and unromanticized view of incarnation, 'taking the form of a servant', a form unpopularly simple, a form accommodated to the particular and frail human condition and context. God reveals himself by the 'scandal' of very specific particular places and times in the vast span of the universe and its history. The word of the Lord, never separable from the Lord himself, speaks in words to humankind. The church learns of God's nature, often in the face of historical experience, by interpreting her experience through Christ as he mediates himself in scripture.

D. AN INTERPRETING CHURCH

But the church also interprets scripture in the light of her journey. This itself is scriptural. She does not learn if she regards her role as teacher as one of pickling or freezing the word of God, of passing it on in the language of the past. Preserving the church means that she has to make the revelation her own in each generation; she has to ponder the revelation in her heart as did Mary. This process also entails self criticism: has the church got her interpretation distorted, and fixed this distortion in her tradition which in turn muffles the word? Anglican ecclesiology is committed to the principle of self criticism, *semper reformanda*. Today it may be that *Faith in the City* and the voices raised in the third world are challenging the interpretation of the Western churches to reappropriate the admonition of James that 'faith without works is dead'. The 'Green' ecological parties are challenging the church to take creation seriously and to protest against the wholesale materialism of East and West in plundering the planet irresponsibly.

The church must be a learning church in more than a wooden way: she has to pass on the faith in ways which relate to current issues. She must interpret it in terms of the current culture, yet without simply restating those cultural mores using biblical and dogmatic imagery as clothing. This is a difficult tension and is the context in which the modernist reacts against the conservative who simply repeats dogmatically the revealed truths in ancient terms. The 'then' and the 'now' interrelate, and the disagreement is over how this happens. The liberal focuses on the present as the criterion of acceptability; the modern Roman Catholic refuses to split them, linking them in an evolutionary growth model after Newman, declining to measure one against the other; the Anglican, Evangelical and Anglo-Catholic, operate with a foundation-superstructure system, the 'then' acting as a measure and content for the present expression of it 'now'.

For Anglicanism the content of revelation will resist fundamentally distorting interpretations of its central core, just as a great play will resist misinterpretation because of its very substance. For a director to focus the interpretation of a production of Macbeth around the scene of the porter at the gate would resist the grain and plot of the play. So attempts to restructure revelation will ultimately founder. The church's learning is learning to interpret what is broadly comprehensible, not licence to plasticise revelation and mould it according to the taste of the day. The church must re-express the truth for today in the light of current questions.

The 'church as servant' fails society if she abandons her doctrinal and ethical norms in favour of the current ethos of the day. Church and her authoritative canonical teaching link together crucially. The creed of absolute personal freedom, autonomy, is leading to agonizing fragmentations in society and in church life. If personal freedom is not seen within the wisdom of the gospel and the law of the Lord, then everyone does what is right in his own eyes.[60] Relationships, notably between wife and husband, seem increasingly at risk because of the cult of independent freedom, cut free from responsibility and the need to exercise freedom within obedience to God. Likewise the plain teaching of the Bible on chastity, heterosexual and homosexual, just cannot be reversed by the church, if she is to be a faithful servant to humanity.

The whole church is a learning and interpreting church; each member of the body of Christ reads and ponders the word in his or her heart. This is the true sense in which authority in the Church of England is 'dispersed', it is dispersed and available throughout the whole people of God, who are thereby open to the voice of the prophets and apostles and can measure the teaching of the ministry accordingly. This process does seem to gain expression in various movements 'from below' coming into the debates of the General Synod, sometimes in conflict with the episcopal consensus. This dispersed biblical authority, combined with the representative synodical structure, forms the true guarantee which allows the church to have her radical, experimental thinkers. All new interpretations of the faith will have to convince the whole church as it seeks to hear and obey the apostles. For the Anglican the fiat of the bench of bishops on matters of faith has to show conformity to this highest authority.

This principle is the reason for the possibility of the Anglican comprehensiveness. It is the often unacknowledged core, the magnetic pole for the adjustment of the theological compass. Because of the apostolic authority, freely available to all, dispersed among greatest and least, there is a knowledge that developments will not breach the proper bounds of the faith. Despite the influence of a great weight of liberal critique, the Church of England remains a trinitarian church with a gospel of salvation from sin and a conservative ethical tradition. That this is so is not because of her theologians, many of whom for some time have attacked this position: it is the content of the apostolic voice dispersed amongst the whole body that produces this conservative power, often so frustrating for the experts. This coherence from the whole body may take time to assert, or reassert, itself and Anglicans need a sense of history when and if they feel that things are taking a wrong direction; the history of the people of God, before, after and during the apostolic age has never been without failure, confusion, question, and wrestling. The church will always need prayerful renewed trust in the word of God as a critical reality in her ongoing life. The notion of splitting from a church for its heresy is therefore an absurd lack of faith, equivalent to a prophet of the Old Testament skulking off into isolation, instead of pursuing his task of proclaiming the word to a difficult people.

The true liberal is no mere awkward destroyer, but an interpretative stimulus seeking to raise honest questions about the faith and life of the church. The fact that sometimes these suggestions can be shown to run clean counter to the opinions of the tradition of faith, as for example over sexual ethics, and that sometimes radical questions are correct criticisms of the church's attitudes and behaviour, as for example the complacency exposed by *Faith in the City*, shows that there is a foundational position with which to dialogue, and which needs this dialogue. The current wrestling with questions of women's ministry is an opportunity not only for the church to acknowledge her patronizing view of women and to ask how to incorporate their gifts into ministry, but also to examine notions of ordination in the light of the normative voice of the apostolic gospel. The truly liberal mind will respect the fundamentals and enjoy the dialogue: the dogmatic 'liberal', the closed-minded reductionist, will not. The orthodox Anglican needs the liberal to point him to current issues and horizons, to prevent the text, the horizon of the past becoming separated from the present. True liberalism respects the orthodox argument and knows that liberal questioning feeds off, and needs, the classical tradition.

This dialogue takes place in the stream of faith in the living God, who provides the hermeneutical bond between the 'then and the now'. The biblical characters and situations are a long way removed from us and may to many seem to be therefore dead as far as we are concerned. 'It is true that in terms of space, time, and culture, they, and the historical epoch to which they belonged, are a very long way from us. But the link between them and us is not found at that level. The link is God Himself. For the God with whom they had to do is the same God with whom we have to do.'[61] This is why the scriptures are not dead examples of religious consciousness occasionally rising to heights which we today might use as examples of what we know to be true. The written word remains powerful and lively, the content lives and speaks, as does that of a play or a novel: we can and do find the whole authoritative and normative. We find the distinction driven between personal and external authority qualified. The word combines both, as the word addresses us and roots within our hearts, setting up the potential for covenant dialogue.

This fact, that the same living God is portrayed in scripture, lies behind the view that scripture interprets scripture, despite and through great gaps of time between texts. This classical doctrine, 'the analogy of faith', rebuts the notion that scripture can be interpreted in any way the reader wishes, each interpretation being as valid as the next. The very content of the whole collection resists this subjectivizing and relativizing move. Ultimately this has to be realized in spiritual experience as well as scholarship.

Here gospel and canon interrelate.

> 'The Christian experience is not something we bring rationally to the Bible to test scriptural truth; it is something miraculously created in us by the Bible to respond to divine power acting as grace; and it can therefore be in no collision with the authority which makes the Bible what it is, the authority of the gospel, of the Redeemer felt and owned as Redeemer.'[62]

That very redemption, of which the apostles were authoritative preachers and teachers, meets us in the Christ whose life and meaning are set forth in the texts as they mutually cast light on one another and, together, upon our journey today. The same redemptive God of grace forms the coherent point of reference uniting the kaleidoscopic diffusion of biblical material. The category of 'word' goes beyond the subject-object divide of thought, goes beyond the distinction of the experiential and the objectively informational. The word, always complex and mediated in contexts and cultures and traditions, reaches into the heart and the mind, treating the human as the whole person and evoking free response. As the personality of the playwright comes from his text to the reader, and the audience of the stage performance, so does the fashioner of the gospel reach out into the church through the words of his commissioned messengers, embedded in the scriptures.

4. Conclusion: the dynamic essence of the church

That is why the scriptures are the church's authority, why she seeks to frame her outlook from them, trying not only to interpret them but to incarnate them. She desires to assimilate or appropriate biblical faith radically within herself. Biblical criticism plays a part in understanding the meaning of the texts and their historical genesis: it touches interpretation but not authority, any more than brain research on the poet affects the status of the great poetry fashioned by that poet. The church is the stager of the play of the drama of redemption in Christ; in her case the play is even more real than the world to which it is played and announced. She has been summoned to draw into the cast all who listen and watch. She is fundamentally the community of the word living and active, hard at times to interpret but not susceptible of censorship and cutting. This is the being of the church, primarily the church audible for it is as she plays out her script, in the spirit of the central dramatic act, that she most truly is what she is. It is as the word is obeyed and embodied in personal life and relations that the Lord's presence becomes plain, and this is so for praxis or social action.

The church is this community, linked across time and space to the Lord who created the world by his word and redeemed it accordingly. She is not a form of the word, but a community of free beings in covenant with him who first spoke the word of love and mercy and steadfast love, enacting that, at supreme cost, in time. She is personal society and social personality, or she will be, because she is reborn by the Holy Spirit to the common life of the crucified and risen Lord, the person of the divine Word. That is her destiny and her being, that is why she must continue the quest for unity in the word and under the authority of the word, both gospel and canon. That is why she cannot do otherwise than spread the word by all means possible, and gear her resources to evangelization. Her being and her function coincide in her being sent by the incarnate, crucified and risen Lord to proclaim and enact the word of life, forming true *koinonia* in Christ by the Holy Spirit. Of this great church, the Church of England forms part. As an old branch of the tree of faith, she often becomes dry, but the Spirit renews and the sap runs afresh in all churches repenting and turned to the Lord.

Her ministry, *as a whole people of God*, is firstly to face her Lord, her centre, to stand upon her living foundation stone. Into the olive tree of Christological faith she now has to graft the hundreds of thousands who have strayed or never heard this good news, never experienced the love and care of Christ, himself the true vine. Because her structures are so bonded into society and claim such historic pedigree, she needs, repeatedly, as Barth says, to consecrate herself afresh to the gospel. If this catholic and evangelical consecration can happen, she stands well placed to proclaim and serve the gospel, to all who are near and far off, of the God 'who has sent the Spirit of his Son into our hearts, whereby we cry Abba, Father.'

Christ being the centre of her life, the Anglican church must increasingly turn 'local ecumenical projects' into one great ecumenical family nationally, the branch of the tree of faith in this corner of creation.

END NOTES TO CHAPTER 6

1. *Doctrines of the Creed* London, Nisbet, 1938 pp. 284–5.
2. ibid.
3. *Models of the Church* Gill and Macmillan, Dublin, 1976 p. 186.
4. *The Household of God* op. cit.
5. *Church Dogmatics* 4/1 p. 650, for example.
6. *The Church and Sacraments* op. cit. p. 141.
7. In his book *Being as Communion* London, DLT, 1988.
8. ibid. p. 18.
9. ibid.
10. *I and Thou* trans. R. Smith, T & T Clark, Edinburgh, 1958 p. 25.
11. *Being and Time* translated by J. Macquarrie and E. Robinson SCM, London, 1962 p. 156.
12. *Perspectives on 19th and 20th Century Theology* SCM, London, 1967 p. 142.
13. op. cit. p. 49.
14. *Being as Communion* op. cit. p. 61.
15. J. Sabbas 'The Holy Spirit in Christ and Christians', *American Benedictine Review* 1969. 20. pp. 99–121.
16. *Sanctorum Communio* (1927), translated by R. Gregor Smith, Collins, London, 1963 p. 202.
17. *Christian Holiness* Lutterworth Press, London, 1960 p. 22.
18. *Life Together* 1949 translated J. W. Dobertstein SCM, London, 1954 p. 18.
19. *Ecclesiastical Polity* book 5, ch. 56, 11.
20. Barth *Church Dogmatics* 3/1 uses this distinction to relate creation and covenant Christologically.
21. *The Christian Doctrine of the Godhead* A. E. Garvie Hodder and Stoughton, London, 1925 p. 479.
22. ibid.
23. *The Faith We Confess* T & T Clark, Edinburgh, 1984 p. 205.
24. *Church Dogmatics* 4/2 p. 722.
25. *Church Dogmatics* 4/2 p. 681.
26. op. cit. p. 249.
27. E. Troeltsch *The Social Teaching of the Christian Churches* vol. 2, trans. O. Wyon, London, George Allen and Unwin, 1931 p. 993.
28. ibid.
29. *The Household of God* op. cit. p. 86.
30. ibid. p. 105.
31. *God's Reign and Our Unity: report of the Anglican Reformed International Commission*, SPCK, London, 1984 p. 71.
32. *Freed to Serve* London, Hodder and Stoughton, 1983 p. 48.
33. op. cit. p. 73.

34. A. E. J. Rawlinson *Problems of Reunion* Eyre and Spottiswoode, London, 1950 p. 164.
35. *Christian Unity: the Anglican Position* Hodder and Stoughton, London, 1948 p. 19.
36. op. cit. p. 175.
37. *The Structure of the Divine Society* London, Lutterworth, 1950 ch. 12.
38. *Report of The Archbishop of Canterbury's Commission on Communion and Women in the Episcopate* 1989 Church House Publishing, London, 1989.
39. See R. T. Beckwith 'The Problem of Doctrinal Standards', in *All in Each Place* ed. J. Packer, Marcham Manor Press, Sutton Courtenay, 1965 p. 125.
40. For a survey on episcopacy in the sub apostolic church, see J. Zizioulas 'Episcope and Episcopos in the Early Church', in *Faith and Order Paper* 102 WCC, Geneva, 1980.
41. p. 188–9.
42. op. cit. p. 227–8.
43. op. cit. p. 228.
44. Reunion p. 189.
45. 'The Crisis Facing the Church of England' *Churchman* 1988. 1. p. 15.
46. *Church Dogmatics* 1/2 p. 831.
47. See the 'Preface', *Crockford's Clerical Directory 1987/8* Church House Publishing, London, 1987.
48. *Liberalism, Modernism and Tradition* O. C. Quick Longmans Green and Co, London, 1922 p. 3.
49. *The Christian Faith* 1830, trans. Mackintosh and Stewart, T & T Clark, Edinburgh, 1928 15 p. 76.
50. P. Avis *Ecumenical Theology* SPCK, London, 1986 p. 7.
51. ibid. p. 39.
52. ibid. p. 40.
53. *Our Knowledge of God* OUP, London, 1939.
54. op. cit. p. 48.
55. *The Shape of Christology* SCM, London, 1966 p. 41.
56. *Problems in the Relations of God and Man* Nisbet, London, 1911 p. 81.
57. *The Concept of the Church* Sheed and Ward, London, 1981 p. 219.
58. *Institutes* ed, McNeil, Westminster Press, Philadelphia bk. 3, ch. 2, par. 7.
59. *Old Testament Theology* vol. 2 Oliver and Boyd, Edinburgh, 1965 pp. 233, 274.
60. For a clear presentation of the origins and effects of the cult of absolute autonomy, see Colin Gunton *Enlightenment and Alienation* Marshall Morgan and Scott Basingstoke, 1985 part 2 especially.
61. J. I. Packer *Knowing God* op. cit. p. 80.
62. P. T. Forsyth *The Principle of Authority* 1913 Independent Press, London pp. 333–4.

GENERAL INDEX